T0311006

# Advance Acclaim

"How do you acquire a lifetime of learning, research, and experience in the most effective art and practice of clinical hypnosis without spending a whole lifetime doing so? In *Process-Oriented Hypnosis,* Michael Yapko distills and shares the very essence of his career-long knowledge and wisdom as a world-leading practitioner, teacher, and writer. His unique contribution with this new volume is in ways to use hypnosis effectively by articulating the specifics of how to be nonspecific. The process for learning this and becoming a more masterful clinician yourself is simple: first, read the book, and second, apply its approaches."

—**George W. Burns**, Adjunct Professor of Psychology, author,
*101 Stories for Enhancing Happiness and Well-being*

"Michael Yapko has explored an element that has become identified as a core Ericksonian approach—the tailoring that follows listening carefully to the words, the phrases, and the expressions of the client, then subsequently adapting the direction of therapy specifically to the needs, wants, and desires of what is revealed and expressed by the subject. Yapko has taken that basic concept and turned the whole picture upside down and inside out. And in so doing, he may have arrived at the most Ericksonian of all approaches—that of looking at the forest and working within the context of the bigger picture."

—**Roxanna Erickson Klein, Ph.D.**, coauthor,
*Hope and Resiliency: Understanding the
Psychotherapeutic Strategies of Milton H. Erickson, MD*

"*Process-Oriented Hypnosis* offers a fresh and approachable vocabulary for many of the process-oriented concepts and techniques that have often been overlooked and all but lost in the teaching and training of modern psychotherapy. *Process-Oriented Hypnosis* reanimates then creatively expands upon these multi-dimensional approaches with the kind of clear emphasis on practicality that is typical of Yapko's writings. This book is long overdue and is a must-read for all therapists, whether they use hypnosis as a context for treatment or not."

—**Stephen R. Lankton**, LCSW, DAHB, FASCH,
Editor-in-Chief, *American Journal of Clinical Hypnosis*

"Once again Michael Yapko is proving himself to be a leader in the field of therapeutic hypnosis in *Process-Oriented Hypnosis: Focusing on the Forest, Not the Trees*. This how-to book integrates practicing psychotherapy with salient and positive principles including ambiguity, expectancy, discrimination, impulses, compartmentalizing, acceptance, responsibility, action, integrity, and foresight—the major principles of modern therapeutic hypnosis. These are, indeed, the trees that make up the forest of effective treatments. Bravo, Michael!"

—**Ernest L. Rossi, Ph.D.** and **Kathryn L. Rossi, Ph.D.**,
codirectors, PsychoSocial Genomics Research Institute and
The Milton H. Erickson Institute of California Central Coast

# Other Books by Michael D. Yapko

# Process-Oriented Hypnosis

A NORTON PROFESSIONAL BOOK

# Process-Oriented Hypnosis

## Focusing on the Forest, Not the Trees

Michael D. Yapko

W. W. NORTON & COMPANY
*Independent Publishers Since 1923*

**Note to Readers:** This book is intended as a general information resource for professionals practicing in the field of psychotherapy and mental health. It is not a substitute for appropriate training, peer review, and/or clinical supervision. Standards of clinical practice and protocol change over time. No technique or recommendation is guaranteed to be safe or effective in all circumstances, and neither the publisher nor the author can guarantee the complete accuracy, efficacy, or appropriateness of any particular recommendation in every respect. All case subjects described in this book are composites. Any URLs displayed in this book link or refer to websites that existed as of press time. The publisher is not responsible for, and should not be deemed to endorse or recommend, any website other than its own or any content that it did not create. The author, also, is not responsible for any third-party material.

For information about permission to reproduce selections from this book, write to Permissions, W. W. Norton & Company, Inc., 500 Fifth Avenue, New York, NY 10110

For information about special discounts for bulk purchases, please contact W. W. Norton Special Sales at specialsales@wwnorton.com or 800-233-4830

Manufacturing by Lake Book Manufacturing
Production manager: Katelyn MacKenzie

Library of Congress Cataloging-in-Publication Data

Names: Yapko, Michael D., author.
Title: Process-oriented hypnosis : focusing on the forest, not the trees / Michael D. Yapko.
Description: First edition. | New York : W. W. Norton & Company, 2021. | "A Norton professional book." | Includes bibliographical references and index.
Identifiers: LCCN 2020041738 | ISBN 9781324016335 (hardcover) | ISBN 9781324016342 (epub)
Subjects: LCSH: Hypnotism—Therapeutic use.
Classification: LCC RC495 .Y369 2021 | DDC 615.8/512—dc23
LC record available at https://lccn.loc.gov/2020041738

W. W. Norton & Company, Inc., 500 Fifth Avenue, New York, N.Y. 10110
www.wwnorton.com

W. W. Norton & Company Ltd., 15 Carlisle Street, London W1D 3BS

1 2 3 4 5 6 7 8 9 0

To Diane with love
44 years later, your smile is still
my very favorite thing to see

# Contents

## Part I: The Foundation of
## *Process-Oriented Hypnosis*

## Part II: The Methods of
## *Process-Oriented Hypnosis*

# List of Tables

# Acknowledgments

While quarantined at home due to the COVID-19 pandemic, I had the opportunity to bring this long-percolating book to fruition. It has provided a nice closure to a project I wasn't sure I'd ever get around to completing. Being quarantined, though, was hardly a welcome condition. The suffering of so many millions worldwide really drives home the point, in the worst of ways, of how inextricably tied to each other we all are. But this is a challenging time that also brings out the best in many people: The courage of the doctors, nurses, and other frontline health care professionals who selflessly care for the sick and dying despite their individual fears of infection or death is inspiring beyond words. All those who gave and continue to give so much, who find courage through the power of their mission, whether it's restocking shelves or sanitizing the facility, show us how much we are capable of when we commit to something greater than ourselves. That lesson of what makes humans become our best selves should never be overlooked by anyone, *ever.*

My wife, Diane, and I have now been happily married for 44 years. This isn't a story you hear much anymore, but it is our story; we're so grateful to have found each other so early on and that we've had the chance to spend our lives together. And what amazing lives they have been! Diane's love, wisdom, and relentless positivity are wonderful gifts she shares generously. And that smile . . .

My family and friends add a richness to my life that I never take for granted. My siblings, Brian, Jerry, Ken, Jackie, and Mitchell, are individually and collectively the wonderful, loving family I would choose to have, not just have by default. And my lifelong best friends, Wendy and Richard, and our "shared" daughter Megan, are my best friends for so many reasons, all of which I hold in my heart.

Many friends and colleagues have given so much of themselves to my personal and professional development. I want to acknowledge two in particular: Jeff Zeig has been an especially important part of my life for more than four decades; I am deeply grateful for his unwavering support and friendship. Jeff has given so much to so many, and I am often awed by his generosity, vision, stamina, and perceptiveness. Erving Polster is a dear friend who holds a special place in my life. He reminds me every day of just how far grace, depth, and a sense of humor will take you in life. Erv is a role model in so many ways, and I am deeply inspired by what he does and, especially, the way he does it.

Two of my most revered mentors are no longer with us but still deserve my note of appreciation here. Jay Haley and William S. Kroger were two of the most brilliant people I have ever known. Both challenged me in the best of ways to keep pushing beyond the limits of my comfort zone, and I am grateful for the many lessons they taught me that I continue to rely on virtually every day of my life. I never had the chance to meet Milton Erickson, unfortunately, but his influence on my work is profound. His unique perspectives supply a seemingly endless array of therapeutic options, encouraging creativity and a deeper appreciation for all that hypnosis can offer.

My editor at Norton, Deborah Malmud, was receptive to the idea for this book from the very beginning and provided valuable feedback. Mariah Eppes, project editor, then guided it through the various stages of development and did so with a clarity and efficiency I appreciate greatly. Karen Fisher was the copyeditor, and she did a wonderful job of smoothing out the book's wrinkles and modeling what a great attention to detail looks like. She improved my work substantially, for which I'm very grateful.

Finally, I want to acknowledge how important my students and colleagues around the world have been in shaping my ideas and perspectives. I am so fortunate to have had the chance to teach to and to interact with talented professionals in many different parts of the world. Each brings a different point of view to even the most basic things in life that then give me reason to pause and give them further consideration. Ideas go through revisions, and the revisions go through revisions. Thank you one and all for all you have given me. I hope you'll see some of yourself in these pages.

Michael D. Yapko, Ph.D
www.yapko.com

# Foreword

In 1984, I was honored to write the foreword to the first edition of Michael Yapko's book *Trancework: An Introduction to the Practice of Clinical Hypnosis*, which has continued to be the definitive textbook for the practice of clinical hypnosis and is now in its fifth edition. In that foreword, I noted that he provided the necessary building blocks to learn and understand the evocative vocabulary and grammar of hypnotherapy. Now, more than 35 years later, I am honored to write a foreword to *Process-Oriented Hypnosis*, which builds on the exemplary contributions this talented therapist and theorist has made in the decades subsequent to *Trancework*.

As one of the world's leading experts in the practice of hypnosis, in this book, Michael extols the value of hypnosis in psychotherapy. Even more, he provides a template for improving psychotherapy, regardless of one's preferred theory and form of practice. Hypnotic processes are inherently woven into every form of psychotherapy, whether or not the practitioner realizes it, and the intentional use of hypnotherapy, even without formal induction, can be immensely beneficial.

We become clinicians because we want to help clients live more adaptively. But there is no right way to provide therapy. As Michael explains, there are many entry points for effective psychotherapy and just as many departure points, because finite patterns and concomitant behaviors underlie human suffering. While pathology has common roots no matter what the presenting problem, the good news is, there are no limits when it comes to human adaptation.

In this edition, Michael outlines general themes that underlie most client problems, including intolerance of ambiguity, lack of control over impulses, and relinquishing personal responsibility. Careful study of these themes and Michael's innovative approach to overcoming them will help clinicians be more effective, regardless of the specifics of the presenting problem.

When it comes to what makes psychotherapy work, Michael and I share many beliefs and orientations, including an emphasis on the utilization of the client's adaptive processes, instead of analyzing client weaknesses. We both maintain that evocative experiences trump psychodynamic understandings, and that the power of communication—as especially evidenced through hypnotic processes—is remarkable. We see trance as a way of awakening people to dormant resources, and not as a method of programming a person to do this or that. Neither Michael nor I are keen on using hypnotic scripts. We believe that therapy is an art, the same way that adaptive living is an art, and should therefore involve creativity, spontaneity, and tailoring to individual needs. And because living happens in the present and is directed to the future, we should be goal oriented in clinical practice.

Michael Yapko is as much an advocate for hypnosis today as he was nearly four decades ago. And his dedication to his art is apparent in both his work as a therapist and his contributions as an author. Join him on his continuing journey in making powerful hypnotic processes part of therapeutic practice. This book will help you become a more effective and creative clinician. It is user friendly, easy to read, and replete with practical suggestions for bettering clinical practice.

Jeffrey K. Zeig
Phoenix, May 2020
erickson-foundation.org

# Introduction

*It is not the strongest of the species that survives, nor the most intelligent that survives. It is the one that is most adaptable to change.*

—Charles Darwin

When I decided to actively pursue a career in psychology as a young college student, my academic coursework and clinical training required my participation in different forms of the therapy experience. The thinking at the time by those in charge was that through your own therapy experiences, group and individual, you could reduce the risk of your personal issues contaminating your work and also better understand what your clients would experience by being in therapy.

I knew about my own issues well before those experiences, though. I knew I was way too perfectionistic, intolerant of mistakes I made, and often pretty harsh in what I would say to myself. As my involvement in the therapy field gradually deepened, I became increasingly concerned that perhaps I wasn't meant to be a therapist when my own issues were so unyielding. Filled with self-doubts and negative judgments about myself, more than once I thought I'd better choose a different profession. How lucky for me that I didn't because of a single interaction!

One day I was talking candidly with one of my mentors, and I disclosed my self-doubts to him. I told him I had this voice inside my head that was forever criticizing me, telling me awful things about myself and how I'd never succeed, and on and on. He listened to me as I told him how bad it made me feel to have this persistent and draining inner voice. Then he hit me with a life-changing thunderbolt when all he said was, "Well, why do you listen to it?"

*Why do I listen to it?* Wow! Everything that I'd learned to that point declared that whatever went through my mind had some significance to be analyzed and worked through. The very idea of not listening to it was astonishingly alien to all I had been taught and therefore would likely never have occurred to me in a million years. Suddenly, there was no need to analyze why I had those issues or what in my background gave rise to them. I now had a genius of a man, for whom I had enormous respect, telling me in so many words that my inner voice could say anything it wanted, but I didn't have to listen to it. For me, this was a huge, shocking, and liberating realization. With that one penetrating question, asked so simply and casually, my whole focus changed from what was wrong with me to discovering what else I could focus on that would better serve me and the clients I hoped to eventually help.

The lesson went even deeper than that, though. I had been so focused on the small stuff, each moment's self-criticism, that I was missing the bigger picture of who I was and what I might be capable of. I realized in that powerful moment that my focus had been terribly misdirected. I had been so wrapped up in trying to change the content of what my inner voice told me and how I reacted to it that I had entirely missed the process of self-talk involved and what I could do to change myself at that higher level.

This insight has paid off in a lifetime of personal and professional dividends. I could and did study the microdynamics of therapy in general and hypnosis in particular, and have written many previous books detailing them. But as valuable as the microview has been, the macroview, that is, the bigger picture, has always been at least as valuable. In my book *Depression Is Contagious*, I said it directly: We don't need a better microscope for understanding and treating depression. Instead, we need a better macroscope, one that can see the bigger picture of what is happening socially and technologically in today's world that has led to the sharp rise in depression such that it is now the world's number one cause of human suffering and disability, according to the World Health Organization (WHO). The problem isn't in people's brains; more often it's in their circumstances. The COVID-19 global pandemic has helped make that point even clearer.

*Process-Oriented Hypnosis* is an invitation to experienced hypnosis practitioners to develop their hypnotic interventions according to the bigger picture. It speaks to common themes in therapy, considers how people develop their problems rather than striving to explain why, and encourages the use of hypnosis to help people shift their frames of reference in more helpful directions, just as I was encouraged to do when told I could have a different response to my harsh inner voice.

This book adds to the many perspectives of hypnosis already in existence.

It is not an introductory training manual for beginning hypnosis students new to the field. To address that need, I have written the richly detailed and widely used hypnosis textbook, *Trancework: An Introduction to the Practice of Clinical Hypnosis* (5th ed.). By making sharp distinctions between being process and content oriented in structuring one's hypnosis sessions in *Process-Oriented Hypnosis,* I hope to bring another level of sound practice to the field.

# Part I

# The Foundation of Process-Oriented Hypnosis

# Chapter 1

# That Problem Sounds Familiar: Repetitions in Therapy

*Each man is an island unto himself. But though a sea of difference may divide us, an entire world of commonality lies beneath.*

—James Rozoff

## The Paradox of Individuality

"You're unique . . . just like everyone else." This statement represents one of the many paradoxes inherent in the practice of psychotherapy. On one hand, it acknowledges the uniqueness of each person that is clearly evident in their physical being, personality, history, and circumstances. On the other hand, it highlights a challenging conundrum: if everyone is special, then is anyone special?

The field of mental health has been wrestling with this paradox throughout its history. The diagnostic classification systems we have developed have encouraged us to respond more to people's labels than to the people themselves, thereby diminishing each person's uniqueness. If you were to assemble a room full of therapists together and ask them if they believe each person is unique as an individual, you will get a unanimous answer: "Of course!" But if you then ask them about how they deliver their treatments, many might tell you about their "10-week program where in week 1 we do this, week 2 we do this, week 3 . . ." and so forth. Each unique client goes through the same cookie-cutter program, and at the level of actual clinical practice the message can be reduced to this: "Here's a size 9 therapy shoe, now go ahead and fit your foot to it."

Similarly, when a psychiatric medication is prescribed as the sole form of treatment (i.e., without concurrent psychotherapy) according to the diagnosis and types of symptoms the patient has, the individual patient is reduced to a neurochemical anomaly to be corrected. The client's uniqueness is again overshadowed by the common denominators of the presumably biological problems they share with similar others.

This is an important issue that sets the stage for what this book is about. While it is ideal to deliver treatments that are as unique as the clients receiving them, it is often a practical necessity to develop standardized programs and therapies that can recognize and treat disorders as efficiently as possible across large numbers of individuals needing help. Delving into irrelevant aspects of what makes someone unique can delay or even prevent delivering timely and effective treatment, yet we still strive to prioritize honoring the individual, as well we should. Thus, we psychotherapists all wrestle with this practical dilemma: How can we acknowledge the uniqueness of each person without having to act as if we've never heard their story before or haven't had to intervene in other cases that were structurally identical?

## How Unique Are People's Problems Really?

Each person who comes to therapy naturally thinks that their problems are unique. Anyone who has been doing therapy for any significant length of time will likely have noticed that while each person is unique as an individual, the problems that individuals present are not all that unique. In reality, the problems that people present to therapists are often remarkably redundant: Here's yet another person suffering with an airplane phobia; here's yet another couple suffering in a distressed marriage; here's yet another person feeling unhappy with their job, and so on. When was the last time you heard a client's story that was new to you?

This is absolutely not meant to make light of anyone's problems, because such problems, suffered by each individual person, can be devastating to them and those around them. They deserve our attention, empathy, and sincere desire to help reduce their suffering, which is why we became therapists in the first place. Rather, the point is that people's problems are repetitive. Occasionally you might hear of some problem that is unlike anything else you've heard before, perhaps even shockingly so, but far more often your new client is telling you a personal story you've heard many times before. The names and faces change, but the stories you hear are quite familiar. Human experiences may be diverse in nature, but they also have a great deal of overlap. Wherever there are families, there are family issues; wherever there are marriages, there are marital issues; wherever there are human bodies, there are health issues, and so on.

Someone's problem may, in fact, have some unique characteristics, some extra little twist to their tale, but these are far more likely to exist on the level of details (content) that are only indirectly related to resolving the presenting problem. Thus, when therapists are able to avoid getting distracted by aspects of the problem that aren't particularly salient to overcoming it, they can better focus on the aspects that are vital to the problem's formation and resolution. This point is one of the primary ways that therapists differ, though, for what one therapist considers central to someone's problem is viewed as only peripheral by another.

## Micro- and Macroviews of Human Experience

What level of consideration, then, is most helpful to the work we do? In recent years, the level of consideration has moved to the microlevel as therapists increasingly focus on abstract and incomplete neuroscience to explain people's problems and their interventions. With precious little evidence to support their claims, many therapists now promise to stimulate neurogenesis and rewire brains. These approaches seem to hold promise and should be explored and developed further. But, with this book, I'm going in a different direction. Instead of engaging in what I call bioreductionism as a treatment model, focusing on the relationship between neurons, I'm encouraging a macroview and focusing on the commonalities of human experience as they underlie people's problems. It's important to say at the outset that this is not an either-or choice of where therapists need to align themselves. Rather, it's a both-and opportunity to recognize that a broader macroview offers at least as many advantages as a microview.

What this book is about, then, is how our therapy clients come to form the problems they present to us with the hope that we can do something that will be of help to them. The focus throughout will be on striving to understand the process, that is, the sequential steps someone follows that culminate in the development of a symptom or problem. The main point is this: When people follow sequences, identifiable steps that lead down a symptom-producing path of experience, anyone following the same steps will end up in the same psychological place. It no longer matters how many degrees they might have, or where they went to school, or what they like to do on their days off. For as long as they continue to do what they do (cognitively, behaviorally, emotionally, interpersonally, etc.) in the same way, the unfortunate outcome can be quite predictable. The problem is in their process.

## Consider an Airplane Phobia as an Example of the Point

Consider a client who presents the problem of an airplane phobia to a therapist. It's a common problem and can be quite costly on many levels (e.g., the missed family events, the self-criticisms for being weak, and the sense of living in too small a personal world self-limited by fears). A therapist might listen attentively and empathetically to the client describe the content of episodes of terror suffered during actual past flights, or sad feelings of regret for important events they missed because they just couldn't bring themselves to get on an airplane.

A content-oriented approach, one that focuses primarily on the details of the client's narrative, might strive to teach the client any of a number of seemingly relevant techniques (such as mindful breathing, deliberate distraction, systematic desensitization, providing factual information such as flying being statistically safer than driving, etc.) intended to, hopefully, counter the anxiety. A content-oriented hypnosis practitioner might perform an induction and then offer empowering suggestions amounting to not much more than a pep talk ("You can do it!"). Or the practitioner might offer simple suggestions of how to "get deeply absorbed in a good book or movie and before you know it the flight will be over . . . You'll be amazed at how comfortable you were and then you can look forward to more comfortable flights."

But a process-oriented approach will have a substantially different focus: How does the client generate unmanageably high levels of anxiety even just thinking about flying? Even though the names and faces of clients who present an airplane phobia differ markedly, the process by which they generate that phobia is amazingly similar.

As someone who flies regularly, I am aware on virtually every flight how different fearful flyers' experience is from my own. I settle into my seat and instantly relax as I think, "For the next 17 hours, no one can call me!" Then I look across the aisle and see someone obviously anxious as they white-knuckle the armrest and practically hyperventilate. In the early days of my career, I'd get up and go ask them what they were doing "in there" (i.e., inside themselves). How did they generate so much anxiety, in sharp contrast to my experience of relaxed flying?

Here's the short answer: Male or female, young or old, high-powered career professional or low-key surfer dude, each followed the same process. They each imagined in vivid detail being held prisoner in their seat as the plane took off, then would clearly imagine the wings falling off, the plane going down in flames in torturously slow motion while they screamed uncontrollably, and then all that was left to see were their body parts strewn all over the ground. It's no surprise that anyone engaging in that kind of horrific imagery would be terrified of flying.

Why would somebody sitting on a plane think about plane crashes? Because you have to as soon as the cabin crew begins their safety demonstration. The more salient question for this book, though, is why all the flyers who are directly warned about cabin depressurization, putting on oxygen masks, following the floor lights to the nearest exit if the cabin goes dark or fills with smoke, and how to "use your seat cushion as a flotation device in the event of a water landing" aren't anxious. How do they process the multiple dangers described in the safety briefing at the start of every flight in such a way as to still be comfortable flying? What specific skills, cognitive or otherwise, make the threat of a possible fatal air crash not seem to be a threat at all?

Thus, the content of the problem is an airplane phobia with all the associated details (such as the person's feelings, history of the problem, previous attempts at resolution, etc.), but the process of the problem relates to how someone assesses risk and how someone is unable to distinguish well between real and imminent threats and merely possible imagined ones. A process-oriented hypnosis session would focus on building these specific skills rather than only focusing on the content of a fear of flying in airplanes or worse, talking about the client's presumed control issues or the symbolism of what the airplane represents in your unconscious.

Clinically, it is well known that someone with a phobia is likely to have multiple phobias, not just one. Altering the process of how someone assesses risk and utilizes their own resources more effectively holds the potential to solve many more problems than just one phobia. We want to be able to improve the way people respond to their feelings of fear when those feelings arise in any context.

## Why Hypnosis?

One of the primary reasons why hypnosis as a treatment tool is so effective is because more often than not, people's problems are ultimately problems of focus. They may focus only on what is wrong and thereby miss what's right. They may focus on the unchangeable past and miss opportunities to create a different and better future for themselves. They may focus on the big picture and miss the salient details (or vice versa) of what actually matters. They may focus on their feelings when they would be better off thinking rationally (or vice versa). Much more will be said about hypnosis and its applications in later chapters, of course, but it's an important point to establish early on that hypnosis is a valuable tool for helping people to shift focal points. Hypnosis, in general, is particularly effective in engaging someone's attention and gently moving it in a more useful direction, one that is consistent with the goals of treatment. That attribute of hypnosis becomes especially important when addressing the repetitive nature of people's problems that arise from their tendency to focus on images, ideas, feelings, perceptions, and so on, that cause them distress. What any good hypnosis practitioner does, like good therapists in general as well, is to say, in essence, "Here. You've been focusing on that and it has caused you significant discomfort. Now, to feel better, you can begin to focus on this instead." And so, the hypnotic induction begins . . .

## The Problems That Sound Familiar

All people face challenges in life that can easily become the source of emotional distress. No one escapes the adversities that can range from relatively small bumps in the road of life to the huge earthquakes that can rock your world. We all face illness, death, failure, rejection, humiliation, prejudice, too many forms of unfairness to count, and so many other reliable sources of emotional and physical pain that can come at us from the outside world. But it's also true that much of the distress people experience isn't externally generated. Instead it's generated by internal forces, whether it's sloppy thinking that gives rise to damaging misperceptions (such as a crippling perfectionism or an endless rage over unfulfilled and unrealistic expectations) or bad behavior that leads to self-loathing or worse (such as alcohol abuse or reckless sexual acting out).

Each individual has personal reasons for and ways of suffering, but the paths of human suffering that people follow are well worn and plainly visible. What follows, then, in this section is an identification of some (not all) of the most common, repetitive problems that people present to therapists in the hopes of getting meaningful help. More important is the brief discussion of each one in terms of what someone, anyone, would have to learn in order to resolve that issue. The role of process-oriented hypnosis in helping people acquire those skills can then become clearer.

## Rigidity

Not long before he passed away in 1980, Milton Erickson was asked this question by one of his students: What do you believe is the basis for most people's problems? Erickson's one-word answer: rigidity. That answer is brilliant in its simplicity and has been a constant source of inspiration for all those therapists (like me) who strive to promote greater flexibility in those contexts that clients find challenging.

What does rigidity mean exactly? It means someone has a response—a behavior, a cognition, an emotion—that doesn't vary even when the context does. In other words, the person doesn't adapt to changing circumstances to their own detriment. The ability to adapt is one of the keys to mental health. When circumstances change but someone persists in a pattern that may have worked before but can't any longer, the result is all too predictably negative. There are many different forms of rigidity a client may display, as delineated in Table 1.1.

It was one of Erickson's primary goals in therapy to create situations, whether through hypnosis or prescribed life experiences (such as task assignments or behavioral experiments), that would make it nearly impossible for his patients to continue doing whatever they were (rigidly) doing. So many of Erickson's case examples, and the case examples of Ericksonian practitioners such as Jeffrey Zeig and strategic therapy practitioners such as Jay Haley, are stories of wonderfully creative interventions that promote flexibility as the obvious counter to rigidity.

The use of hypnosis can itself be a model of flexibility. When you do hypnosis, you are saying, in essence, "We can relate to each other in a variety of ways

---

### TABLE 1.1. FORMS OF RIGIDITY

- Cognitive rigidity (tenaciously held beliefs despite contrary evidence and reflexive thoughts containing obvious cognitive distortions)
- Behavioral rigidity (persisting in behavior despite it being ineffective)
- Emotional rigidity (awareness and decisions made only according to feelings)
- Perceptual rigidity (reflexive patterns for interpreting the meaning of events)
- Identity rigidity (a self-definition that precludes the possibility of change)
- Relational rigidity (a fixed and ineffective style of relating to others)
- Contextual rigidity (an automatic response to a type of situation)

---

and on a number of different levels. You can discover things about yourself that you didn't know, and your view of yourself can change as a result. You can learn new skills and new ways of seeing and doing things that can result in you feeling better about yourself." These messages are embedded in any hypnosis session, whether content or process oriented, and they hold great therapeutic possibilities.

Virtually all of the process-oriented hypnosis sessions provided in this book address rigidity in one way or another. Each aims to counter at least one form of rigidity and usually more than one. Carefully reading the session transcripts will make this readily apparent to you.

## Trauma (at Any Age, but Especially in Childhood)

Trauma can take many different forms, of course, and can range from what many therapists call the "small t" traumas (e.g., not being picked for the sports team or being passed over for a promotion) to the "Big T" traumas (e.g., childhood sexual abuse or combat-related injuries). As mentioned above, no one escapes suffering the adversities of life, but exposure to trauma is especially hurtful. No one goes looking for it—it finds you. It can easily overwhelm people and lead to a wide variety of enduring emotional, behavioral, and physical difficulties. These are typically amplified when the trauma occurs at an early age, before there is any substantial means of protecting oneself or processing its significance insightfully.

The field of trauma therapy has grown exponentially in recent years. The variety of approaches that are advocated by the experts in that field range from physically to psychologically based, and each has great potential value in reducing the sequelae of trauma and deserve careful study.

The number of skills that one must develop if one is to overcome a history of trauma makes recovery a formidable therapeutic endeavor. Dealing with guilt, shame, rage, fear, and avoidance provides plenty of serious issues to address sensitively in therapy. But no matter what therapeutic approach one might choose to employ, there is one especially important skill that anyone with a history of trauma will have to develop. That skill is compartmentalization, the subject of Chapter 9. From a process-oriented perspective, what keeps trauma going in someone's life is when the past continues to bleed into the present, contaminating now with what happened then. That means reacting to current people, situations, feelings, and perceptions from the past trauma's frame of mind. It is a safe prediction that until the client can fully separate past from present and respond on the basis of now, not then, trauma symptoms will persist.

Different therapies facilitate compartmentalization in different ways, but they all do it in one way or another out of necessity. Compartmentalization means separating different elements of subjective experience from one another. This is the textbook definition of dissociation, and dissociation is the foundation of hypnotic responsiveness. You can do hypnosis without doing relaxation processes, but you can't do hypnosis without facilitating some degree of dissociation. Thus, hypnosis for helping resolve the distress of trauma should be a part of every clinician's repertoire, in my opinion.

Hypnosis in general has shown a remarkable capacity for both quelling and instilling automatic or nonconscious responses in people, empowering them in the process. Hypnosis to stimulate new automatic responses and to alter what "the body remembers" are realistic outcomes to expect from process-oriented hypnosis sessions that encourage these possibilities. Enhancing the acquisition of self-regulation or self-management tools is what hypnosis does best.

# Anxiety

At the time of this writing, the COVID-19 global pandemic is the near-constant focus of virtually everyone. The numbers of infected people and deaths worldwide are staggering and are still on the rise. No wonder that the number of antianxiety drug prescriptions in the U.S. has increased so greatly during this time! People are asking anxiety-provoking questions of their government leaders and medical specialists: When will this pandemic end? Will there be a vaccine? When will we be able to go back to work and resume a normal life? These are all reasonable questions, and it is understandable why people are asking them. They want answers. But none are forthcoming because the onset and course of the virus are ambiguous, at least for now.

People are also asking anxiety-provoking questions of themselves: How am I to cope with the pandemic's effects on me and my life? How will I survive financially? What will happen to my job? How do I explain what's going on to my young children? What am I supposed to do while being stuck at home all the time?

People generally prefer certainty to uncertainty and predictability to chaos. On a national level, well before the pandemic hit, you could already see the distressed response of Americans to today's turbulent political and social climate when surveyed about their level of emotional upset. The American Psychological Association's 2019 Stress in America survey of Americans, published on November 5, 2019, and posted on the APA website, starkly revealed that the majority of Americans feel anxious, depressed, and fearful about life in America today, particularly in regard to mass shootings, health care, and the next presidential election.

Therapists all over the country had reported the large uptick in their clients' stress levels before the pandemic because of the uncertainty about our collective future. There's nothing like big existential but currently unanswerable questions to make the future seem ominous: Will democracy survive in America? Will we be able to save the planet before climate change and overpopulation doom us all? This isn't just an American phenomenon by any means. Although the APA has identified and quantified stress in America, as I travel around the world conducting clinical trainings, the stress is quite apparent virtually everywhere I go. I'm sure my international colleagues share the same observation.

Beyond the anxiety associated with these huge issues, anxiety at the individual level is statistically the most common reason for people seeking therapy, which was especially amplified by the COVID-19 global pandemic. Many factors contribute to anxiety, as is true of any condition, but none are more significant than how the individual responds to ambiguity. People are anxiously wondering what will happen, how they'll cope, and what they should do.

Ambiguity means there is no single clear meaning of an event, no clear cause-and-effect relationship, no clear path to follow or decision to make, no certainty to be had. Whatever is going on in the client's world (the content), they are cornered by their need to have clarity in a circumstance where there simply is none to be had. Without that clarity, even small risks can seem huge, and paralyzing self-doubt can take over.

Someone who is going to learn to manage anxiety will need to acquire specific skills, including the ability to first recognize the ambiguities evident in a specific context in order to begin to define what is known and knowable and what is unknown and unknowable. More simply, do people know when they're asking unanswerable questions? Too often, they don't, so they get angry at authorities who they think should have the answers even though they can't, or they become ruminators who analyze endlessly while looking for an answer they believe they'll find if they just keep looking or thinking about it.

Searching for the answer to unanswerable questions (such as whether there is life after death or why the tornado hit your home but spared your neighbor's) is a colossal waste of time and energy and drives up symptoms of both anxiety and depression. Furthermore, we need skills in assessing risks realistically, or else we could convince ourselves that if we go outside, we might get hit by a meteor. We can make almost anything seem life-threatening if we imagine how that would happen in enough detail. As the psychologist and anxiety expert David Barlow said (personal communication, December 11, 2009), so much of what anxiety is about is overestimating risks and underestimating resources.

Hypnosis as a means of helping people recognize and develop their resources is critically important in the treatment of anxious individuals. We want people to know what their resources are so that they don't underestimate them or miss opportunities to use them in self-empowering ways. Recognizing ambiguity is the first step toward eventually better tolerating ambiguity, a vitally important life skill we want to help develop that has not only treatment value but also prevention value.

Therapists routinely proclaim clients have innate resources that they're not connected to or using. This is true. Why aren't they using them? Because the resources are dissociated, meaning there is no internal or external trigger to access them. This is what hypnosis does exceptionally well: It connects (associates) people to their resources and helps them use the resources effectively. Empowering anxious people to bring even objectively scary circumstances from unpleasant and unmanageable into the realm of unpleasant but manageable is a big deal. This is considered in greater detail in Chapter 5.

## Helplessness

One of the most important perceptions people can hold that will exert a strong influence on their quality-of-life decisions is about their power (or lack thereof) to change either themselves or their circumstances. Usually, when people come into therapy, they're not feeling powerful. They usually feel stymied by unknown forces in their self-help efforts, helpless to know what to do.

Helplessness is powerlessness. People who are powerful have choices, while people who are powerless have few or none. But power is about perception. People routinely overestimate how much power they have ("I'm going to make you care about this") as well as underestimate it ("I can't do anything about how I feel"). It is a goal of therapy in general to help people make more realistic appraisals of how much power they have in a given circumstance. More often than not, this takes the form of helping someone who feels helpless to discover that they have more ability to influence what happens than they realize.

The ability to discrimate meaningfully between what is and what isn't controllable is vitally important to someone who reflexively retreats into helplessness whenever they encounter a formidable challenge of one sort or another. Taking responsibility for oneself, being action oriented rather than passive, and better discriminating what is and isn't controllable are all skills that can be helpfully integrated into process-oriented hypnosis sessions, as you will see in later chapters on these subjects.

## Hopelessness and Apathy

The perception that nothing can be done because any effort to change or improve things will simply be wasted is the essence of feeling hopeless. The resistance that therapists routinely analyze and confront in the course of therapy is often driven by the client's perception that there's really no sense in trying. This is especially prominent in the experience of depression. It is fair to say that the mantra of depression is, "Why bother?" The corollary questions, then, are, "Why bother to go for therapy? Why bother to read my therapist's recommended books? Why bother to do my therapist's recommended homework assignments when I already know I'm a hopeless case?"

Hopelessness and apathy are thus entwined and together highlight how critically important it is to address this terribly impaired view of the future and what's possible. Knowing how much people's expectations—their orientation to the future—shape their experience and treatment response, it becomes a major goal to help build positive expectancy. The hypnotic phenomenon of age progression can be utilized for just that purpose. This is the subject of Chapter 6, but other chapters also enhance the recognition that building positive expectations in a variety of ways is essential to good therapy.

## Coping Skills

Smoking, drinking, drugging, overeating, sleeping too much, sleeping too little, spending money you don't have, watching too much porn, self-mutilation . . . whew! There are clearly lots of ways someone can make their difficulties even worse simply because of how badly they're coping with them in self-destructive ways. Primitive attempts to cope with stressors, whatever they might be, can lead people into the realm of addiction when what was meant to be a quick and easy way of avoiding a problem instead became the problem. Similarly, a poor coping skill doesn't have to lead to addiction; it just has to divert the person from the path of managing themselves and their problems skillfully and lead to self-loathing instead.

The skills necessary to cope with stressors well, whether external stressors (such as job pressures) or internal (such as exercising compulsively to have a perfect body), can be well-defined and facilitated hypnotically. These include (1) the ability to compartmentalize experience, effectively creating a safe emotional distance from the stressor(s) in order to reduce its emotional impact; (2) building the expectancy that you can grow and outgrow the need for what was intended to be helpful but instead became damaging; (3) building the impulse control to think beyond the moment and make a better choice about what to do, thereby encouraging foresight as well; and (4) building a sense of integrity about your actions, setting and adhering to a standard of behavior you can feel good about. All of these goals of a process-oriented hypnosis are addressed in detail in later chapters.

## Relationship Skills

Our relationships help define us: We're someone's kid, sibling, spouse, partner, parent, boss, employee, and more. How many roles we each occupy at a given time! How well do we manage those roles?

Therapists routinely have the experience of listening to someone describe the terrible abuses they suffered at the hands of their parents. These are the stories of parents who were emotionally sterile and unavailable, the parents who were manipulative and self-serving in using the weapons of guilt or withdrawal of affection to get their way, parents who were cruel in the beatings they gave for truly minor infractions, and on and on. Every therapist listening to such stories has wondered silently, "Why did this person's parents have children when they were so woefully inadequate to the task of parenting?" That's a good question, and too often the answer is simply "because they thought they were supposed to" or, worse, "because they forgot to go to the drugstore."

Every relationship has requirements for maintaining its health. Clear definitions of what the relationship is about are the starting point, but the real keys lie in how people define the rules, the guidelines, for how to interact. This is easier said than done. Everyone needs approval, for example. How much approval seeking is okay, and when does it become excessive? ("Am I okay? Am I okay? Do you think I'm okay? What about now? Do you still think I'm okay?") How much conflict avoidance prevents unnecessary petty arguments, and how much does it prevent important discussions of serious issues where a difference of opinion might uncomfortably arise?

The skills that go into building healthy, positive relationships are on the decline, unfortunately. Too many people are far more into their smartphones than smart people, and self-absorption has made relationships of only secondary or even tertiary importance to them. The cost of these interpersonal deficiencies shows up in troubling ways: The rise in acts of violence against minorities in recent years shows a clear lack of empathy and respectful acceptance of others' differences, two of the key relationship skills to bring into your valued ongoing relationships. Taking responsibility for yourself and owning up to and apologizing for hurtful mistakes you've made is another. Knowing how to define and maintain your own personal boundaries and accept the boundaries others establish for themselves is a vital way of modeling integrity. Acting with integrity by doing what you say you're going to do in order to build trust in others is yet another key skill to develop.

Another consideration is this: What happens when your role changes through the loss of a relationship? For example, when you've been a caretaker for an elderly parent who passes away, who are you now? The sense of loss and the grief such an event fuels can be understandably devastating. But, consistent with the above, it requires a rewriting of one's self-definition. For the person who says, "I'll never get over this . . . I'm no one without that person in my life," the grief can be intense and indefinite. Hypnosis to encourage a shift in identity, an acceptance of the loss, and an expectancy that there will be a gradual rebuilding can be profoundly helpful in such instances. That same process of redefining yourself at developmental transition points in your life defines flexibility in yet another important way.

Most of the time when you do hypnosis sessions, you're encouraging people to focus internally almost exclusively. Once you enter the social or interpersonal arena, though, many of your suggestions will be encouraging a greater external awareness, especially of who you bring into your life and why while also growing clearer about your level and quality of impact on other people. You'll notice this other-oriented quality of suggestion in many of the later chapters' session transcripts.

## Final Points

It has always seemed tinged with cruelty to me when a desperate client in distress asks a therapist for direction ("What do you think I should do?") and the therapist replies, "Well, what do *you* think you should do?" The quaint philosophy of careful neutrality that guided such evasive responses has gradually eroded, and most therapists now describe themselves as eclectic and active in structuring treatment. That's good progress for the field, in my opinion.

What it tells me is that being active in catalyzing progress in therapy has become the norm. The desire to do that as quickly and efficiently as one reasonably can makes sense to me. I attribute that perspective to the influence of my friend and mentor, Jay Haley, who used to say, "The problem with people in therapy is that they're in therapy. Therapy isn't a normal context for living; the goal should be to get people out of therapy and fully into their lives as soon as possible." I think Jay was right about that.

This is what set the stage for me wanting to develop ways of getting to the heart of the client's issues more quickly and efficiently without getting bogged down or diverted by unnecessary details (the content of the problem). Focusing on the process and identifying which skills are needed to help clients accomplish what they came to therapy to accomplish makes this possible.

# Chapter 2

# The Distraction of Content and the Salience of Process in Treatment

*You can't do big things if you're distracted by small things.*

—Anonymous

## Shifting From a Content to a Process Focus

One of the key issues that I address in this book concerns how to provide effective interventions without making unnecessary and potentially hazardous interpretations. Some therapies have already managed to do this. The solution-oriented approaches have been valuable in this regard, demonstrating the effectiveness of approaches that bypass the pitfalls of interpreting meanings and focusing instead on encouraging behavior and shaping the context in which it appears. The strategic therapies of Haley and Erickson further provide a welcome foundation of pragmatism that steers clear of making interpretations in order to intervene effectively. Through approaches such as these, the focus is on changing how the client does the symptom rather than interpreting its deeper meaning. Consider the following case example.

Bill came to therapy asking for help with his anxiety problem. It seemed ever present in his awareness, but it spiked in certain situations, almost always social ones where he felt certain he was being judged negatively by others. As a result, Bill was overly self-conscious, fearful of rejection, and socially awkward as he struggled to say and do the right things around people.

Now, what is salient to Bill's problem and what is merely distracting content? Think of all the different therapeutic paths we could go down just from this short description: Should we explore his need for approval and what in his attachment history amplified that need so greatly? What about treating his neurologically wired-in fear response? Or his grief from all the relationships he's lost and the resulting self-blame and low self-esteem he suffers? Should we focus on his anger at people for not giving him the acceptance he wants? Should we analyze his unconscious fear of intimacy as the basis for doing things to drive others away? Should we tell him he's just an introvert and that he should accept that in himself? What about teaching him to recognize and correct his cognitive distortions about himself and others in social situations? What about . . . ?

There are therapists who would agree with any one of these interpretations and then proceed to build the therapy around it. I would disagree, as you might predict. None of those viewpoints speaks directly to the process of how Bill generates his social anxiety.

I asked Bill a few questions about his perceptions of himself and what his ideas were about his discomfort around people. I was especially interested in his reply to my question about how he knew what others were thinking. While he was formulating his answer, Bill was startled when I challenged him directly to read my mind in that very moment. Of course, he couldn't, and he was confused by my demand. But he sensed that I was making a point he needed to grasp.

Listening to stories of Bill's social failures wasn't necessary. Listening to stories about how his parents treated him when he was growing up was an unnecessary distraction. Listening to him vent his frustration and anger at how judgmental people can be is another unnecessary distraction. Listening to him describe his sadness at how isolated he feels even in a crowded room is yet another irrelevancy. Asking him why other people's approval is so import-ant to him while advising him to approve of himself is irrelevant. Everyone wants approval, including you. It's not pathological and worthy of analysis. The salient questions are, how far will you go to get approval and what will you do with it when you get it?

So, what is salient to Bill's case? Bill goes through a series of steps, a sequence, when he interacts with others. When he first initiates an interaction or responds to an initiation from someone, he then focuses internally as he asks himself whether he's being interesting or worthy of someone's attention. Next, he rapidly concludes he isn't and that the other person is judging him negatively. Now he feels rejected, so he naturally acts rejected (brittle and sar-castic) and, finally, ends the interaction on a self-critical and anxious low. Why he does this, what his history is of doing this, and what it might mean may be of interest to some therapists but are unnecessary distractions to helping Bill. My intervention was straightforward and involved the use of a process-oriented hypnosis session.

After startling Bill with my playful yet serious demand that he read my thoughts in that moment, I paused for a long time, long enough to let him wonder what that was all about. Then I invited Bill to close his eyes and just listen attentively to what I had to say. My voice became softer, slower, more soothing, hypnotic. Bill remem-bers me talking about how people learn to walk and talk and how he thought about his own experience of learning to do such basic things. There's nothing threatening or challenging about having learned some pretty basic things in life, so Bill gradually became more focused and relaxed as he listened. Then he heard me say something about how people are born with the capacity to imagine and how it's our ability to imagine that leads to amazing creations in technology and art and so many other areas. I said people can use their imaginations in many different ways, from thinking about beautiful but imaginary places to thinking about imaginary expla-nations for why the world is as it is. He remembers me saying some-thing to the effect that old myths about gods of the sea and the moon and the sun used to be considered true stories that explained why things are as they are and that people reacted to them in that way. At first, Bill wondered why he was listening to my stories about mythological gods and people's ancient beliefs, but he found them compelling, and they held his attention. Then I began talking about the myths that each person lives by, those things we were either told or told ourselves a long time ago that we believed . . . but now have a chance to revise and modernize. Bill heard me say something about the misconceptions people form about other people, making snap judgments about them with no more information than their own hastily formed superficial conclusions . . . people who think they can read or somehow know other people's thoughts . . . living out the myth of being all-knowing. Now he can realize that no one can do that, not even him with his extensive experience in pretending he can read minds. I focused him on how important it is to just carefully notice people and to cultivate a rich and enjoyable sense of curiosity about them . . . and how easy it would be to turn his attention from the inside to the outside . . . to engage with people comfortably when he has the chance to demonstrate his interest in them through the questions he asks so he can learn what's on their minds instead of only imagining what's on their minds. . . . Bill reported later that it was as if all of a sudden during this session he felt this huge burden lifted from him. Suddenly people seemed so easy to understand: Observe them, ask questions, and make it easy for them to answer—and then listen to the answer! Learn something about what matters to them, discover whether it's easy or hard for them to share themselves, see if they have a sense of humor. Bill remembers thinking, "I can do that!" The next thing Bill knew, I was talking about how he could open his eyes and bring back a new knowledge he could use to be surprisingly comfortable around other people.

To this day, Bill credits that single hypnosis session with turning his life around. In that one session, his focus shifted dramatically from his imaginations about what people were thinking (and then actually believing himself) to actually engaging with people in order to find out. I saw Bill for a few additional sessions to improve his social skills (such as how to know what and when to self-disclose, how to begin and end conversations, how to recognize interpersonal boundaries, and so forth). Empowered with new confidence and a better feel for people now that he's no longer so internally focused and engaging in mind reading, he's a different man—a much happier, calmer man. Hypnosis was an experiential vehicle for teaching perspectives and skills in ways that were gentle, supportive, and easy to integrate.

## Asking How to Get to What Matters

As you can appreciate, it is easy to get lost in the content, that is, the details of the elaborate stories our clients tell us. They provide us with powerful narratives that share the hurts they suffer that elicit our empathy, the traumas they endured that elicit our sympathy and compassion, the triumphs that move and inspire us, and all the other details that make their stories so compelling. The content is valuable, but only to the extent that it provides the therapist with some insights about the process.

How much content does a therapist need to listen to before understanding the process well enough to know where to intervene? How do you know when you have enough problem content and a strong enough therapeutic alliance with the client to move into the intervention phase with a well-defined therapeutic goal?

Presumably, you have likely developed a style and method for interviewing your therapy clients. In this section, I encourage a relatively simple modification to your interviews by adding one or two more questions designed to elicit greater clarity about how—not why—the client develops and maintains symptoms. Specifically, the goal of asking pointed "how" questions is to develop an understanding of the steps in the symptomatic sequence in order to be able to introduce effective interruptions to its unfolding. Consider my how question to Bill in the case above: "How do you know what other people are thinking?"

Asking how someone knows something they profess to know or how they made (or will make) an important decision tells you what they focus on and therefore what they miss or exclude from the process that generates unwanted results. For example, when Bill focuses on his feelings, how he knows other people are judging him negatively is only because that's what his feelings tell him. I used hypnosis to shift him from being so internally oriented to being more externally oriented by encouraging him to focus much more on the other person in the interaction and on what he could learn about them through careful observation and asking inviting questions instead of mind reading. Bill's case example is simple, yet this structure of helping people with social anxiety applies to countless people.

When a client has made a choice (including the typically unintentional choice not to choose) in some vulnerable area and suffered some unexpected consequence that causes distress, it reveals a flaw in the decision-making process. Clients don't know where the flaw in the process was, just as Bill didn't. He reacted reflexively, and typically had no idea there was some decision to be made about where to focus his attention or how to know when he was engaging in mind reading.

Thus, when the clinician asks the how questions, such as "How do you decide which thoughts or feelings to keep to yourself and which ones to express?" or "How do you know whether to accept this limitation or strive to transcend it?," the most common response is confusion and the reluctant admission, "I don't know." As therapists, we want to know what that flaw is so we can teach a more effective decision-making strategy and thereby help the client avoid duplicating the same mistake in similar future episodes. Thus, treatment also provides opportunities for prevention (for a detailed description of the merits of "how" questions in clinical interviewing, see Yapko [2016]).

A wonderful book called *The Knowledge Illusion: Why We Never Think Alone*, by Steven Sloman and Philip Fernbach (2017), isn't a therapy book per se but has enormous relevance for therapists. It makes the same point about the merits of how questions from a different perspective on helping people come to realize that they don't know as much as they think they do. Sloman and Fernbach wrote:

> The human mind is both genius and pathetic, brilliant and idiotic. People are capable of the most remarkable feats . . . and yet we are equally capable of the most remarkable demonstrations of hubris and foolhardiness . . .
>
> People often lack skills that seem basic, like evaluating how risky an action is, and it's not clear they can ever be learned . . . Perhaps most important, individual knowledge is remarkably shallow, only scratching the surface of the true complexity of the world, and yet we often don't realize how little we understand. The result is we are often overconfident, sure we are right about things we know little about . . .
>
> Our point is not that people are ignorant. It's that people are more

ignorant than they think they are. We all suffer, to a greater or lesser extent, from an illusion of understanding . . .

We can't possibly understand everything, and the sane among us don't even try. We rely on abstract knowledge, vague and unanalyzed. (2017, pp. 3, 4–5, 8, 10)

The great American humorist Mark Twain once said, "It ain't what you don't know that gets you into trouble. It's what you know for sure that just ain't so." He was only half correct.

# Chapter 3

# The Process of Hypnosis: Paying Attention with Intention

*Out of hypnotic training comes skill in observing people and the complex ways they communicate, skill in motivating people to follow directives, and skill in using one's own words, intonations, and body movements to influence other people. Also out of hypnosis come a conception of people as changeable, an appreciation of the malleability of space and time, and specific ideas about how to direct another person to become more autonomous.*

—Jay Haley, *Uncommon Therapy*

There are two distinct, but closely related, sides to the type of interventions I'm advocating in this book: the strategic and the hypnotic. In the first two chapters, I focused on the strategic side of the equation first by highlighting the repetitive nature of people's problems while encouraging you to think of the skills someone would need to have to resolve them, and second by drawing a sharp distinction between content and process in interviewing in order to more clearly define the targets of treatment.

In this chapter, then, I want to turn our attention to the hypnotic side of therapeutic intervention. First, I want to address the foundational question, "Why hypnosis?" Most clinicians have not had training in hypnosis, which I find most unfortunate for reasons I'll specify shortly. Worse, there is a common bias against learning hypnosis, which, if you've never seen it or had clinical training, is typically only thought of as a sleazy form of entertainment. Anyone who practices hypnosis can tell you about how much time they spend having to debunk myths and correct people's misconceptions (for a detailed consideration of the typical misconceptions and how to respond to them effectively, see Yapko [2019]). Thus, the clinical merits of hypnosis seem like a good place to begin this chapter's focus on evolving skills with process-oriented hypnosis.

# Why Learn and Practice Hypnosis?

The merits of hypnosis have been well articulated in the clinical and research literature. It is well beyond the scope of this book to review the large body of empirical studies affirming its added value for a wide variety of treatments, but I can summarize some of the key points about what makes hypnosis valuable here.

## Evidence-Based Applications of Hypnosis

Hypnosis is at least as much about art as it is science. I'd say the same about psychotherapy. But hypnotic processes clearly have enough structure to define and measure their impact on therapeutic outcomes. Toward that end, the objective evidence supporting the use of hypnosis across a wide variety of medical and psychological conditions makes for a compelling case for including hypnosis in a client's treatment plan (see Elkins [2017] and Yapko [2019] for in-depth reviews of this literature).

## The Inevitability of Utilizing Suggestion in Any Treatment, Not Just Hypnosis

The study of hypnosis provides an in-depth consideration of the power of communication, both verbal (especially) and nonverbal. As health care providers in whatever capacity we conduct our work, we are offering ideas, perspectives, and directives to our clients that range from subtle suggestions (e.g., "This will help you feel better quite soon") to high-pressured commands (e.g., "You must do this practice every day or you won't get better"). "Focus on your breathing" is a suggestion. "Sit comfortably" is a suggestion. "Listen to and really focus on what I say" is a suggestion. "Meditation will help you" is a suggestion. "Go to the drugstore and fill this prescription" is a suggestion. Therefore, it's important to be knowledgeable about the many different forms that suggestions can take and how to choose from among them what is most likely to be acceptable to the client. No matter how well-structured or clever a suggestion might be, if the client doesn't accept it, then it really doesn't matter.

## Hypnosis Highlights the Subjective Nature of Experience

In offering suggestions to someone, you can use content or process suggestions. Content suggestions provide specific details (e.g., "You can visualize being in a beautiful garden surrounded by bright and fragrant red roses in full bloom"). Process suggestions carefully avoid the use of details (e.g., "You can think of a special place"). One insightful way of characterizing the differences in style is evident in the language Milton H. Erickson Foundation director and hypnosis expert Dr. Jeffrey Zeig (2014, 2019) uses: It's the difference between imposing on someone what to do (or think or visualize) versus eliciting the person's own experience from within. Obviously, a process-oriented hypnosis is built upon the notion of eliciting hypnotic responses rather than imposing on the client to comply. The style in which suggestions are delivered will be almost entirely permissive in nature, suggesting possibilities but demanding nothing. A careful reading of the session transcripts included in this volume will affirm this point.

It is a basic truth: meaning is in people, not the words you use. This is the basis for a process-oriented hypnosis: People can only use their subjective experience (i.e., their experiences, views, style of processing information, etc.) to make sense of the things you say during a session. The idiosyncratic nature of people's interpretations of your words assures you that people will form conclusions you didn't intend and react in ways you didn't expect. Most of the time these disconnects aren't all that problematic . . . but they can be. Part of good training teaches how to handle such delicate instances sensitively and skillfully.

The other key point about subjectivity is that people can have very meaningful experiences in hypnosis that are neither rational nor measurable in any objective way. The client who enjoys "floating peacefully through space and time" isn't really doing that from the clinician's perspective, of course. But for the client who has that subjective experience, it can be profoundly meaningful and integrated as a helpful self-regulating resource to access during times of stress.

### Hypnosis Highlights the Malleability of Experience

People in hypnosis process information differently, and they are able to access abilities they otherwise don't know how to access. During hypnosis, people can experience marked shifts in subjective experience, as detailed in Table 3.1.

The shifts that can take place in any and all of these facets of the client's experience highlight the point that is so essential to any therapy, regardless of the modality one employs: Your experience can change. Given the power of rigidity to keep clients stuck in some distressing pattern, described in Chapter 1, the value of the flexibility that hypnosis encourages cannot be overstated. Even something as simple as deliberately doing a breathing exercise that significantly reduces one's level of anxiety can be transformative. What seemed unchangeable did, in fact, change, and in light of that experience you will have to redefine yourself as more empowered than you previously realized. This is why even single-session interventions can have a deep and lasting impact. It's also why the pervasive myth of hypnosis diminishing people's sense of control rather than enhancing it is so very unfortunate.

---

**TABLE 3.1. POSSIBLE SHIFTS IN SUBJECTIVE EXPERIENCE DURING HYPNOSIS**

**Physiology** (breathing slows, muscles relax, etc.)
**Sensory perception** (temperature, weight, distance, etc.)
**Cognition** (thoughts clearer, slower, detached, etc.)
**Affect** (happier, sadder, more curious, etc.)
**Behavior** (self-help, new behavior, proactive, etc.)
**Temporal orientation** (past, present, future focus)
**Self-definition** (more resourceful, self-aware, self-controlled, etc.)
**Relational definition** (more attuned, empathetic, compassionate, generous, etc.)

---

## Paying Attention with Intention: What's the Goal?

What does hypnosis actually do? It amplifies and/or deamplifies specific elements of experience. It generates associations (i.e., connections to) and dissociations (i.e., detachments from) regarding whatever might be suggested. In each of the session transcripts, you'll see how suggestion is used to associate people to some new awareness or resource and/or dissociate them from some established link that is problematic for them (e.g., this place leads to that memory).

Association and dissociation are two sides of the same hypnosis coin. As soon as you suggest associating to *this*, you're also suggesting dissociating from *that*. Hypnosis is built upon the experience of dissociation, and it is arguably the therapist's greatest ally in treatment. If you consider the role of detachment in virtually every therapy, you can appreciate this point. For example, in cognitive-behavioral therapy (CBT) we often encourage people to adopt the perspective that you are not your thoughts ("Just because you think it doesn't make it true"). In acceptance and commitment therapy (ACT) we might encourage people to externalize their thoughts ("Picture your distressing thoughts written on a sign carried by a marcher in a parade and watch it just go by harmlessly"). In emotion-focused therapy (EFT) we might ask the client to identify the intentions of the feelings beneath their behavior, and so on across many different therapeutic approaches.

Thus, how you think about hypnosis (and people, and therapy, and life, and . . . ) will naturally determine how you apply hypnosis. The first lesson anyone studying hypnosis is likely to learn is this: What you focus on, you amplify in your awareness. The salient clinical question is, What do we want the client to focus on, and why? Given the hundreds of therapies out there, this is clearly a primary distinguishing characteristic between therapists.

Regardless of your orientation though, the use of hypnosis is predicated on defining a goal of one sort or another. Hypnosis is an unapologetically goal-oriented approach; it truly is attention with intention. How you establish the goals of treatment is your own subjective process, and the encouragement I provide throughout this book is to better distinguish distracting content from salient process and then build the hypnosis session accordingly.

## Building Process-Oriented Hypnosis Sessions

Whenever you choose to do a hypnosis session with someone, there's a reason why. You have (or should have) a goal in mind, a point you want to make experientially, or an experience of some kind you're hoping to facilitate. Whatever your intent might be, there's an innate structure to hypnosis sessions that provides a means for achieving that goal.

Calling it an innate structure means that whenever you design and deliver a session, it will have all or most of the components listed in Table 3.2.

The generic structure in Table 3.2 provides a skeleton framework for your session, a foundation on which to build the specifics of your approach. Your decisions as to (1) how to define the session's goals; (2) what content you will include, such as which induction to employ and in what suggestion style (i.e., direct or indirect, authoritarian or permissive, etc.); and (3) what problem theme to address with which kinds of suggestions will produce the wide variations in one client's treatment compared to another. So even though you may be treating five different people for anxiety, let's say, what you actually say to each one will vary dramatically depending on their individual needs and patterns of self-organization according to your assessment (e.g., cognitive style, problem-solving style, perceptual style, etc.).

The generic structure components are probably self-explanatory to you as

---

### TABLE 3.2. THE GENERIC STRUCTURE OF HYPNOSIS SESSIONS

- Orient the client to hypnosis
- Induction procedure
- Build a response set
- Introduce therapeutic theme no. 1
- Introduce metaphors on the theme, generally moving from less to more direct
- Optional check-in point: interaction regarding derived meanings
- Introduce therapeutic theme(s), no. 2 (3, etc.)
- Introduce additional metaphors per theme
- Optional check-in points: interaction regarding derived meanings
- Posthypnotic suggestions for integration (contextualize relevant learnings)
- Closure
- Permissive disengagement

an experienced hypnosis practitioner (if not, see Yapko [2019]). However, there might be a few exceptions I want to make clear.

## Response Sets

When I use the phrase "build a response set," I'm acknowledging that most people can't produce hypnotic phenomena such as analgesia or regression instantly on demand. Most people need time to build their hypnotic responsiveness over the course of a session. Thus, paying attention to the deliberate building of response sets is simply a way of increasing the likelihood of catalyzing a positive response to the hypnotic experience. Here's one way to do that: Before asking your client for a specific response, such as analgesia, you allude in a general way to such responses that naturally arise in the course of daily living (e.g., "There are times when someone can be so absorbed in their gardening they don't even notice that they've cut themselves"). The response set moves the client in the direction of generating the desired hypnotic response but not yet suggesting a specific response.

## Therapeutic Themes

When I use the phrase "therapeutic theme," I'm referring to the distilled therapeutic message you're attempting to get across or the frame of mind you're trying to help the client build. What do you want to say to this person that is meant to be helpful? What is the client's misperception or self-limiting belief you want to help them detach from? What empowering resource(s) do you want to associate the client to? By a "distilled message," I mean the essence of your therapeutic advice; in 25 words or less, what do you want to say to this person? I can crystallize the therapeutic messages of each of the 10 chapters of process-oriented hypnosis sessions in this book as follows:

- Learn to recognize and tolerate ambiguity (Chapter 5)
- The future is filled with possibilities (Chapter 6)
- You can learn to make better choices (Chapter 7)
- It's important to anticipate consequences before you act (Chapter 8)
- This part of your experience can be separate from that part (Chapter 9)
- You can be more accepting of how things are instead of fighting against them (Chapter 10)
- You are responsible for the choices you make but not the choices others make (Chapter 11)

- What you do is often more important than what you think or feel (Chapter 12)
- You can develop a code to live by that you feel good about (Chapter 13)
- You can learn to think preventively (Chapter 14)

When you are clear about what the helpful message is you want to convey, then you have established the topic of your therapeutic theme. You can decide whether to use more direct suggestions or more indirect suggestions, as in the use of metaphor, perhaps. The next decision in this regard is how many themes you want to address in a single session. Each of the sessions I've provided have multiple themes embedded within them, and they show a clear progression of ideas as they move toward a resolution. You could quite literally take just one theme, though, and build an entire session around it. The best way to decide how many themes to address in a single process-oriented hypnosis session is to assess your client's attentional style and level of stimulus need. Some people have long attention spans; others have shorter ones. Some people need a lot of stimulation to hold their attention (i.e., more themes), while others are perfectly content to have one idea presented to them and that's enough for today.

## Checking in With the Client During the Hypnosis Session

When I use the phrases, "check in; interaction regarding derived meanings," I'm highlighting how important it is to find out what the client is getting from or understanding from your session. As you've learned, meaning is not in the words you use; rather, meaning is in the person who relates to your words in inevitably idiosyncratic ways. Thus, you can give someone a direct suggestion to go take a walk outside when they feel themselves getting stressed, and all the person hears is a dismissive "Take a hike!" Or you can tell someone a great story about another client with a similar problem, and all they hear is that you talk about your clients in your examples. Then the client gets wrapped up in anxiously wondering whether you'll be using them as an example, and thus never hears whatever the point of your story is.

Talking at clients and hoping they absorb some intended message is an older-style practice of hypnosis, missing the importance of making the session interactional. Some practitioners are afraid that if they check in, they will be disruptive. This is an unnecessary concern; while there may be a momentary lightening of the hypnosis, it is counterbalanced by the value of the feedback you get that allows you proceed even more intensively than before. After all, you're not a mind reader, no matter how skilled you might be. If you want to know what's going on with your client, how they're interpreting your suggestions or what they're experiencing, there's one surefire way to find out—ask! But ask neutrally, that is, without presuppositions about their experience, as in, "Can you describe what you're experiencing?" or "Can you describe what you are aware of?" Questions such as, "What are you feeling now?" or "What thoughts have come to mind?" are leading questions because they orient the client to assessing then reporting on their feelings or cognitions. It is generally best to stay neutral and allow the client to describe their experience without any prompting. Only by checking in with the client during the session can you have any sense as to whether they are deriving anything useful from your session and thereby have the chance to make midstream corrections to your approach if necessary.

## Individualized Versus Scripted Approaches

As the final section of this chapter, I want to address the elephant in the room. Those who know my previous works know that I strongly advocate tailoring the hypnosis session to the client's individual needs. In fact, here's what I wrote on the subject in my hypnosis textbook, *Trancework*:

> Many books and clinical trainings on hypnosis advocate the verbatim use of prepared scripts that have been written for all types of general problems, such as overweight, smoking, phobias, and so on. This suggests that the script is the therapy: reading these words to the hypnotized client will be what effects the cure. The use of scripts promotes the misconception that hypnosis in clinical practice can be standardized and that each client can receive identical treatment as long as they have the same presenting complaint. Reading the same script to all smokers as if they are the same simply because they all share a bad habit is an obvious gross oversimplification. When such an approach fails, typically the client gets blamed, rather than the scripted approach.
>
> The use of scripts robs hypnosis of its real potency, the strength derived from the recognition and use of each individual's unique experiences and needs. Spontaneity and flexibility are essential for best results in doing hypnosis. Even when a therapeutic strategy is worked out beforehand, as good treatment planning may require, a skilled cli-

nician will still incorporate the spontaneous responses of the client into the procedure. (Yapko, 2019, p. 40)

I further wrote, "Using impersonal scripts suggests the power is in the incantation rather than in the quality of the relationship between clinician and client" (p. 49). Clearly, my view is that using verbatim scripts is not as desirable as constructing and delivering more individualized sessions.

So why am I providing 10 full-session transcripts in this volume? While I advocate for a more individualized approach to eliciting hypnosis, I am also aware that when learning a new skill set, in this case doing hypnosis sessions with minimal content, it helps to have models that illustrate those skills. I do not provide these session transcripts so that you will read them verbatim to your clients. Rather, I provide them as a generic structure upon which you can elaborate. I think the artist Picasso got it right when he said, "Learn the rules like a pro so you can break them like an artist."

Stephen R. Lankton, a highly experienced and perceptive clinician and the editor in chief of the *American Journal of Clinical Hypnosis,* took on the issue of using scripts in an editorial in a recent issue of the journal:

Being an *expert* in a martial art requires that one follow heuristics and not follow scripts. Human behavior changes quickly, and the clinician's appropriate responses must also adapt and change quickly. Yet, the key word in that sentence is "expert." No one begins as an expert.. . . . Students learning piano practice chords and scales, ballet students learn fundamental classic postures, yoga teachers learn well defined asanas and scripted dialogue, and future math geniuses begin by learning the rules of algebra, trig, matrix geometry, and calculus. In other words, beginning students in any field of art or science are tasked to follow well defined rules, programs, and scripts. Experts aren't meant to robotically act or recite these basic forms (other than in an educational setting), they are meant to elaborate, individualize, and build upon them. (2020, p. 173)

The session transcripts provided in later chapters can best be viewed in this light: You are encouraged to use and further develop your expertise and go beyond the words and ideas I've shared. But my hope is that these will inspire you and help you to break the rules like an artist.

# Final Point

In this chapter, I have identified many of the nuts and bolts of clinical intervention involving a process-oriented hypnosis. It bears repeating that no book, no person, no scientific study can tell you exactly what to say or when and how to say it best to a particular client. Ultimately, the only person that can give you the salient feedback about what works is your client. And what works for one individual may be quite different from what works for another. It can be a great help to know that using your words to stimulate the client's inner associations, that is, to build new subjective understandings and linkages, is what makes for successful sessions. That's true for therapy in general and equally true for process-oriented hypnosis as well.

# Chapter 4

# Targeting Symptomatic Sequences with Kind and Gentle Interruptions

*Human resources are like natural resources; they're often buried deep. You have to go looking for them; they're not just lying around on the surface. You have to create the circumstances where they show themselves.*

—Sir Kenneth Robinson

## Setting the Stage for Process-Oriented Hypnosis Sessions

Is the goal of therapy to reduce pathology or to expand wellness? There is a substantial difference between focusing on what's wrong with someone and focusing on what's right with someone. Whatever problems the client might have, they are more than their problems. They are more than their history, more than their feelings, and more than their biology. The primary challenge in doing therapy well is this: How do we help our clients expand their focus beyond their symptoms and encourage them to use more of their resources in life-enhancing ways?

Anyone who practices clinical hypnosis does so with the firmly entrenched and therapeutically invaluable belief that people have many more abilities than they consciously realize. Hypnosis engenders an entirely optimistic appraisal of people in practitioners because of the things that happen in sessions that are often nothing short of amazing. I can't count how many times I've either watched or conducted a demonstration where the client is doing something that seems so improbable (such as controlling blood flow to a particular body part or suddenly and dramatically breaking free from some lifelong burdensome perception) that all I can think to myself is, "No way!" Except, there is a way, and they're showing it to me right then and there.

Hypnosis creates a focused, energized, high-powered context for people to explore, discover, and use more of their innate abilities. Hypnosis isn't the therapy, and hypnosis itself cures nothing. Rather, hypnosis is the vehicle for connecting (associating) people to the abilities and realizations that ultimately serve to help them. More to the point, it isn't the experience of hypnosis itself or the spoken words that are therapeutic. Rather, it's what happens during hypnosis in terms of developing new and helpful associations that has the potential to be therapeutic.

All of the session transcripts in the remaining chapters have therapeutic potential through offering suggestions that revolve around these practical questions:

1. How can we, the client and I, cocreate a safe and growth-oriented context that promotes experiential learning?
2. How can we identify which underdeveloped or latent resources may be accessible in a given individual's experience of hypnosis?
3. How can we structure the development of new therapeutic resources previously unknown and undeveloped in the client?
4. How can we bring these new or previously inaccessible resources forth at the times and places they will best serve the client's needs?

These four questions offer a sound framework for organizing your interventions and give greater substance to one of the simplest ways to describe the process of therapy: pattern interruption and pattern building. After all, any intervention will strive in some way to help the client stop or do less of some problematic response while encouraging the client to start or do more of some more effective and life-enhancing response.

What this chapter is about, then, is introducing these pattern interruptions and new patterns to build in ways that are kind and gentle. The reasons why kind and gentle matter are likely to be self-evident, but all build on the recognition that people learn best and grow in the healthiest of ways when the environment supports them in doing so. I especially like the way Milton Erickson used to describe good therapists. To paraphrase, he said, "A good therapist is the weather . . . someone who provides a good climate for change."

Toward that end, in this chapter I address five such kind and gentle approaches routinely embedded in process-oriented hypnosis sessions: (1) dissociation, association, and automaticity; (2) accessing and contextualizing resources; (3) reframing; (4) therapeutic metaphors; and (5) seeding assignments. It is important to point out that in the same way the power of a suggestion isn't in the words but is in the person's response to those words, the power of these techniques is in the person's response, not the technique itself. Thus, the issue of responsiveness to hypnosis is of obvious importance.

## Addressing Hypnotic Responsiveness

The mere fact that the client is focused or absorbed in the experience of hypnosis does not mean they will necessarily respond to or integrate anything the clinician has to say. The clinician provides opportunities for the client to absorb something meaningful by employing carefully worded suggestions that have the potential to be helpful. The new understandings, the new associations or links the client forms while attending to the clinician's suggestions, represent the potential benefits of treatment during hypnosis. No matter how deeply hypnotized someone might be, if the suggestions aren't relevant and meaningful to the client, they will have little or no therapeutic effect.

There aren't very many things about hypnosis that all experts agree upon, but this is one of those few points of agreement: People vary widely in their ability to respond meaningfully to hypnosis. Why that is and what it means about individual differences is the subject of serious scientific debate, with reasonable hypotheses asserted by a wide array of experts that may challenge and even contradict each other. Even the terminology associated with this issue is open for discussion. Are we talking about hypnotizability? Suggestibility? Hypnotic susceptibility? Hypnotic responsiveness? Hypnotic talent? Capacity for absorption? Attentional style? All of these terms are used by different experts who share the goal of wanting to define, describe, explain, and measure the differences between individuals' responses to hypnosis. The topic is inherently fascinating but also has implications beyond the practice of hypnosis. Why are some therapy clients so responsive and others less so? Is this a fixed trait or is it malleable?

It has become quite clear that, despite the great many attempts in the last

100 years to measure and predict hypnotic responsiveness with scores of well-conceived so-called hypnotizability tests, no one can predict with any certainty whether or how someone will respond to your hypnotic methods. If you want to find out how someone will respond to hypnosis, then do hypnosis.

For me personally, I think the most practical position to take regarding the differences across individuals in the context of psychotherapy is one of therapeutic curiosity. As I begin a session, very often my first words, even preceding the induction itself, are, "I don't know." I might say, "I don't know what the most comfortable position is that will allow you to sit most comfortably. . . . I don't know at just what moment you'll find that you want to let your eyes close. . . . I don't know just what you'll discover during the course of this session that can be meaningful and helpful to you. . . ."

You'll notice the presuppositions and indirect suggestions in these "I don't know" suggestions, but I'm also making a statement that is undeniably true: I really don't know. And it's a statement that reflects my curiosity about you and what you'll do, when you'll do it, and how you'll do it. How valuable is it to the therapeutic alliance to have your client feel you are genuinely curious about them and that you have faith that they can respond well and grow from the experience? Many clients will describe how they feel held by the therapist in the experience, meaning valued, supported, and treated as capable in ways they couldn't see in themselves until then. So, as you move from the interview to the induction of hypnosis phase, you can be curious about the client's hypnotic abilities and how you might help him or her connect to those abilities. This is a way to positively reinforce the development and use of whatever natural hypnotic talents the client might have to whatever degree they have them.

## Dissociation, Association, and Automaticity in Process-Oriented Hypnosis

Dissociation has too often been considered by clinicians only in terms of psychopathology, where it has been applied by individuals in ways that are terribly disruptive to their lives. However, as is generally true of all hypnotic phenomena, what is harmful in one context can be helpful in another. When therapeutic dissociations are encouraged in hypnosis, they amplify some element of experience and thereby simultaneously also deamplify another element of experience. If I suggest that you look over here and amplify that in your awareness, at the same time I'm diverting you away from looking over there and deamplifying that in your awareness.

Dissociation is defined as the breaking down of global experiences into their component parts. As I briefly mentioned earlier, dissociation involves a separation of subjective elements of experience from one another. When there is some association, or link, between two or more elements of experience that are detrimental (e.g., the sound of a siren instantly takes you back to when you had a terrible accident), gently interrupting that connection is a worthy therapeutic goal.

Table 4.1 offers examples of dissociation on different dimensions of experience that highlight their potential therapeutic value. Consider how each form of dissociation could be of benefit in helping someone overcome a related issue.

As soon as you begin an induction and encourage clients to detach from their usual experience of themselves (e.g., "You can detach from the external environment now as you turn your focus inwardly"), you're suggesting dissociation. As soon as you start to talk to people about different parts of their experience (e.g., "Part of you feels optimistic about progressing and another part of you is curious about just how that will happen"), you are suggesting dissociation. Each of the dissociation types listed in Table 4.1 has the potential to be useful in helping the client subjectively move away from what is hurting

---

### TABLE 4.1. VARIETIES OF THERAPEUTIC DISSOCIATION

- *Cognitive* elements (as in separating thoughts from feelings)
- *Physical* elements (as in separating the painful limb from the rest of the body)
- *Behavioral* elements (as in separating someone's behavior from its underlying intentions)
- *Temporal* elements (as in separating the painful past from the hopeful future)
- *Relational* elements (as in separating someone's minor flaws from their overall worth as a person)
- *Emotional* elements (as in separating feelings from choice of action)
- *Self-definition* elements (as in separating one's income level from one's sense of worth)

or limiting them and moving toward (i.e., associating to) some other quality of experience that can help them. Careful analysis of the session transcripts provided throughout the remaining chapters will provide many examples of dissociative and associative suggestions. You'll likely notice how gently these suggestions are offered throughout.

What makes dissociations in hypnosis so integral to the therapeutic process? Dissociation allows for the automaticity of hypnotic responses, meaning the involuntary or nonvolitional nature of people generating hypnotic phenomena. It is nothing short of extraordinary, for example, to offer clients suggestions for complex experiences such as age regression or sensory alterations and have them spontaneously produce such experiences without any sense of conscious or intentional effort. Automaticity leads the client to subjectively report, "It just happened." Neuroscientists have taken on the challenge of explaining how that impressive response "just happened." So far, a definitive answer has been most elusive.

Related to the automaticity of suggested responses arising during the course of a session is the automaticity of responses following the hypnosis session. As you might recall from Chapter 3's delineation of the sequential components of a generic hypnosis session, posthypnotic suggestions are an integral part of the process. You'll see them included in every one of the session transcripts and for good reason: posthypnotic suggestions encourage a carry-over from the session into the rest of the person's life. It's the primary vehicle for gently but deliberately extending the gains made during the session into those situations where the client would most benefit from them. And it helps generate the therapeutic progress clients report following hypnosis sessions when they say, "It just happened."

## Accessing and Contextualizing Resources

The process of hypnotically accessing and contextualizing resources brings to life the belief that people have more strengths and resources than they realize. This is particularly valuable when clients are preoccupied with their symptoms and feeling powerless, the antithesis of feeling resourceful. It is truly a positive psychology in action.

The essence of the strategy is to listen to clients do what they naturally do, which is tell you their story, their personal history. As you listen to them describe significant events and relationships, you can easily find examples of strengths they've used in the past that they never really thought of as strengths (e.g., they liked playing sports or doing crafts as a kid but never thought about what that says in terms of their competitive spirit or creativity). So you hear their story and identify resources from their experience that they evidently used well, which may be the very same resources that would be helpful to counter the problem situation. This is the phase of accessing resources. When you identify and actually name those resources and extend them into the problem situation as a better way of managing it, this is the phase of contextualizing resources.

Age regression is used to recall or revivify some meaningful episode from the past; resources are identified and named, such as courage, creativity, or perseverance; and then age progression is utilized to gently integrate those resources into some trouble spot in such a way that the resources would lead to new helpful perspectives, reactions, and behaviors. Table 4.2 provides a more detailed but generic structure for this empowering process.

When people associate to (reconnect with) their own resources, inarguably present in their history from the examples they unwittingly shared with you

---

### TABLE 4.2. A GENERIC STRUCTURE FOR HYPNOTICALLY ACCESSING AND CONTEXTUALIZING RESOURCES

- Induction procedure
- Build response set regarding memory (orient to general experience)
- Age regression to a specific memory
- Ideomotor signal (such as a raised finger) indicating memory retrieved
- Suggestions to facilitate verbalization
- Verbal interaction regarding memory
- Identify specific resources in past context as you listen to the memory description
- Consolidate resources (name the resources that were evident in the memory)
- Orient to the future and extend those resources into desired contexts
- Posthypnotic suggestions for integration
- Closure and disengagement

through their personal narratives, it is often a moving and transformative experience for them. It is an exceptionally kind way to orient people to the realization that they are stronger than they think and not as helpless as they may have come to believe. This is the empowerment that process-oriented hypnosis can provide.

## Reframing

The meaning of an event or a communication is determined in part by the context in which it appears. Its meaning is also determined in part by the meaning someone assigned to it. When there is a mismatch between what actually happened and how someone interpreted it, the result can be most unfortunate. In fact, this is the basis for the various cognitive approaches to therapy, most notably CBT. In these approaches, it is a constant theme of therapy to tell clients in no uncertain terms that their thoughts about the events and people in their lives are partially or entirely incorrect, that is, the product of so-called cognitive distortions.

What necessitates helping people shift their interpretations and subsequent reactions (i.e., emotions, behavior) is encapsulated in a single word: ambiguity. This is the topic of Chapter 5, the first intervention chapter, because the phenomenon of ambiguity is at the core of life experiences, both good and bad. Ambiguity means there is no innate meaning, no single interpretation that fully or even adequately explains some issue or occurrence. When dealing with something concrete and definable (e.g., "This is a chair"), ambiguity isn't much of an issue. But when the issue or occurrence is abstract and can be interpreted in many different ways (e.g., "How do you conceptualize spirituality?"), the ambiguity will inevitably lead to differences of opinion—different perceptual frames—in what it means. Sometimes the opinions one forms can be quite self-damaging, and these become the targets of therapeutic intervention. They are the hurtful or self-limiting viewpoints about self, others, life, the universe, everything that become the basis for reframing in hypnosis. When the same action or event can be interpreted in a number of plausible ways, helping the client let go of an interpretation that hurts in order to accept one that helps is the process of reframing. You can clearly see the role of dissociation and association in this approach.

With the turn of a phrase, especially during hypnosis, liabilities can be turned into assets, traumatic events can be converted into learning experiences, weaknesses can be turned into strengths, and so forth. Reframing can be accomplished with a single remark, or can involve a lengthier, more experientially absorbing hypnotic experience. Any approach that encourages the client to have a different perspective on the problem involves a reframe. As soon as you say, "You can look at it this way . . . ," you're attempting a reframe.

An underlying assumption in doing reframing as an intervention strategy is that every thought, feeling, or behavior has some positive value somewhere, but not everywhere. More often than not, clients' problems arise when they reflexively use only their feelings or past experiences to guide them and miss the cues from the environment that would have told them, "Not now. Not here." This is a primary means of teaching discrimination strategies to the client, the subject of Chapter 7.

People typically have good intentions (e.g., always being generous to others), but then employ a strategy that works against them (e.g., being painfully taken advantage of by manipulative or abusive others). By taking an experience that the client views negatively (e.g., "I guess I'm just an easy mark") and commenting on how and why that same experience might actually be an asset to him or her somewhere else (e.g., "Your generous nature will be appreciated, not abused, by the people who feel grateful rather than entitled"), one can change the client's attitude about that experience. It's then no longer a problem of being too generous; rather, it's reframed as a problem of being too generous with the wrong people. The problem can be solved by learning to distinguish who is and who isn't deserving of this generosity. Reframing is particularly helpful when suggestions for new and better alternatives are gently offered for replacing whatever perspective the client held that wasn't working very well. The reframe says, in essence, "It isn't that you're pathological; it's the way you're going about it that's ineffective in that context." It sets the stage for the hypnosis sessions that suggest, "You can do something different when what you're doing isn't working."

Finding a way to turn a minus into a plus, or vice versa, if appropriate, is a basic part of clinical work. It's an exceptionally kind way of helping people get past frustration and self-condemnation as they come to learn how to read situational cues better and that their perceptions can be more malleable.

## Therapeutic Metaphors

In this section, the focus is on stories delivered during hypnosis as a vehicle of therapy. These stories, known as therapeutic metaphors in the domain of hypnosis, can be told for a variety of reasons that all serve to help move the client forward in the direction of a goal. The stories have direction and purpose.

The use of therapeutic metaphor is a core component of most modern hypnotic processes, a lasting tribute to the influence of Milton Erickson on the field of hypnosis. His use of folksy teaching tales with his patients was a great innovation at a time when other hypnosis practitioners were uniformly direct and authoritarian in their methods. Erickson viewed stories as a kinder and gentler way of making a point than the more common approach in his era of adopting the demeanor of an authority who will straightforwardly tell you what to do and who is not to be questioned. Erickson's observation is a pretty simple one: Most people don't like to be told what to do even when it's clearly in their best interest. So, the ability to tell stories that in some ways parallel the client's experience such that they can learn from the story is an easily integrated pattern interrupter and pattern builder in process-oriented hypnosis.

It isn't quality that necessarily defines a good story for therapy. Any story that has a message worth telling, no matter where it comes from, has potential therapeutic value. It can be a piece of gossip or a funny or sad story on the nightly news. But a story only has value as a teaching tool to the extent that someone is able and willing to engage with it. Otherwise, the story passes through our awareness with no substantive connection, and so the message is lost. This is why the context—the weather—the therapist creates is crucial in determining whether a story goes over well or just crashes and burns (metaphorically speaking).

Hypnosis lends itself to creating a context of meaning. Hypnosis can give a story an aura of gravitas that may not be present in just a casual telling of that same story outside of hypnosis. Hypnosis encourages focus, and the premise for the hypnotic interaction is that the clinician has something to say that's worth focusing on and absorbing. The implicit message is, "I'm telling you this story for a reason." This is what activates the therapeutic value of stories through a process called the search for relevance. The client accepts the premise that there's a reason why you're taking the time during the hypnosis session to tell a story. The client accepts the premise that there is a personal relevance that needs to be acknowledged at some level. This is one of the many paradoxes in hypnosis: "I'm going to tell you a story that isn't about you. But it really is about you, which is why I'm telling it." The search for how the story might be relevant and helpful begins.

Generally speaking, the most common use of metaphor in the context of psychotherapy is to suggest potential solutions for resolving the client's problems. It's as if you are saying, "Here's the dilemma the person in the story faces that, not coincidentally, parallels the dilemma you face, and here is how they resolved it . . . so maybe you could do something similar."

There is a great deal to be said about constructing and delivering therapeutic metaphors well (see Burns, 2001, 2007; Yapko, 2019, for in-depth considerations of this topic). Suffice it to say here that good stories aren't personally threatening to the client and can engage them in considering new perspectives and possibilities. They are not only gentle and indirect; they are also process oriented, as you will see in the session transcripts that follow.

## Seeding Assignments

Realistically, when so much of therapy involves education and specific skill building, there needs to be some vehicle for helping clients acquire the education and skills they need and then actually use them in their everyday lives. Homework assignments are a primary vehicle for promoting the acquisition and integration of new perspectives and skills beyond the therapy room. They are intended to encourage new behaviors, the development of specific new skills that have been undeveloped or underdeveloped, test out the accuracy of one's perceptions, and amplify particular thoughts, feelings, and behaviors that the clinician judges important to the therapy. Homework assignments operate on the level of actual direct experience, a more powerful level than the merely intellectual. Homework helps people integrate new learnings on multiple levels. And by doing homework, the client has to expend effort, increasing the likelihood that they will place a greater value on the therapy.

A large body of research evidence makes it clear that clients have a faster rate and better quality of result when therapies include the use of structured homework. There are many different types of homework assignments such as role-plays, symptom prescriptions, ambiguous function tasks, skill-building tasks, and externalization strategies, to name just a few. The challenges to the clinician are about knowing what to assign and when, taking care to make sure the assignment is safe, relevant, acceptable, and instructive for the client. But when clients aren't inclined to be proactive in their own behalf, even waiting passively for you to fix them, getting the client to carry out homework assignments can be difficult.

Negative expectations that inspire a "Why bother?" attitude can easily preclude a willingness to do the assignment, so building a positive expectancy is important (see Chapter 6). Strategic therapist and family therapy pioneer Jay Haley called this process of introducing the homework assignment during the hypnosis session "seeding" (1973, p. 34). By orienting the client to the necessity of doing things differently in order to get better outcomes and using illustrative metaphors to that effect, the clinician can plant the seed that frames action as desirable and likely to produce positive results. This is a powerful means for motivating client action (see Chapter 12). The clinician can think in these terms: Where can I send the client and what can I ask them to do that will help them acquire the perspective and skills to help catalyze therapeutic progress?

The literature of strategic, action-oriented therapies contains a treasure trove of creative and helpful homework assignments. These can be useful in helping clinicians generate relevant homework assignments that can teach specific skills (such as coping, problem solving, and social skills) to clients needing help developing such skills. During hypnosis the client is oriented to the aims of the skill and the benefits of acquiring it, perhaps even doing an age progression to a time of actively carrying out the assignment, what might be called an experiential rehearsal. Posthypnotic suggestions for doing the assignment and being curious about what will be experienced or discovered are invaluable. Then, after the hypnosis session ends, the clinician can assign the real-life skill-building task.

## Closure

I clearly hold a professional and personal value that leads me to emphasize the process-oriented strategies I've presented here as kind and gentle. I am a firm believer that people, all people, can do better than they're doing, can aspire to more. Human potential, to me, isn't just an empty phrase, it's a call to action. When so many people are struggling in their lives for any of a number of reasons, including the aftereffects of a global pandemic, economic recession, political instability, social division, and so many other debilitating events that affect us all directly and indirectly, the need for mental health professionals of all types has never been greater. The need for kind and gentle methods that can inspire and heal has also never been greater.

# Part II

# The Methods of Process-Oriented Hypnosis

### A Note About Generic Session Structures

In each of the following 10 chapters, I provide session transcripts that are richly detailed yet must still be considered generic. They are meant to illustrate how a process-oriented hypnosis session might be structured and delivered while addressing a particular issue, but I do not intend for them to be read to the client verbatim. Instead you can consider ways you might adapt the session to the needs of individual clients. Not only will the content of your verbalizations vary according to the unique attributes of each individual client, but the steps themselves may vary according to what needs more or less amplification in the client's experience. As always, it is a matter of clinical judgment what a particular client is likely to respond to best. The more feedback from the client a clinician uses in formulating an approach, the more likely the interaction can be tailored appropriately.

# Chapter 5

# Recognizing and Tolerating Ambiguity

*Don't ask the meaning of life. Life is asking the meaning of you.*
—Viktor Frankl

## The Case of Lisa

Only 13 years old, Lisa is already wise beyond her years. A smart, sensitive girl, Lisa has been brought to therapy by her father, who is quite concerned about the high level of anxiety she is experiencing. Lisa has "always been a bit of a worrier," Dad reports, but lately her level of worry has been reaching new heights. He's not sure why but speculates that maybe she is suffering some aftereffects of her mom and dad having divorced three years earlier. Though difficult for her at first, he thought she adjusted reasonably well to the back-and-forth of their shared custody.

Interviewing Lisa, she was open and engaging, seemingly quite happy to have the chance to talk to someone about what was bothering her lately. She came right out with it when she said, "I'm stuck at home now because of the coronavirus lockdown. My school is closed. I can't see my friends in person, and all I can think of is how the virus is going to kill everybody I love." She got teary-eyed for a moment, but just a moment, and then asked directly, "What if everyone I love dies? What if I get the virus and I'm the one who gives it to my mom and dad, and they die? What if I don't know I have the virus and I give it to people, and they die? What if . . . ?"

With each "what if?" question, Lisa became increasingly agitated and finally had what amounted to a mild panic attack. There was no mistaking how anxious and afraid she was.

Is this about her cognitive distortion of catastrophizing? Is this about a crippling fear of death, either her own or that of her parents? Or a further loss of the unfulfilled need for secure attachments? Is she an adolescent dealing with identity issues of dependence and independence? Is this a delayed grief reaction to her parents' divorce? Or a fear of an imminent loss of control? Or what?

How Lisa generates her anxiety was demonstrated clearly right in front of me. Long before the COVID-19 pandemic, she was already a "worrier," as described by her dad and as she affirmed. Previously, though, her worries were more mundane: "What if I fail the math test? What if my new teacher doesn't like me? What if the other kids on the soccer team don't think I'm good enough?"

Now that her worries have risen to a life-or-death set of questions related to the coronavirus, Lisa's anxiety level has risen right along with them. The content of Lisa's anxiety relates to the virus and who might die and how she might be the unwitting cause of their death. The process of how Lisa generates her anxiety is straightforward: She asks unanswerable questions about all the uncertainties associated with the pandemic and then fills in the knowledge gaps with her greatest fears, making them seem both real and imminent. No wonder she's overwhelmed emotionally. And this has been her pattern all along, whether wondering if she'll pass the math test, will be liked by her new teacher, or whether her teammates will think of her favorably.

Lisa's questions are not pathological. Her concerns are legitimate. But she has already developed a ruminative coping style, facing the ambiguities of life by endlessly asking herself scary questions that she has no ability to answer definitively. Because she is unable to answer these "what if?" questions definitively, the questions hang in the air as imminent threats to her well-being and the well-being of those she loves. It overwhelms her emotionally by seeming to be both horrible and entirely unmanageable.

Rumination as a coping style is the target of the process-oriented hypnosis session. What she ruminates about, the issue du jour, will routinely change across circumstances, but the pattern of asking "what if?" questions and then spinning those same questions around and around will persist without treatment. Learning to recognize and tolerate ambiguity, developing clarity about what can and can't be answered, requires a shift of focus: instead of imagining things being horrible and unmanageable, the focus turns to identifying what resources you have to cope with the uncertainty and eventual outcomes. By amplifying awareness for her resources, Lisa can learn to answer the "what if?" questions with some variation of, "If that happens, it would be bad . . . but I'll manage it." It's a big and healthy leap to go from "I can't handle it" to "I hope I don't ever have to handle it, but if I need to I will." That level of self-awareness and self-trust as an effective problem solver is the aim of using process-oriented hypnosis to help anxious and ruminative clients learn to recognize and tolerate ambiguity.

## The Role of Ambiguity in Quality of Life

The field of psychological testing has developed many tests over the decades, including that class known as projective tests, which includes sentence completion tests, the enigmatic pictures of the Thematic Apperception Test, the Draw-a-Person Test, and, perhaps most famous of them all, the inkblots of the Rorschach Test. The Rorschach Test presents the test subject with a series of inkblots on cards and asks the person to describe what they see in the inkblot. The inkblots don't have any innate meaning but invite projections from the test subject. Where else but from within the client's own mind through the mechanism of projection can these interpretations of and reactions to the inkblots come from? The Rorschach is a pretty old test, but it still offers us this valuable insight: In the face of uncertainty about an ambiguous stimulus in the form of an inkblot, people will *reflexively* form interpretations about the inkblot's meaning. But the pattern of making meaning—the process of projection—goes well beyond mere inkblots. It shapes much of one's life experience, including the symptomatic experiences that distress people and may even bring them into therapy.

Consider your response to this question: What is the most ambiguous stimulus every human being faces? When I ask this question of groups of people, usually therapists, they might offer answers such as, "what happens after we die," or even just "other people." These are good answers and bring into sharp focus how different people's projections can be about the meaning of life experiences.

Ernest Hilgard, one of the great founding fathers of experimental hypnosis, once described hypnosis to me as "believed-in imagination" (personal communication, August 14, 1988). That is an astute framing on his part, capturing both the essence and spirit of hypnosis. To go a step further than just the hypnotic interaction, though, one could also say that everyone's view of life is similarly a product of "believed-in imagination."

That's why my own answer to that question is life: Life is the most ambiguous stimulus we all face. One could even say life is an experiential Rorschach blot! Life doesn't have an innate meaning. We give it meaning through the choices we make. Out of all the things you could have done with your life, why did you make the choices you made that have brought you to where you currently are in your life? All of the choices we make—what job to take or what profession to pursue, whether to be single or married, whether to work out regularly or just eat more pizza on the couch—these are all choices we make in the face of the uncertainty in the question, what do I want my life to be about? Some people's response to the Rorschach of life is never to even ask that question.

From the ambiguous stimulus of life, one person forms a belief that life is wondrous and joyful, while another forms the belief that life is a miserable burden to endure. These represent two radically different believed-in imaginations that have specific and measurable mental health consequences for each individual. We give it meaning through the choices we make and then we live with the consequences that follow, for better or worse.

From this vantage point, it is easy to see how ambiguity may well be the most powerful and pervasive risk factor of all known risk factors for a wide variety of mental health issues. Ambiguity in this context refers to the lack of clear meaning associated with one's various life experiences. Events occur; we observe them occurring; but what we most often don't know with any degree of certainty is what, if anything, they mean. The great majority of events in life do not have a clear and inherent meaning, leaving each of us the task of having to establish for ourselves, through the mechanism of projection, our own subjective interpretation of what the meaning or significance is of the event. The quality of the meanings we form with our projections provides them with their emotional valence, the degree of comfort or distress they generate and the decisions that they lead us to make.

Beyond real events that may be ambiguous, imagined events may also invite our projections: We have a job interview next week, for example, and we imagine the interviewer forming a negative impression that precludes our getting the job, thereby raising our anxiety level about the interview. Or we imagine being on an airplane that crashes and thereby generate a sense of panic about the prospect of flying. Daily life experience presents us with endless opportunities to project meanings that can generate depression, anxiety, low self-esteem, destructive relationships, and much, much more.

## Coping with Ambiguity . . . Badly

In Chapter 2, I highlighted the point that people tend to know much less than they think they do. That observation becomes especially evident when people form firm, unyielding opinions about things they can't possibly be certain about because certainty doesn't exist there. How can you be certain as to what God's plan is for the Middle East? Or why reincarnation isn't possible? Or what Abraham Lincoln would have done if he'd lived? Much more personally, how can you know with certainty that you're capable of being perfect and that you must be self-hating until you are? How can you know for certain that you won't get a job you're actually well qualified for, so there's no need to apply for it?

Why can't people willingly and with self-awareness sidestep the vulnerability of their own beliefs? Consider as an example the so-called cognitive distortion of jumping to conclusions, the error of reaching a conclusion despite the lack of any supportive evidence. Why jump to conclusions if not merely to have a conclusion? But the salient question is, why have so strong a need for a conclusion? What is it about ambiguity that is so uncomfortable and compelling in the force it generates to reach a conclusion, even at the risk of reaching an incorrect one or, worse, one that actually causes emotional harm? From this vantage point, you can appreciate why the ability to recognize when a question is unanswerable in an objective sense (e.g., is there a God?) and then to accept "I don't know" as a legitimate answer instead of just making up something that you choose to believe is exceptionally sophisticated.

For the person who is deeply uncomfortable with ambiguity, it poses another risk: the negative coping style called rumination. Rumination means spinning around the same thoughts over and over without getting anywhere. It's endless analysis at the expense of taking sensible action. Rumination is based on the subjective perception that if you analyze the ambiguity long enough, clarity will emerge. Thus, people who ruminate think that they are taking action, but that is only illusory and most often simply perpetuates asking even more questions that can't be answered (e.g., "What if I always feel this way?").

Rumination is very strongly correlated with increased symptoms of anxiety and depression. The topic of taking action and how action is a necessary counter to passivity is explored in depth in Chapter 12.

## Typical Problems Derived From a Lack of Tolerance for Ambiguity

The types of problems that people might present for treatment that reflect an inability to recognize and tolerate ambiguity can seem quite diverse, and may include such problematic patterns as:

- Jumping to conclusions without evidence just to have a conclusion
- Rigid thought patterns of feeling certain about things you can't possibly be certain about
- Inability to admit not knowing something
- Feeling anxious or nervous about what might happen that will be overwhelming
- Feeling unable to cope with some stressor
- Spinning around the same thoughts without reaching a meaningful conclusion
- Expecting and even demanding that things be as they were, resisting the need to adapt
- Excessive reassurance seeking from others
- Overreliance on others' opinions about what to do
- Overanalyzing actions and conversations for their true meaning

These patterns represent the kinds of problems clients might present that all reflect a lack of tolerance for ambiguity. The content of what they want help with is what they will naturally describe to the therapist, but it is up to the therapist to recognize the client's inability to recognize and tolerate ambiguity as the process needing intervention.

## Defining the Salient Therapeutic Targets

For as long as an individual is unable to tolerate uncertainty, they will be motivated to continue forming meanings about life experience with little or no insight into the interpretive process, and thus suffer the mood and other consequences (e.g., anxiety) when these meanings are negatively distorted yet accepted as true. Thus, one of the most basic goals in treating therapy clients in general, and anxious and depressed clients in particular, is to teach them how to recognize and tolerate ambiguity. This goal even precedes identifying specific cognitive distortions or irrational beliefs in the client. Before teaching someone to avoid jumping to conclusions (or personalizing, thinking dichotomously, or forming any other cognitive distortion), that person would have to become more comfortable with having no conclusions, that is, reduce their drive to have a definite answer. By addressing the issue of ambiguity in therapy and making it a primary target of a specific process-oriented hypnotic intervention, the larger goals of therapy, such as teaching rational thinking skills, as in cognitive therapy, can be well facilitated.

The primary therapeutic goals of a process-oriented approach, therefore, are to (1) learn how to quickly recognize ambiguity in situations; (2) be on guard against one's own tendency to interpret such events in some patterned and hurtful way that may not be objectively true; and (3) develop a tolerance for ambiguity that permits comfort with not knowing. Not knowing what's

---

**TABLE 5.1. GENERIC SESSION STRUCTURE FOR RECOGNIZING AND TOLERATING AMBIGUITY**

**Induction**

| | |
|---|---|
| **Response set:** | Uncertainty |
| **Theme 1:** | The value of knowing and not knowing |
| **Theme 2:** | Accepting not knowing |
| **Theme 3:** | What you focus on, you amplify |
| **Theme 4:** | Recognizing and interrupting the process of projection |

**Posthypnotic suggestions for integration**
**Closure and disengagement**

right or what's true in a given context can be either empowering or victimizing, depending on one's perspective. Not knowing can be an empowering spur to finding out. Table 5.1 provides a generic structure for using hypnosis to encourage a client's developing greater comfort with uncertainty.

## SESSION TRANSCRIPT

### Induction
You can begin by taking in a few deep relaxing breaths. . . . Orient yourself now to internal experience for a while. . . . Right here, right now, what I most want to encourage is you having an experience that's worthy of your time . . . worthy of your attention . . . an experience that allows you to discover something of value about yourself, about life, about something that's meaningful. . . .

### Building a Response Set Regarding Uncertainty
Of course, here at the beginning, there's really *no way for you to know* just what I'm going to be suggesting, just what possibilities I'm going to encourage. . . . And can anyone looking at you . . . really know . . . the depth of your experience? . . . It's so limited . . . to think in terms of measurements or even brain scans. . . . Someone monitoring your brain . . . as you *grow more relaxed* . . . might correctly point out . . . how one part of your brain becomes more active . . . or another part becomes less active . . . yet have no knowledge at all . . . of what you're actually experiencing inside. . . . And in that respect, . . . it's what's so wonderful . . . about being connected to your own experience . . . the privilege of being the only person *anywhere* . . . who knows what it feels like for you . . . to *breathe comfortably* . . . to feel your body . . . *growing more relaxed* . . . and there is something special about that . . . of all the things that define you . . . as an individual . . . physically separate and distinct from others . . . and unique in your history. . . . But as always . . . what we see is a product of the lens we look through . . . the framework of our values and biases we use quite unconsciously . . . to see ourselves . . . or to see the world around us . . . whether it's the lens of biology . . .for explaining ourselves . . . or the lens of humanities. . . . What lens do *you* use at a given

moment . . . and with what realization as a result? . . . And your usual ways of viewing and experiencing yourself . . . afford you the chance to develop many understandings and insights about yourself . . . and about life. . . . But you know and I know . . . there are things about ourselves . . . we don't know. Things we do know, we don't really understand. . . . That little bit of mystery . . . that little bit of uncertainty . . . is something each of us builds a relationship with. . . . It's a curious thing . . . how you come to know . . . what you don't know . . . times you discover that what you thought you knew turned out to be incorrect . . . and likewise . . . how you come to know . . . and come to terms with knowing . . . that there are some things you'll never know. . . . Now, it's a curious thing to me that we spend so much of our lives striving to know . . . *desperately* at times striving to know . . . and for some people, it turns into a mission . . . to try and know the unknowable . . . the people who want to know whether you can weigh a human soul . . . or the people who want to know whether you can measure . . . how much you love your family. . . .

## Theme: The Value of Knowing and Not Knowing

Wanting to know is a powerful driving force . . . that helps us better understand the world around us . . . and the people in it, too . . . including ourselves. . . . But as you may discover, there's also a value in *not* knowing. . . . There are lots of examples that I can give you where it's a great advantage to realize you don't know . . . and an even greater advantage to know that you're not going to know. . . . As comfortable as I would want you to feel right now with knowing where this session is going . . . it might well begin to occur to you what a great skill it is to be equally comfortable not knowing. . . . After all, you don't know which ideas I'm going to introduce to you will be the ones that help transform aspects of how you live. . . . You don't know which ideas I'm going to offer you will prove to be enlightening. . . . What a pleasure not to know . . . and to have a sense of curiosity and willingness to discover. . . . When you get so comfortable not knowing, it allows you a universe of possibilities . . . to explore new viewpoints . . . to seek out new explanations for things you think you already understand. . . . There may be something that you can think of now that you know you don't currently know the answer to . . . perhaps a question that you can openly acknowledge to yourself that you don't know the answer to . . . and you may not ever know

the answer to . . . questions that may be by their very nature unanswerable . . . that you can be really glad, really glad . . . that you can achieve a
measure of acceptance . . . that no answer will be forthcoming. . . .

### Theme: Accepting Not Knowing

But whether you realize it yet or not . . . I'm really addressing a deeper
issue . . . a much deeper issue. . . . It's an issue of how *you* handle uncertainty. . . . Now you know and I know uncertainty is inevitable in many
areas of life. . . . Isn't it interesting the range of reactions that people
have, the people who strive to avoid uncertainty because it scares them
when they fill uncertainty with fear . . . while other people embrace
uncertainty . . . absorbed in the curiosity of wondering what will happen
without any dread that comes from anticipating the worst. . . . Uncertainty is an invitation for greater structure . . . the structured information gathering you can do to answer a question *if* it's an answerable
question . . . or the structured acceptance of what can't be answered,
at least not right now. . . . Consider one of your most basic questions
in life, a question that has nagged at you for years . . . and now you get
to ask yourself, "Is this an answerable question? Is there *any* amount of
research that could answer that question?" What a relief when you discover there are questions that can't be answered. . . . There are no data
to explain to someone why life isn't always fair. . . . There are no studies to explain why someone was injured or killed in a freak accident. . . .
There is no good explanation for why an innocent child is harmed by
abusive parents. . . .

### Theme: Recognizing and Interrupting the Process of Projection

Yet people make up explanations in such situations. . . . Too many people
are happy to have explanations for things that can't be explained with
actual facts just so they can have an explanation, even if it's wrong. . . .
Consider a simple example. . . . I'm sure you've had the experience of calling someone . . . getting their voice mail . . . and leaving a message. . . .
And when the person doesn't call back in a time frame you think reasonable . . . you might naturally wonder what it means . . . whether the person is simply busy . . . or whether their voice mail is working properly . . .
or whether the person is avoiding you for some reason . . . or any of many
other possible reasons. . . . And how can you know what the real reason

is? . . . But it's human nature to speculate about what things that happen mean . . . and the real skill is knowing when you're merely speculating . . . and when you have real evidence to support your interpretation. . . . After all . . . you don't want to react to something on the basis of an incorrect interpretation . . . and all the speculations about why that person didn't call back are normal . . . and reflect our desire to make sense out of things that don't seem to make much sense. . . . And whether you want to understand something like why someone doesn't call back . . . or something much more complex, like how to build a successful career or build a happy marriage . . . it's one of human beings' greatest strengths that we strive to understand and make sense of the things that go on around us. . . . And the fact that you can generate so many different explanations for why someone doesn't call back . . . gives you an opportunity to realize you don't know why they didn't call back. . . . You can make lots of guesses . . . but you really don't know for sure . . . and when you don't know how to explain something . . . it's perfectly all right just to say you don't know. . . . After all, no one really expects you to know why someone else doesn't return a phone call. . . . It's a gift of honesty and clear thinking when you can say "I don't know" instead of making up an answer that might well be wrong . . . and even hurtful to you. . . . Before you reach a conclusion . . . *any* conclusion, you can learn to ask yourself, "How do I know?" And if your answer is, "I just feel it's so" or "I just think so" . . . then you can know that you're forming a conclusion with no apparent real information. . . . That doesn't mean you are wrong, necessarily, but it increases the chances of being wrong. . . .

## Posthypnotic Suggestions for Integration

And each time throughout the day you encounter this situation where the meaning isn't clear to you . . . or, better yet, when you can even anticipate such an ambiguous event before it happens . . . you can recognize there are many different ways to interpret that event . . . and many different ways to think about events that have yet to occur . . . and you can instantly remind yourself you don't know what it means, at least not yet . . . and so your skill level grows in being able to recognize the uncertainty in many life situations . . . and grows in being able to comfortably accept that sometimes you don't know and may not ever know why or what it means . . . and grows in your trust in yourself to handle the uncertainties of life with a sense of calm confidence and clarity about what you do and don't know *before* you react. . . .

### Closure and Disengagement

Now, out of all the things that I've talked about . . . far be it from me to predict what will be enduring in your awareness. . . . But you can certainly decide that for yourself as you start to bring this experience to a comfortable close. . . . Take whatever time you want or need to process your thoughts and feelings . . . in order to absorb the deeper implications. . . . And then when you've had enough time and feel like you're ready to . . . you can start the process of gradually reorienting yourself at a rate that's comfortable and easy. . . . Take your time, and when you're ready, you can let your eyes open, feeling fully alert and feeling refreshed.

# Chapter 6

# Building Expectancy

*People don't come to therapy to change the past. They come to therapy to change the future.*

—Milton H. Erickson

## The Case of Carmen

Carmen's life hasn't been easy. Raised on a cattle ranch, she was one of four kids, all of whom were expected to work hard to help out before and after school. Her childhood had some happy times, to be sure, but not enough of them to satisfy her wish that her childhood had been more carefree. When she finished high school, she did what the small-town girls where she lived usually did: she got married and had two kids of her own. By age 54, she was long single following an amicable divorce over 10 years earlier, and her kids were grown and gone. For the first time she felt like her life was truly her own.

Carmen had always had the dream of going to college and developing a profession for herself. She doubted her ability to do so, though, especially in what she considered to be her "advanced years." Her kids encouraged her to go for it, apply to a college, maybe a junior or community college, and get the ball rolling. Carmen firmly said, "Maybe," and never got as far as applying. Finally, her oldest son, without her knowledge, filled out an application in her name, and no one was more shocked than Carmen was when she received a letter of acceptance to the local community college, where she could begin pursuing an education and develop her goals. Carmen's first reaction when she found out what her son had done was to become furious with him. That passed rather quickly, though, as the conversation now turned to how she could possibly make this work. What did she know about taking college classes? What could she do at her age to study and learn and remember, especially when almost all the other students were less than half her age? Her kids were wonderfully persuasive, to their credit, and they helped her get registered and develop a class schedule. Before she knew it, she was sitting anxiously in the front row of a lecture hall, pen and notebook at the ready.

Carmen was shocked to discover that she could be attentive and actually learn. She didn't think she had it in her. And as for all the young people surrounding her, she dismissed them as no real competition after all because she was one of the few that actually wanted to be there.

Jumping ahead some years, Carmen found a passion for counseling. She applied to a graduate school program she was sure she'd never be accepted into . . . but she was. Now at age 59, she had a master's degree in counseling, she had ambition, and she had total paralysis related to actually going to work using her degree.

Seeking therapy to get unstuck seemed sensible to a counseling program graduate, so she did. Disclosing her history of seeming to always freeze up when she had the chance to move forward in some area of her life, she wondered why she suffered with this difficulty. The content of her problem was delaying or avoiding taking a step forward in her own behalf, whether in getting out of a bad marriage (her husband pushed through the divorce), going to college, going to graduate school, or taking a job.

Was this about poor self-esteem? An unconscious fear of success (or failure)? An unconscious need for self-sabotage or punishment? A crippling perfectionism? Or what?

The process of Carmen's problem was that whenever she dared to establish a goal, she reflexively formed the expectation that the goal was unreachable because of her presumed personal shortcomings. She expected to fail and, based on that perspective, why bother to try?

Her current situation, the one that brought her to therapy, was wanting to get a job in her chosen field. But she stopped herself from applying for a job by asking these questions: Who's going to hire me at my age? Who's going to want a 59-year-old intern with no experience? Why did I get a degree anyway? What was I thinking?

Carmen needed some help to get clear that she's not the one who decides whether she's worth hiring. She's not the one who decides whether they're willing to take on a 59-year-old intern. She's not the one who decides for anyone what they're willing to do. The use of hypnosis to build the expectation that there are people out there for whom age isn't the primary consideration generated a marked shift in her viewpoint. Hypnosis was used to help build the realistic expectation that effort would be rewarded, just as it had been in previous cases when she (or someone on her behalf) took action and succeeded despite expectations of failure. Facilitating a sense of optimism that her future was filled with possibilities directly countered her negative expectations. A session utilizing hypnosis to build expectancy was all it took. Less than a month later, Carmen called to say she was thrilled she had found a great job where she'd be learning a lot. She summarized the lesson well that had been told during the hypnosis session: "The best way to predict the future is to create it."

## The Role of Expectancy in Quality of Life

The effects of our expectations on our experience can be profound. The power of expectation has been demonstrated in numerous places and called by many names, and virtually all models of psychotherapy emphasize the value of positive expectations in enhancing treatment results. Probably the most widely used term is "self-fulfilling prophecy," describing how our behavior is unconsciously aligned with our expectations, whether good or bad, increasing the likelihood of their eventual fulfillment. Addressing the issue of expectations—both yours and the client's—makes good clinical sense and helps build the therapeutic alliance.

Depressed clients in particular, people who suffer hopelessness and despair and thus have lots of negative expectations, show us how vitally important positive expectations are for eventual recovery. The clinical challenge to therapists is the necessity of building hopefulness out of hopelessness. Hypnosis is an ideal mechanism for helping to accomplish this goal for a variety of reasons I will address in this chapter. I have previously described some hypnotic strategies serving this purpose in a number of publications (Yapko, 1992, 2001, 2010a, 2010b), and in this chapter I provide another one that is entirely process oriented. Helping clients cocreate a compelling vision of what's possible in their lives is one of the most important things that can happen in therapy.

## The Effects of Hopelessness on the Therapeutic Process

Hopelessness is a cornerstone of depression but is by no means exclusive to depression. People can feel hopeless about anything going on in their lives and/or anything that's going on in the world at a given time. When someone presents for therapy and conveys their sense of hopelessness, the first things a clinician might assess are how pervasive and personal the sense of hopelessness is for the client.

Pervasiveness speaks to how generalized the client's sense of hopelessness is: Do they feel that everything in their life is hopeless, or just the specific problem domain for which they seek help from you? The more pervasive the person's sense of hopelessness, the wider the target area for treatment, making it necessary to address the issue of how to help the client go from an overgeneralized and unrealistic perspective to a specific problem or class of problems to address. Feeling hopeless about everything is simply too broad a perspective to hold, and the cost of doing so in terms of suffering a crippling despair is a terrible consequence.

The personalization of hopelessness addresses the issue of whether the client sees the problem as beyond anyone's ability to solve, or whether the inability to solve the problem is a reflection of their own incompetence or lack of personal resources. It makes a substantial difference in the clinical picture whether someone is able to recognize that a circumstance is beyond their own or anyone else's ability to resolve versus thinking it's a reflection of their own shortcomings. The latter is a much more painful perspective to hold and is more likely to be the case in therapy clients.

Unlike the past, which has already happened and can be reviewed, albeit with our imperfect memory, and the present, which we can tune into and be mindfully aware of as it unfolds from moment to moment, the future hasn't happened yet. Therefore, it doesn't have the ready availability and concreteness of the past and present orientations. The future is abstract and ambiguous. As first described in Chapter 5, it is another experiential Rorschach inkblot of sorts, an ambiguous stimulus that invites our projections to give it shape and substance. The quality of those projections can shape our treatments and our clients' clinical response to those treatments and, even more significantly, one's entire quality of life.

Hopelessness is obviously a statement of negative expectancy for the future. In the therapy context, it is a powerful factor that quite literally influences every phase of treatment response. That's why it is imperative that every therapist, regardless of theoretical orientation and style of practice, recognize and respond proactively to the need to build a positive expectancy, the core message of this chapter. To be specific about how expectancy affects the process of therapy, let's consider each component of treatment.

The first stage is the client making contact to request help. It is well known that the majority of people who need mental health treatment don't receive it. There are a number of reasons why people don't seek out the help they need: Some are afraid of the stigma of being "mentally ill" (a phrase I personally detest); some don't have any insight as to the nature of their own problems and believe "that's just the way I am" or "that's just the way life goes"; and others—perhaps most—feel hopeless that anyone can say or do anything that would make any difference. It's a straightforward question: Why would I seek help from someone if I don't believe help is possible?

That perspective can easily be compounded by the belief that treatment will involve endless sessions spent talking about your childhood or being told to take drugs you don't want to take for your "illness." Expectations clearly play a huge role in deciding whether to seek help. Furthermore, expectations shape the concern related to seeking treatment, namely staying in treatment. How many clients drop out of treatment after just one or two sessions because their sense of hopelessness was never sufficiently challenged by the therapist? How a therapist conducts the first therapy session or two can make a great difference in whether or not the client continues in treatment. The process of building expectancy described later in this chapter speaks to this critically important issue.

The next consideration is how hopelessness affects the rate of treatment. If someone goes ahead and seeks treatment despite their misgivings, how can they possibly progress quickly if they believe progress isn't possible? The negative expectation that change is unlikely creates a barrier that can partially or wholly block good therapeutic input, leading the client away from success and thereby confirming their negative expectations—the self-injurious self-fulfilling prophecy.

The issue of treatment cooperation is directly affected by the client's expectations as well. Most therapists encourage clients to make use of reading materials, typically self-help books (i.e., bibliotherapy) and/or structured homework assignments intended to facilitate the acquisition of ideas and skills taught in therapy. It is a constant cause of frustration to therapists how often the client does not do the suggested readings or assignments. To the hopeless client, though, the prevailing perspective is, "What's the point of doing the reading or homework assignment when nothing is going to come of it?" Expectations help determine whether the client will cooperate with the treatment plan.

Expectations influence not only the rate of recovery, but also the degree of recovery. In the clinical literature, researchers can consider therapies successful if a client moves just a couple of points on some symptom measurement scale. For the client who continues to have symptoms, despite their being fewer or less severe than before, will the therapy be considered a success? Perhaps, but the expectation that the problem will never go away serves as a predictor of whether the treatment's success will be partial or complete.

Finally, the client's hopeless expectations that "this problem will never go away" or "even if the problem goes away for a while it'll just come back again" help predict the client's vulnerability to relapses. No treatment can be considered complete without addressing the issue of relapse prevention, and clearly expectations about the permanence of a symptom in one's life or the sense that "it's gone forever" will be a major determinant of what the future brings.

When expectations play such a pivotal role in the therapy process, it seems imperative that every therapist become adept at creating a context early on in therapy to help the client develop positive expectations for treatment. The process-oriented hypnosis session contained in this chapter is an experiential means for helping to serve this purpose.

## Realistic and Unrealistic Hopelessness

Hopelessness may be realistic or unrealistic depending on the circumstances. What we discover so often in the therapy context is people who reflexively assume there is nothing they can do to change their circumstances and so retreat into hopeless passivity. How well someone can distinguish realistic from unrealistic hope is a critically important skill to have in order to make sound and effective decisions.

Hope may be a good thing, but it can also be hurtful, again depending on the circumstances. Hope that you can make your life better is usually very helpful as a foundation for actually doing so. But hope can be destructive—after all, every person who gambled away a desperately needed paycheck was hopeful. Every person who stays in an abusive relationship is hopeful their partner will change.

Since expectations are the filter through which we make evaluations, the quality of those expectations—how realistic or unrealistic they are—makes a difference. When clients have unrealistic expectations for therapy, for example, how likely are they to be disappointed when they discover their therapy experience didn't live up to their expectations? This is how we judge almost everything, even our closest relationships. As relationship experts will tell you in no uncertain terms, marital satisfaction is highest when your partner does what you think they should do. But what happens when someone holds an unrealistic expectation, but clearly doesn't realize it? I have a favorite cartoon that shows a clearly unhappy woman telling her obviously perplexed partner, "If you really loved me, you'd win the lottery!"

From the start of treatment, then, helping establish realistic expectations for the therapy experience is imperative. The hypnosis session provided in this chapter speaks to the need for the client to evaluate (with the therapist's help, of course) whether their expectations are realistic, not just for therapy but for whatever issues they face. A lot of frustration and disappointment can be prevented in this way, yet another good reason to make addressing expectancy a formal stage of early treatment.

## Typical Problems Derived From Negative Expectancy

The types of problems that people might present for treatment that reflect negative expectancy may include such patterns as:

- Depressed mood
- Being reactive rather than proactive in managing life situations

- Giving up on oneself (resignation)
- Apathy toward oneself and/or life in general
- Rigidly believing that effort is pointless
- Predetermining that they will never succeed (failure is inevitable)
- Suicidal ideation and/or behavior
- Refusing to consider or try potentially helpful alternatives
- Believing their problem is genetic and unalterable in any way
- Being frequently disappointed that people or situations don't live up to their expectations, leading to social withdrawal and isolation
- Nocebo responses to medication or therapy

What specifically the person feels hopeless about is the content, but the target of building expectancy is the process of how the person comes to believe and maintain the belief that their problems cannot be overcome.

## Defining the Salient Therapeutic Targets

When negative expectations contaminate life experience, it becomes clear that addressing the issue of expectancy will be important. Telling someone steeped in negative expectancy to "try and look at the bright side" may be well intended but is an exceptionally weak piece of advice. It's the equivalent of telling a depressed person to cheer up. It's a worthy goal but telling someone what to do doesn't enable them to do it. Experience is a much more powerful teacher, and the experiential learning of a process-oriented hypnosis session can be invaluable in this regard.

The therapeutic targets, then, include (1) helping the client look ahead, not behind, disrupting the pattern of using the past to predict the future. A principal cause of negative expectations comes from past failures (e.g., "I'll never be happy because I never have been"; "I'll never have a good relationship because I've never had one"; and the twisted logic of negative expectancy when saying, "I won't be happy until my parents treat me better when I was a kid!"). Other targets include (2) separating past failures from future possibilities; (3) redefining the future as having opportunities not yet known but inevitable; (4) scaling global hopelessness down to an individualized plan of action; (5) distancing someone from their expectations long enough to help them distinguish between realistic and unrealistic expectations across all life experiences; and (6) motivating a willingness to take action with the message that sensible effort can pay off. Any and all of these messages can be contained in a session on building expectancy, amplifying which ones are most essential at the time. Table 6.1 offers a generic strategy for helping the client build positive expectancy.

---

### TABLE 6.1. GENERIC SESSION STRUCTURE FOR BUILDING EXPECTANCY

**Induction**

| | |
|---|---|
| **Response set:** | Expectancy |
| **Theme 1:** | Expectations shape experience |
| **Theme 2:** | Your expectations can mislead you |
| **Theme 3:** | What you focus on, you amplify |
| **Theme 4:** | Developing realistic goals to pull yourself forward |
| **Theme 5:** | You have personal resources you can use in new ways |
| **Theme 6:** | Looking and moving forward |
| **Theme 7:** | Planting seeds for the future |
| **Theme 8:** | Looking ahead to positive possibilities |

**Posthypnotic suggestions for integration**
**Closure and disengagement**

---

## SESSION TRANSCRIPT

### Induction

You can find yourself a comfortable place to sit, a place that is free of unnecessary distractions . . . and then you can arrange yourself in a position that is comfortable for you. . . . The important thing right now is to make sure that your body has good support . . . because you can *realistically expect* that as your body gets really relaxed, it naturally tends to feel heavier . . . and it helps to relax when you can be physically comfortable *effortlessly.* . . .

Once you have settled into a comfortable position that you can easily sit in for a while . . . you can let your eyes close. . . . That way you can start to build an internal focus . . . a focus within yourself . . . so that you can find inside yourself . . . those parts of you . . . that most need to experience comfort . . . relaxation . . . the experience of being soothed . . . and also inspired . . . as you build a greater degree of focus over the next few minutes . . . on the helpful ideas introduced here. . . .

### Building a Response Set Regarding Expectancy

And especially on the important realizations they can bring to you. . . . In that way you can fully *expect* . . . to absorb new possibilities . . . new things you can do that can be helpful to you . . . new skills that you can develop and use in many different life situations . . . on your own behalf . . . new perceptions that can give rise to a stronger sense of your emotional growth. . . . Out of all the things that there are to focus on at this moment . . . you can begin this process of evolving a meaningful vision of your future by first turning your attention to . . . the feelings of sitting comfortably. . . . It's an easy thing to do to notice how each breath that you take in . . . can allow you to grow more comfortable . . . more relaxed within yourself. . . . And as your comfort deepens . . . you can appreciate that you have some time right now . . . of absolute freedom . . . the freedom to just be. . . . Nothing you have to think about. . . . Nothing you have to analyze. . . . How comforting to be able to have some quiet time to yourself . . . to enjoy the freedom of not having your thoughts spinning around in different directions. . . . It means that little by little . . . your thoughts can begin to get more focused. . . . Your mind can grow more comfortable . . . just as your body can get more comfortable. . . . And little by little, the experience develops . . . more completely and more fully . . . of being deeply relaxed . . . wonderfully comfortable . . . and it's an interesting thing to observe in yourself . . . where your attention goes when it doesn't have to go anywhere. . . . It's one of the most pleasing things about the experience of hypnosis. . . . There is a certain quality of freedom embedded within each hypnosis session . . . the freedom to let your mind wander if you'd like . . . the freedom to either entertain—or dismiss—any particular thoughts or sensations as you choose. . . . And that's part of what you learn about yourself . . . your individual way of experiencing these sessions . . . whether you find it easy to focus . . . whether you're able to build a meaningful experience of absorption simply because you choose to. . . . And you can probably appreciate how different the experiences of hypnosis are for different people . . . and even how different it is for you from one time to the next. . . .

## Theme: Expectations Shape Experience

And so much of what you experience is directly related to what you *expect* to experience . . . and that's true across so many life experiences. . . . You expect to not enjoy a new restaurant your friends want to try, and you don't . . . or you expect not to like someone new at your job, and you don't. . . . How easily things can live *down* to your expectations . . . especially when they're tainted by an arbitrary and undeserved negativity . . . undeserved because you haven't experienced it yet. . . . And, likewise, how easily things can live *up* to your expectations . . . when reflecting a sense of optimism and a well-practiced ability to notice what's *right*. . . . So as you enjoy this hypnosis session . . . it can be helpful to be aware of your expectations for yourself, whatever they might be . . . as you anticipate how well you'll be able to focus now . . . and how easily you'll be able to absorb new ideas. . . . And it's that anticipation I'm going to speak about . . . encouraging you to consider the question of *how* your expectations come about in the first place . . . for *whatever* you have yet to actually experience . . . and the question that follows . . . as to how you know whether your expectations are accurate and useful . . . or whether they contaminate your experiences . . . by reaching unfounded conclusions well ahead of the actual experiences yet to unfold. . . . It's a valuable skill to be open to new experiences . . . to approach them with what has been called a beginner's mind . . . a mind without prejudice or expectation. . . .

## Theme: Your Expectations Can Mislead You

As you well know, the world is filled with diverse cultures . . . people leading very different lives from your own. . . . There are peoples and places so different and unfamiliar across the earth that can remind you that there are lots of different ways of going through life successfully, happily. . . . And some of those cultures are extremely different and others only mildly different. . . . It's a really powerful experience to spend time in other places . . . where your ideas and your expectations of how things should be and how people should live are quite different from how these people actually do live. . . . And yet you discover that even though their lives aren't as you expected . . . they're still living well and enjoying life in their own way. . . . They still love family and music and celebrations and good food, whatever they think of as good food, even if you don't happen to think so. . . . And this experience highlights how our expectations can sometimes be quite irrelevant to what actually happens. . . . And there are experiences that *you've* had in your own life that turned out to be so different from what you expected. . . . It can be a simple example, such as when you felt obligated to go to a social gathering that you were really not in the mood to go to, perhaps even dreading having to go . . . but you went and much to your surprise you ended up having a great time, even though you didn't expect to. . . . You had some enjoyable conversations with interesting people . . . and the food was good . . . and the music was good . . . and you ended up genuinely enjoying yourself. . . . Other simple examples, such as never trying a food that just didn't seem appealing to you, especially when you were a child . . . and then eventually you tried it and came to love it. . . . Or another example of going to meet a person you weren't expecting to like, and perhaps didn't like when you first met, who eventually became special to you . . . a person you really came to like or even love despite your original negative expectations. . . . And if you think about it, your life is sprinkled with those kinds of experiences . . . where something turns out to be quite different than what you were expecting and even much *better* than you expected . . . and it's good to allow for that possibility. . . .

### Theme: What You Focus On, You Amplify

And as always, what you focus on shapes so much of your experience. . . . So the first principle in learning to move forward in your life is *what you focus on, you amplify.* . . . And what an extraordinary thing it is to be able to focus your attention on what's useful . . . and life-enhancing. . . . So often people don't think to do that . . . so they focus on what's wrong instead of what's right . . . or they focus on things in the unchangeable past instead of a wide-open future filled with the chance to make positive choices. . . . Now there are many different things that I can talk about that are important in helping you learn to feel good . . . but right now it can be quite valuable to think about . . . the mind . . . *your* mind. . . . After all, that's what we're dealing with . . .

*your thoughts . . . your* feelings . . . *your* way of looking at things. . . . And you already know how enormously complex the mind is. . . . There isn't anyone who understands all of it. . . . The fact that your mind is so complicated . . . is precisely why . . . you can have unexpected reactions . . . confusion about your feelings at times . . . mixed feelings about things or people . . . why you can have conflicting motivations about things you want to be able to do but then don't . . . how you can consciously feel hopeful about your future being compelling and meaningful . . . and at the same time . . . be concerned that your hopes may not be realized. . . . Having these mixed feelings and reactions is so very, very normal . . . which can be a relief to know. . . .

### Theme: Developing Realistic Goals to Pull Yourself Forward

And you know there are different levels of awareness we all have . . . things that we're aware of on the surface level . . . and deeper things that can be hidden even from ourselves. . . . And some of the most powerful experiences that you are capable of having . . . take place at levels much deeper than just what you're aware of . . . much deeper. . . . And whether you call that deeper part of yourself . . . the *un*conscious mind . . . or the *sub*conscious mind . . . or your *deep* self . . . doesn't really matter. . . . It's just very important for you to know . . . that there is a deeper part of you that can learn . . . and can absorb . . . new understandings. . . . And it's that deeper part of yourself . . . that you can gradually come to know more about and better understand. . . . I know . . . and you know, too, of course . . . that you want things . . . to be better in your life. . . . You want to feel better . . . and not just feel better but actually *be* better . . . in deeper and more enduring ways. . . . And feeling and being better can indeed happen . . . when you begin to do things . . . differently . . . when you go beyond the old and the familiar ways of thinking and behaving that haven't served you as well as you might have hoped. . . . So, you're beginning to learn . . . about your mind . . . especially its ability to focus and get absorbed in new possibilities . . . and you're starting to learn about the relationship . . . between the things that you think now. . . . and feel now . . . and do now . . . and what happens later . . . the eventual results of the choices that you make. . . . And what would you like to experience differently? . . . You can start to become clearer about what you want for yourself. . . . You can gradually develop a wonderful and detailed image of what your life *could* look like . . . and how it could feel good and satisfying to you . . . (10 second pause). Now I don't know if you could create that kind of wonderful vision right now . . . this moment. . . . But whether you could or couldn't *yet* . . . you can understand how important it is to have things to strive for in your life . . . the kinds of things that pull you forward in your life and give you a strong sense of purpose. . . . And even if you're not sure right now what those things might be . . . that kind of powerful personal vision can begin to evolve for you over time . . . as you begin to learn more about what matters to you . . . and what you are capable of . . . that you don't even realize just yet . . . because you already know that there's nothing more powerful than a person with a vision. . . . Now, what is vision? . . . It's a future possibility . . . a possibility that is so motivating and compelling . . . that it leads you to start doing positive things *now* . . . that gradually make your vision possible . . . eventually . . . steps you begin to define and follow that lead you in a meaningful direction . . . that provide you with a level of satisfaction and at the same time keep you wanting more for yourself . . . a complex mix of feelings, of feeling good about where things are going and at the same time wondering what more there may be to discover and experience. . . .

**Theme: You Have Personal Resources You Can Use in New Ways**
You can use your own experience to better grasp the point. . . . After all, there are important things in your life . . . that you have accomplished. . . . If you have a job or a profession . . . you didn't get it by accident. . . . You developed skills and applied for it and created the possibility of actually getting it. . . . If you have a high school diploma or a college degree . . . you didn't get it by . . . sending in two dollars and a cereal box top. . . . No, you got it by *consistently* going to class . . . *consistently* taking and passing tests . . . *consistently* writing papers and turning them in . . . and were there times that you didn't want to go to class? . . . Of course there were times that you didn't want to go to class . . . but you focused on the greater goal of graduating and went anyway. . . . And by fulfilling that most important task, what you discovered is that . . . your feelings of a lack of interest in going . . . may come and go . . . but the diploma stays. . . . The college degree stays . . . It's a very valuable realization . . . that the goal of eventually graduating from

school . . . kept you going . . . even when you really didn't feel like it . . . or when the job was tough at times, you stayed with it and somehow made it work. . . . That's the power of vision . . . the ability to see *beyond* the discomfort of the moment . . . by making the goal the clear priority. . . . When the goal matters more than temporary discomforts like fear or doubt . . . that's when people surprise themselves in the best of ways by accomplishing what seemed unlikely. . . . The wisdom of Nelson Mandela is worth sharing here . . . for he said, "It always seems impossible . . . until it's done!" . . .

## Theme: Looking and Moving Forward

And his extraordinary life and achievements, despite suffering in terrible conditions, shows us all the power of that observation. . . . There are ordinary people who become extraordinary when they take action by setting a goal . . . a *realistic* goal . . . and strive to achieve it. . . . You can take that valuable principle . . . and *you* can apply it in such a way . . . that whatever it is that may have been hurting or limiting you in the past . . . you can turn your attention and actions away from. . . . After all, you can't really move forward by looking backward . . . any more than you can drive a car forward while only looking in the rearview mirror. . . . And you can now begin to develop a new vision for yourself . . . a reason to learn some new skills . . . change some of the things that you say and do that would help move you forward . . . slowly and gradually . . . doing more things for tomorrow's successes than getting lost in whatever discomfort you might have had today. . . .

## Theme: Planting Seeds for the Future

You know, it's a very common metaphor among therapists to talk about the unconscious mind . . . as fertile soil . . . and to tell people that through therapy you can plant seeds . . . that will grow into something healthy and beautiful. . . . It's a useful metaphor, and it's also literally true. . . . And you're planting new seeds right now . . . through this session. . . . Now, fewer and fewer people live on farms these days. . . . Most people don't take the time to grow things that will flower or produce fruits or vegetables. . . . That's because most people live in cities. . . . And there are many good things about city life . . . but there is also something lost by living in a city . . . because in the city the lifestyle emphasis

people tend to acquire is on things happening "right now." . . . That's
very different than the perceptions you develop when you grow up
on a farm . . . when every day . . . your approach to life requires you . . .
to think in longer-term ways. . . . You can easily learn to think in terms
of planting seeds . . . preparing yourself . . . for the changes about to
come . . . in your life. . . . There are so many powerful and great things . . .
that can happen in your life . . . and the challenge is defining what's
worthy of your efforts . . . and defining the steps to follow to reach your
goals . . . and discovering what you know as well as what you know that
*isn't really so* . . . that you can leave behind as you move forward. . . .

**Theme: Looking Ahead to Positive Possibilities**
And when you realize that . . . at a very deep level . . . as you're starting
to . . . then you can nurture your feelings of . . . optimism . . . that things
can change. . . . Things can improve. . . . You *can* and undoubtedly will
learn things that you didn't know before. . . . You can practice developing new skills . . . that you didn't have before. . . . And so . . . I can safely
predict . . . that there are important experiences . . . that you're going to
have in your life . . . that will be wonderfully valuable. . . . And they will
really teach you something about what it means to shift your focus to
observing what's right . . . and to notice more of the things around you
that are worth noticing . . . the beauty of a sunset . . . the joyful playful-
ness of people's pets . . . the polite smile or kind word of a stranger. . . .
There are lots of experiences ahead of you . . . good things to look forward to that haven't happened yet. . . . There will be places that you will
go . . . that you haven't been to yet . . . places that will be powerful in one
way or another . . . places that will generate happy feelings . . . places
where you'll feel good. . . . And I can safely predict . . . that you will meet
people . . . that will influence you in important and wonderful ways . . .
that you haven't met yet . . . people you will find inspiring that bring out
some of the best in you . . . people that will care about you . . . people
that will become friends . . . people that will become teachers . . . people
that you haven't even met yet . . . that will contribute . . . to the higher
quality of your life. . . . There will be favorite movies of yours that haven't
even been made yet . . . and there will be new songs you will love that
haven't even been written yet . . . and the future—*your* future—is filled
with possibilities worth exploring and discovering. . . .

## Posthypnotic Suggestions for Integration

Now whoever it was that said there are no guarantees in life . . . there
are only opportunities . . . clearly had the right idea. . . . Opportunity
speaks to the future . . . and the future hasn't happened yet . . . but the
future is coming . . . and how you shape it to your liking begins with
the choices you make today. . . . You can begin to make better choices
*now* . . . that will bring you more of the things that you want for yourself
in the future. . . . And then that rich, vivid, detailed image . . . *your* vision
of *your* future . . . can be what pulls you forward in your life. . . . You can
*expect* . . . to find yourself . . . starting to do some things differently . . .
and I think you'll be happily surprised to discover . . . that you *are* starting to do some things differently . . . in ways that are more in line with
your evolving vision. . . . And it is the power of the future . . . to draw you
in . . . in ways that can feel great . . . that can guide your daily choices . . .
choosing carefully what to say and do . . . for the results you want
tomorrow . . . the next tomorrow, and all of your tomorrows. . . . And so
you can nurture these seeds of optimism that you're planting today. . . .
You can let them grow. . . . Let them grow. . . . Now you can take whatever time you want to or need to . . . to absorb these important ideas
and possibilities . . . and to integrate at a deep level . . . the strength of
these messages about possibilities. . . . and the future . . . and growth . . .
and change. . . .

## Closure and Disengagement

When you've had enough time to enjoy this experience of comfort . . .
then that's when you can bring this experience to a comfortable
close. . . . So, when you're ready to bring yourself out of hypnosis. . . .
you can start to reorient yourself at a rate that is gradual and comfortable . . . slowly alerting yourself. . . . And when you're ready . . . you
can reorient yourself completely . . . and allow your eyes to open and
fully alert yourself . . . bringing back with you the best feelings . . . of
feeling relaxed and comfortable . . . and wonderfully optimistic . . . as
you remind yourself . . . in the nicest of ways . . . that the future hasn't
happened yet . . . but you can make it deeply fulfilling . . . one day at a
time . . . one decision at a time. . . .

# Chapter 7

# Making Better Discriminations

*In the sky there is no distinction of east and west; people create distinctions out of their own minds and then believe them to be true.*

—The Buddha

## The Case of Peter

Peter looked as tired as he said he felt. Only 36, Peter acknowledged that he was feeling a lot older than his chronological age. He said he was working way too many hours, especially during these days of uncertainty and doubt in the minds of so many. Huge and consequential issues concerned every citizen of the United States, as surveys about the national mood revealed. Health care, gun control, deep and sometimes violent political divides, and more ratcheted up people's anxiety and depression. As a psychologist in clinical practice, Peter was in the front row seeing it all up close.

Peter came to therapy for help in addressing his high level of stress and fatigue. He felt sure he was doing good work, but just too much of it, and he was sure he couldn't sustain that level of intensity without some predictably bad consequences. People were hurting, and he wanted to help, but he knew—intellectually, anyway—that the demand exceeded his supply.

Before I had a chance to ask, Peter spontaneously provided some personal history. He described how even as a boy he was "psychologically aware." He described himself as a "responsible" and "empathetic" child, traits he has always valued in himself that also served to steer him into his career as a psychologist. Asked to say just a little about his family when growing up, Peter described his parents as "die-hard liberals" who were "social activists." They heavily emphasized the value of being of service to others, the importance of seeing things from other people's perspective, and the value of giving of one's time and energy to others. He had two siblings, a brother and a sister, and he said, "It's no surprise that we are all professionals in service-oriented professions." He said quite sincerely, "I admire my parents for what they modeled and expected of us," and I believed him.

I asked Peter what he did for fun. He joked, "What's that?" Then he said, "Playtime has never really been my thing. I guess I'm always so aware that there's more to be done that that's where my time and energy goes. Don't get me wrong, though. I like being productive, and I like that sense I'm doing something meaningful instead of just watching TV or going on yet another first date. But wasting time on my leisure just seems so needlessly self-indulgent."

Given Peter's personal values for being productive and giving of himself, even to the point where it sometimes hurts, Peter seemed to have a blind spot that is not uncommon among health care professionals. Clinicians routinely report that they haven't taken vacations in a very long time, that they work long and sometimes inconvenient hours to accommodate their clients' needs, and that they probably give more than they really should.

So, what about Peter? Does he have poor personal boundaries that need firming up? Is he emotionally needy for his clients' approval and even admiration? Is he unconsciously trying to repair some unresolved attachment issues? Is his self-esteem entirely defined by his professional status, and the more he works the better he sees himself? Or what?

Peter's dilemma is understandable, of course. It's not pathological to want to be of service to others. On the contrary, it is wonderfully compassionate and typically motivated by a genuine desire to reduce human suffering. But when you have grown up with the clear message that your worth comes from what you do for others, most or all of your life experience is then geared toward that value system. What goes undeveloped or underdeveloped, then, is the other side of the equation: There is also value in what you do for yourself.

The content of Peter's problem is stress from working too much. With one how question, the process of how he chooses what he is going to do became glaringly apparent. The question was formulated by his statement, "Wasting time on my leisure just seems so needlessly self-indulgent." The how question posed to Peter was this: "How do you determine whether doing something for yourself is selfish or taking care of yourself?"

Peter paused, tried to process the question's meaning, then asked me to repeat the question. When I did, he had this clear look of confusion on his face before he slowly admitted, "I guess I don't. Anytime I do something for myself, it feels selfish. It doesn't feel good even though it's supposed to, so I guess that's why I don't do things for myself very often."

Hypnosis was used to help Peter start to make a sharp distinction—a meaningful discrimination—between what is selfish and what is simply taking care of self. He had never made this distinction before and now could begin to develop the salient skills for doing so: establishing a work schedule that allowed for free time, learning how to limit the number of sessions he did in a day or a week to prevent burnout, getting practice in saying no more easily when it would serve him well to do so, initiating leisure activities with friends and so forth, all the while feeling good about getting ever clearer that taking care of self is not equated with selfishness. It can be, of course, but isn't necessarily. There is a difference!

Peter was a quick learner. The discrimination strategy addressed in hypnosis really stuck with him powerfully. Based on that experience, he immediately implemented some changes in his use of time and energy, which he later shared with me. He was doing fun things and not giving a second thought to the idea that he was being too self-indulgent. He said he felt better than he had in a very long time.

## The Role of Discrimination in Quality of Life

Cognitive psychology, the study of how people think, has given rise to new understandings about how people gather and use information. This includes how people decide, usually at a level outside of awareness, what is salient to pay attention to in a given environment and, likewise, what is essentially irrelevant. When people get sidetracked into irrelevancy, paying too much attention to what doesn't really matter and too little attention to what does, their misplaced focus naturally leads them away from making optimal decisions. Furthermore, when someone's perspective is so global or overgeneral that they simply don't know how or what to decide in a situation requiring a decision, they are far more likely to make poor decisions on the unfortunate basis of hurt feelings, old history, misconceptions, or blind faith.

It is a fundamental truth in living that the quality of your decisions shapes the quality of your life. The importance of having meaningful strategies for making effective decisions on a situation-by-situation basis cannot be overstated. Simply reacting on the basis of the feeling of the moment is too often the path to later regret: How could I have done that? What the heck was I thinking? How can I live with these awful consequences?

Cognitive psychologists and cognitive neuroscientists use the term "discrimination" to describe the process of making distinctions between different situations that give rise to one's reactions. For example, your reaction will be entirely different if you believe someone stepped on your foot by accident than if you believe they did so deliberately. Your ability to discriminate an intentional act of harm from a moment of unintentional carelessness fully shapes your reaction of either anger or tolerance.

When someone faces some challenging situation and has a choice about whether and how to respond, do they realize that a choice is even available? Reflexive responding—the predominant tendency of people to just react to some circumstance with neither insight nor foresight—clearly says no. If and when a person recognizes an opportunity to make a meaningful choice, does that person have the ability to choose wisely? Only if there is a well-defined and effective template for making good choices, one that considers more factors than just an impulse, or the familiarity or emotional comfort of a reaction. Using hypnosis as a vehicle for helping people go beyond reflexive responding is an exceptionally good use of hypnosis.

In this chapter, then, I consider one of the patterns of thought involved in how people make important life choices, the ones that shape their responses to life circumstances, especially those choices that carry the potential to really make a critical difference in their emotional well-being and quality of life. The emphasis is on how one decides to do this, not that, in especially vulnerable situations, that is, those that hold great potential for causing psychological distress. In developing a process-oriented hypnosis session, the goal is to help our clients develop what are called discrimination criteria, the key factors that help one determine which path to take to respond effectively to some particular situation.

## Global Cognition and Symptomatic Experience

The pattern of thought I'm referring to is called global cognition, also known in more everyday terms as overgeneral thinking. Some individuals are quite detailed and linear in their thinking, while others are more general. The salient metaphor for global thinking is "can't see the trees for the forest," that is, seeing the big picture only at the expense of the associated details. How does global thinking give rise to many of the most common problems people suffer, and what does this imply for effective treatments? Global thinking has been shown to impair problem solving and exacerbate the tendency of depressed individuals to selectively show greater recall for negative memories when depressed. A similar link between overgeneral thinking, memory, and post-traumatic stress disorder (PTSD) and depression has been established as well (Callahan, Maxwell, & Janis, 2019; Hallford, Austin, Raes, & Takano, 2018).

The implications of global thinking and the lack of discrimination skills for understanding how people develop problems are profound. When people are unable to determine whether it's this or that, focusing on one criterion to the exclusion of other available information, they run the risk of responding to someone or some situation in an inappropriate or ineffective way. The resulting discomfort is what brings people into treatment. Here are three examples to illustrate the point:

- Depressed people commonly feel helpless to improve their lives. They globally assume they have no control over situations, and so do nothing proactively to improve them. They focus on their feelings of helplessness and thereby miss the controllable opportunities to make things better. Such a person needs a discrimination strategy to help them determine when they have control and can make a positive difference with sensible action steps and when they are, indeed, helpless and have no control over circumstances, and no amount of effort will make a difference.

- Anxious people commonly worry about what might go wrong that will hurt them. They globally assume they will be overwhelmed and dread the prospect of facing whatever they fear. They focus on and amplify challenges as being beyond their abilities to manage and pay little or no attention to their personal resources for coping. Such a person needs a discrimination strategy to help them determine when something is indeed a serious problem and when something is only an inconvenience.
- People with relationship problems are often hurt by the actions of their partner and feel angry and disappointed. They globally focus on what they want from the person that they're not getting and not on what this person is objectively capable of providing. Such a person needs a discrimination strategy for knowing whether their expectations for the person are realistic or unrealistic.

## Typical Problems Derived From Global Cognition and a Lack of Discrimination Skills

The types of problems that people might present for treatment that reflect global thinking and the associated lack of ability to make meaningful discriminations are quite diverse and cross into many different areas of life. If you consider the number of decisions that you need to make in the course of a single day—big and small—you can easily see why having good discrimination criteria readily available to guide you is so important. Here are some of the common presenting problems that reflect global thinking (at the very least in the problem context but perhaps nearly everywhere else as well) and a lack of effective discrimination criteria:

- Overgeneral problem presentation (e.g., "I just want to be happy")
- Emotional overreactions
- Inability to identify one's feelings (lack of emotional differentiation)
- Poor personal boundaries
- Indecisiveness

- Poor problem-solving skills
- Avoidant coping style
- Inability to think critically or in detail about issues
- Overgeneralizations about oneself ("I'm too anxious to ever learn to relax"), other people (i.e., stereotyping), or situations (e.g., "I'm not safe at the grocery store because I had a panic attack there once")
- Global and rigid self-definition based on one's diagnosis (e.g., "I'm a phobic")
- Holding beliefs or philosophies that have no exceptions (e.g., "Everything happens for a reason")
- Inability to compartmentalize experience
- Inability to think linearly or sequentially (e.g., fails to see cause-and-effect relationships)
- Little or no insight

These patterns represent the pervasive and serious effects of a global cognitive style and the resulting inability to make important distinctions. What the client presents for therapy as the problem reflects the content-related results of their issue (e.g., "I feel guilty all the time" or "I'm a depressive"). The goals of the process-oriented therapist are to identify the exact role of global thinking in the problem content and then to teach the client how to go from overgeneral to specific in resolving the problem. The process-oriented hypnosis session provides a means for teaching the salient skills to achieve these goals. Such sessions also encourage better discriminations beyond the current concerns, and thus have a preventive component as well as a treatment component.

It's important to point out that global thinking isn't globally (i.e., always and everywhere) a problem. Like any pattern, its value is ultimately determined by the context in which it appears. Some things are enhanced by a global perspective ("Isn't the sunset beautiful?"), while for others a global perspective is clearly problematic ("How can my checking account be overdrawn? I still have some checks left!").

## Defining the Salient Therapeutic Targets

In terms of problems, people are inevitably global regarding the things they don't know about or understand. The task of the clinician becomes one of providing a structured means not only to identify the overgeneral thinking of the client, but also to identify and teach specific strategies to effectively counter it and thereby limit its detrimental effects. Most typically, therapists do this when they define treatment goals in specific and concrete terms and then encourage the client to take active steps toward achieving them, an intervention process termed behavioral activation. Catalyzing meaningful action is the topic of Chapter 12.

On an individual level, the client who suffers some distress and perhaps even pursues therapy to help alleviate this suffering has little insight into the specific rigidity that fuels the distress. Here's how it works: If I adopt the global view that "quitters never win" and therefore believe that "one should never, ever give up," then I will continue to "try, try again" without ever considering—much less exploring—the possibility that my effort may be wasted because no amount of effort—not just by me but by anyone—can make a difference in a particular circumstance.

In life, there are many, perhaps too many, situations we face where we simply can't make a meaningful difference. But if you believe that one should never give up, you will continue to try—and fail in such instances. The costs of failure may be ruminative self-doubt, despair, depression, and high levels of interpersonal conflict with those who say "Give up already," thereby causing possibly irreversible damage to the relationship. The rigid and global philosophy of never giving up precludes identifying the exceptions to the rule, that is, when giving up is actually the wisest thing to do. The key discrimination question then becomes, "How do you know when to persist in pursuit of some goal and when to stop trying?" A related discrimination question is, "When you established the goal in the first place, how did you determine whether it was a realistic goal?"

People get lost in their global philosophies (e.g., "always follow your heart") as they strive to live by them, making decisions and pursuing courses of action based upon them. What typically drives people into therapy, then, is when the person directly and painfully experiences the restrictions associated with that belief or perspective. Global thinking unintentionally prevents a critical examination of the belief that would highlight its applicability in some circumstances but not others. Global thinking leads the person to believe the philosophy is entirely (i.e., globally) sound. If and when it fails, it is not typically regarded as a situational failure of the philosophy or belief. Rather, global cognition usually leads the person to view the shortcoming as their own, what surely must be a personality defect, character weakness, or psychologically motivated reason to fail. It just doesn't and wouldn't occur to most people that the problem is caused by a rigid adherence to a belief or philosophy that is counterproductive to the realities of the specific circumstances they're in.

People aren't aware of their blind spots—they don't know what they don't know, nor do they know if what they do know is erroneous. All they know is that what they've been doing isn't working, their problems or symptoms are seemingly out of control, and they don't know what to do. They may well realize that their efforts are counterproductive yet persist because they feel they have to do something.

When a client has made a choice (including the typically unintentional choice not to choose) in some vulnerable area and suffered some unexpected consequence that causes distress, it reveals a flaw in the decision-making process. The client doesn't know where the flaw in the process was. They reacted reflexively and typically had no idea there was some discrimination to be made. Thus, when the clinician asks these key discrimination questions, "How did you decide that was the best decision to make?" and "When making a choice, how do you decide whether it should be A or B?" the most common response is confusion and the reluctant admission, "I don't know."

## Discriminations Representing Repetitive Issues to Address in Therapy

The discriminations listed below are some of the most common issues underlying common client presentations. They are repetitive themes of therapy. You can probably imagine pretty easily what the range of presenting complaints might be for each of these.

- How do you know whether this situation is in your control? (People not controlling things they could or, conversely, trying to control things they can't)
- How do you know whether you are responsible for this situation? (People feeling guilty when they shouldn't or, conversely, not feeling guilty when they should)
- How do you know when you can follow your heart? (People following their feelings when they shouldn't or, conversely, not listening to their feelings when they should)

- How do you know whether this a sensible risk? (People exaggerating slight risks or, conversely, minimizing significant risks)
- How do you know whether you should hold on? (People holding on when they'd do better to let go or, conversely, letting go when they'd do better to hold on)
- How do you know what to self-disclose? (People revealing too much to the wrong audience or, conversely, not revealing or sharing enough with the right audience)
- How do you know whether your expectations are realistic? (People getting attached to a specific outcome of how things should be or, conversely, having no idea of what they might want from a situation)
- How do you know when something is personal? (People who take things personally that aren't or, conversely, people who don't take things personally that are, indeed, personal)

The process-oriented hypnosis session, then speaks to the specific discrimination issue underlying the presenting problem. The clinician has to be able to provide specific discrimination criteria (e.g., "Before you accept someone's blame and feel guilty as a result, here's how you can know whether it's truly your responsibility or you're just being blamed for someone else's mistake") that the client can integrate and use to solve the current dilemma as well as manage future episodes. Table 7.1 provides a generic structure for helping clients evolve the skills for making better discriminations.

---

**TABLE 7.1. GENERIC SESSION STRUCTURE FOR MAKING BETTER DISCRIMINATIONS**

**Induction**

| | |
|---|---|
| **Response set:** | Discriminations |
| **Theme 1:** | New experiences create new opportunities |
| **Theme 2:** | We learn what to value as we grow up |
| **Theme 3:** | Socialization can blur important distinctions |
| **Theme 4:** | Developing the ability to make better discriminations |

**Posthypnotic suggestions for integration**
**Closure and disengagement**

### Induction

You can begin this focusing session by taking in a few deep, relaxing breaths . . . and orient yourself now to internal experience for a while. . . . Certainly you're becoming experienced enough . . . and self-aware enough . . . to know more and more about what's comfortable for you . . . how much time you need or want . . . to build the higher qualities of a meaningful focus for yourself. . . . Using your *deeper* knowledge can make it easy for you to be comfortable . . . easy for you to get more *deeply absorbed* inside with each passing moment . . . as you discover that the outside environment becomes less important for the moment . . . and so gradually recedes into the background. . . . It can be quite interesting to notice how your level of attention grows in intensity as time goes on . . . and what you focus on begins to change. . . .

### Response Set Regarding Discriminations

And out of all the things there are to notice . . . at a given moment . . . such as the routine sounds of the environment . . . or the sensations of comfort increasing within you . . . or the sound of my voice . . . there are things that are relevant . . . and there are things that are irrelevant . . . to creating a meaningful experience of comfort for yourself right now . . . many different things which naturally pass through your awareness. . . . And that in itself is a rather curious statement . . . deciding what's relevant and what's not . . . what's worth focusing your attention on . . . and what isn't . . . and how very calming it is . . . to just let things that really don't matter right now sail on by . . . passing effortlessly through your awareness. . . . And it can be an easy thing to allow . . . because there's no particular pressure . . . no mandate . . . about what you're supposed to do. . . . You can just comfortably recognize what's routine in your thoughts . . . or experience . . . that is *so* routine . . . that it's just not worth paying attention to right now. . . . Those can drift into your awareness . . . and then drift right out again . . . as your attention turns to new ideas and possibilities . . . that encourage a *deeper* understanding . . . of what's worth paying attention to . . . especially when you're needing to make a good choice . . . of where to place your focus . . . and where to

invest your energy and resources . . . as you recognize opportunities to
make important distinctions with insight . . . and foresight . . . just as you
did moments ago . . . when you chose to be comfortable and turn your
attention inward . . . and create a wonderfully comfortable space . . . and
get *absorbed* in a different way of experiencing yourself. . . .

**Theme: New Experiences Create New Opportunities**
And when people are exposed only to the familiar . . . such as the same
picture on the wall in your home that you no longer notice because
you pass by it every day for years . . . or the routine sounds of the environment you work in you that you've stopped noticing simply because
they're always there in the background. . . . People tune out the familiar. . . . You know as well as I do that what tends to capture people's
attention is what's new or what's different . . . the unexpected things
that happen in the space of a moment . . . perhaps the things someone
says or does that catch you off guard . . . quite often in the form of a
happy surprise . . . such as the unexpected phone call from someone
you've been thinking about but haven't talked to in a long time . . . or
the surprise compliment or kind gesture someone gives you for no particular reason that you really appreciate . . . or the things someone says
that you never really thought about before that inspire you in the best of
ways. . . . And the invitation being offered to you here and now . . . is to
allow yourself the luxury . . . of being able to notice things within yourself . . . that you don't usually pay much attention to . . . such as where
your mind goes when it doesn't have to go anywhere in particular . . .
or which parts of you drift off most easily and offer you a wonderful
sense of detachment from the usual. . . . And that's what provides a
window into your inner experience . . . allowing new understandings to
emerge . . . and just how different an experience *this* can be . . . giving
rise to different ideas, different understandings. . . .

**Theme: We Learn What to Value as We Grow Up**
And that's what gives you a chance now to consider the value of new
ideas . . . and new understandings . . . when you come to realize . . . that
some of the things that we learned while growing up . . . and things
we then come to think we understand about ourselves and the world

around us . . . sometimes turn out to not be very helpful to us . . . things
you were taught through direct messages or even just by watching and
listening to influential others . . . who had a perspective that once may
have seemed right without question or seemed to at least have made
some sense. . . . Well, nobody, I mean *nobody,* escapes the power, the
influence of socialization . . . that process of learning how to become a
person that we all go through. . . . You grew up around people . . . parents, teachers, relatives, friends . . . and they each shared their values
through the things they said and did . . . what they emphasized and
what they de-emphasized in the way they acted and the things they
said. . . . And you started learning very early in your life . . . what was
deemed important . . . what was valuable to pursue. . . . Socialization
is a very powerful force. . . . Consider how much it shapes our perceptions of what we think we know or how we think we should act. . . . And
then at some point in your development . . . as you grow more experienced and more aware . . . you might come to recognize that things you
thought were true weren't . . . and ways that you thought you should
act, you shouldn't . . . because situations change . . . and new responses
are needed. . . . And you start to become aware of your ability to choose
which beliefs to hold onto as still relevant . . . and which ones to discard
as no longer relevant . . . if they ever really *were* relevant at all. . . . You
take charge of yourself as you evaluate which things to reaffirm as still
important and which things to dismiss because they just don't work for
you anymore. . . .

### Theme: Socialization Can Blur Important Distinctions
And when you learn from significant others . . . what's important to them
that they believe should be important to you, too . . . you learn a style
of responding to life experiences. . . . For example, if you have parents
who are perfectionistic . . . who are quick to point out and criticize even
small, meaningless mistakes or less than perfect grades in school . . . but
rarely, if ever, compliment what you've done well . . . then you learn to
focus your attention on what's wrong in almost every life situation . . .
and rarely, if ever, on what's *right.* . . . You'll be quick to notice your inevitable flaws simply . . . because you're human . . . but not acknowledge
your strengths. . . . Such people don't learn to distinguish between an
unrealistic perfectionism and a realistic sense of what's plenty good

enough. . . . Or if you grow up learning to always put others' needs and wishes ahead of your own . . . taught that your worth only comes from what you do for others . . . then you might learn to be generous and sensitive . . . but you don't learn how to do caring things for yourself . . . because it seems self-indulgent and even selfish. . . . Such people don't learn to distinguish between selfishness and taking care of self. . . . And there are things you learned growing up . . . ways you were taught to be and values you were taught to live by . . . that were so deeply ingrained in you . . . that you hadn't really realized their significance before. . . . Perhaps you knew about them . . . but there's an important distinction between knowing something and *realizing* something. . . .

### Theme: Developing the Ability to Make Better Discriminations

And we all encounter pieces of wisdom handed to us in the form of old sayings . . . such as "you're never too old to learn something new" . . . but what can be confusing at times is the piece of wisdom that contradicts that wisdom . . . when someone says . . . "But you can't teach an old dog new tricks" . . . or the common advice some people give when they tell you to "follow your heart" . . . and the opposite advice of others who say, "*Don't* follow your feelings because they can too easily deceive you." . . . And how do you decide which piece of conflicting advice to follow at a given time? . . . The ability to recognize that there are at least two sides to consider . . . is one of the most important new understandings that you can develop. . . . And as you learn more and more about *how* to decide when it's best right now to do *this* but not *that* . . . each time you need to make an important choice insightfully . . . it can lead you to make better and better decisions as you move through your life . . . decisions you can feel good about . . . that start with making important distinctions between options that can generate good consequences. . . . And there are so many of these important distinctions to make each day . . . such as determining what is and isn't in your control in some situation . . . or what is and isn't your responsibility in some area of your life . . . or when to listen to your feelings and when to override them . . . when to open up to someone and when to keep a sensible distance . . . all the while growing in yourself a richer and deeper understanding that socialization may lead you to see only one side of something. . . . And your newly emerging awareness allows you to see the choice embedded in each situation . . . so that you can better choose between this possible response and that one. . . .

### Posthypnotic Suggestions for Integration

It's the experiences that you have each day that present a choice to you . . . to do what's familiar because you've always done it that way . . . or to recognize an opportunity to do something different. . . . By recognizing that you're making a distinction that you hadn't considered before . . . that leads to a different and more *effective* response . . . you simply hadn't made before . . . a new process is emerging within you . . . that makes it so much more reflexive to choose wisely with foresight and insight. . . . And when you emerge from this valuable experience . . . and you can see the choices available in different environments . . . you can enjoy discovering that it is so *empowering* for you to evolve the confidence in your own judgment to make the necessary distinctions that lead to more satisfying and enriching outcomes . . . a future of making good choices based on making the distinction between possibilities using the best information you can have at the time . . . in order to choose what will work best . . . produce the best possible result . . . in a particular situation. . . .

### Closure and Disengagement

And you have some decisions to make right now as we bring this session to a close . . . about what you really want to hold on to from this experience . . . and what distinctions you realize now you most need to learn to make . . . and even at just what moment you've had enough time to process these ideas and possibilities and are ready to end this session. . . . But first, take whatever time you want or need to process your thoughts, feelings, reactions to fully absorb the useful things that have occurred to you. . . . And when you've had enough time to process . . . and you're ready to bring this experience to a comfortable close . . . you can start to do so by slowly reattaching to your body . . . and to the environment as your awareness of your surroundings grows. . . . You can feel increasingly alert and energized now . . . and when you're ready, you can let your eyes open and reorient completely. . . .

# Chapter 8

# Developing Impulse Control

*Men are rather reasoning than reasonable animals, for the most part governed by the impulse of passion.*

—Alexander Hamilton

## The Case of Charlotte

Seventeen-year-old Charlotte was somewhat of an enigma, no more so to anyone else than to herself. She was in her senior year of high school, getting excellent grades, and was socially connected to a nice network of friends. She was awaiting a reply to her university application and felt confident she'd be accepted and move on to a new and exciting phase of life as a university undergraduate. She sounded like she was on top of the world, so I waited for her to get to why she was in my office asking for help. I didn't have to wait long. Suddenly, her exuberant demeanor was gone, her tone became hushed, her eye contact went away, and she was clearly trying to figure out how to say what she wanted to say. Finally, instead of telling me, she showed me. When she rolled up her sleeves to expose her forearms, both had easily visible scars.

Charlotte watched me closely for my reaction. I think she was relieved to see I didn't have much of one. I've seen the residuals of self-harm too many times before to be shocked by it, sometimes in people much older and sometimes much younger than Charlotte. I waited for her to initiate the conversation, and she returned the favor by waiting for me to do the same. Finally, I just asked her directly: "What's that about?" She paused, trying to come up with a sensible reply, and finally just said, "I don't know. I don't know why I do that. I just do. It's as if something builds up inside of me and I just feel this weird urge to cut myself and when I do the urge goes away, at least for a while. I think it might just be my way of handling stress."

Charlotte engaged in self-harming behavior. What's that about? Was it an act of self-hate? Was it thinly disguised suicidal behavior? Was it a passive cry for attention or help? Was it anger turned inward that was really meant for her parents? Was it a faddish behavior in today's young people to wear as some kind of badge of honor, and she just wanted to fit in with that crowd? Was it the residual of unresolved trauma? Or what?

I asked Charlotte a few pointed questions about her internal experience: "How do you know when you're stressed? How far ahead of time do you know the feeling is building and you're going to cut yourself? How do you decide where to cut yourself and how deeply to cut? How do you view the cuts and scars after you've made them? How do you explain the cuts and scars to your friends? To your parents? To your doctor? Are you connected to others who do this same kind of cutting?"

It was as if Charlotte, bright as she was, had never thought of these things before. Her answer to each question was some variation of "I don't know" or "I'm not sure." How could such a smart young woman be so oblivious to what's going on inside? Her lack of what is termed "emotional differentiation" means her feelings were so global, so jumbled up together, that she couldn't even begin to untangle them in order to develop realistic self-regulation strategies.

The content of Charlotte's problem is whatever is currently stressing her, whatever is going on in the moment that gives rise to the impulsive desire to cut herself. The process is her poor coping style in which she faces some stressor, real or imagined, and jumps to the self-harm behavior to manage it. She shows no pause to develop either insight or foresight regarding whatever's going on or how she's feeling and how best to manage it. She simply feels and responds to the impulse to cut herself.

Using hypnosis to encourage impulse control, it was important to first depathologize her behavior by asserting that people do what they know how to do to cope, even when sometimes it works against them. But people can develop new understandings and new skills that go along with different levels of personal growth. Charlotte was led to realize that she was groomed to focus outside herself, especially on getting great grades and participating in purposeful activities outside of school to embellish her value to prospective universities. In so doing, she was detached from (dissociating) developing a strong and clear internal awareness. Using a sports metaphor, she was all defense and no offense, a point she understood easily. The task now was to eventually be able to answer questions requiring insight, such as being able to identify, name, and report on her feelings as a big step toward learning to manage them skillfully. If you can't identify it, how can you manage it?

The suggestion was embedded throughout the hypnosis session that she was learning the topography of her inner world, the things that she would know about herself that she'd never realized before. This would evolve as her response began to change quite dramatically to what she previously thought of simply as a "buildup" of an unspecified nature. Now, she was told, "When you start to become aware of a buildup of *any* kind inside, it's a buildup to *greater self-awareness*, a buildup to *greater personal insight*, a buildup to the *foresight* to know that you can do more to help yourself than harm yourself." The suggestion that "the impulse to harm can give rise to the *stronger impulse* to pause . . . and be self-aware and choose a helpful response you can be proud of" helped establish a new and positive association for Charlotte.

The process of self-discovery and a developing a renewed self-definition can certainly be relatively quick, but not instantaneous. Charlotte had six sessions spread out over several months. It was easy to utilize the natural transition she was about to go through, with moving on from high school to college and all that she would be leaving behind, including outdated behaviors, and all that she'd be growing into, such as more mature and safe relationships, including her relationship with herself. The cutting behavior stopped almost right away, but her recognition of the sometimes-confusing elements of her inner world took her some time to develop. She was given values clarification exercises to help her define her priorities and ways to act that would be consistent with them as well as additional hypnosis sessions to reinforce that thoughts and feelings can come and go, but she can think ahead far enough to know when a particular thought or feeling is going to take her someplace she really doesn't want to go. Charlotte learned that she's much more than her impulses. Seeing her after her first semester away at college, she was absolutely radiant. She hadn't cut herself again and was proud of how she had handled some pretty delicate situations with, in her words, "insight and foresight."

## The Role of Impulse Control in Quality of Life

Two common phrases people use to describe the consequences of their actions are, "I don't know what made me jump in and do that, but I'm so glad I did!" and its opposite sentiment when people lament, "I don't know what made me jump in and do that, but it was a huge mistake I deeply regret." Both these statements reflect actions taken in the spur of the moment, deeds done impulsively without the benefit of either insight or foresight. Clearly, there are times when the consequences turn out to be favorable, but at other times the consequences can be painful and the source of regrets that endure for a lifetime. When impulsive actions hold so much potential for harm to oneself and others, the need for a means to manage one's impulsivity skillfully becomes obvious. This chapter focuses on the role process-oriented hypnosis can play in facilitating this skill.

## Temporal Orientation Shapes Life Experience

Each person forms a relationship to the dimension of time, called a temporal orientation. How that relationship is defined and prioritized, whether consciously or nonconsciously, plays a huge role in the way people go about living their lives. Consider, for example, what defines one person as ambitious while striving to climb the career ladder with a clear vision of what their goals are, while someone else apparently lacks ambition altogether and is perfectly content to live in their parents' basement and play video games all day. They have two very different relationships to the construct of time, one ambitiously future oriented, the other passively tied to this moment's entertainment. If you think about different people's lifestyles and how the element of time features within them, it is generally not difficult to see who is living in a way that more heavily favors one sphere of time over another.

What the orientation in time leads someone to specifically do (or not do) represents the content of their experience. How their temporal orientation influences their choices or reactions represents the process. It is a powerful realization with significant clinical implications that every problem we treat inevitably has an element of time embedded within it. Consider the following examples.

Depression is largely a past-oriented phenomenon that prominently features a hashing and rehashing of nearly every hurt, rejection, humiliation, and failure that an individual has suffered. If the depressed person thinks about the future at all, it typically involves extending the troubled past into the future (as discussed in greater detail in Chapter 6), literally saying such things as, "I'll never be happy. Why? Because I never have been. I'll never have a good relationship. Why? Because I've never had one." And the ultimate past-oriented conundrum: "I won't be happy until my parents treat me better when I was a child!" You can probably predict the effect of bringing a past-oriented problem like depression to a past-oriented therapist. A useful clinical guideline suggests that when the structure of the attempted solution matches the structure of the client's problem, it's generally a formula for stagnation. From a process-oriented point of view, helping the client interrupt the pattern of using the negative past as a reference point to predict the future and build the pattern of establishing new goals and defining and taking the steps necessary to reach them is vital.

Anxiety disorders are future oriented, typically featuring a focus on what could go wrong, even catastrophizing and predicting that things will go wrong with devastating consequences that are terribly frightening. Thinking the future holds imminent disaster is what drives phobias, leading people to believe that their safety is threatened. Psychologist David Barlow from Boston University, a major figure in the anxiety field who has spent his life researching anxiety's many causes and treatments, framed anxiety in a simple and compelling way I also shared earlier. Paraphrasing, he said, "Anxiety arises from people *over*estimating risks and *under*estimating their own resources." It is an orientation to the future that predicts harm that one is helpless to stop and inadequate to manage. From a process-oriented perspective, helping people learn to discriminate real threats from imagined ones (i.e., enhanced risk assessment) and connect them to their personal resources for an increased sense that the challenges they face can be managed is at the core of good treatment.

Impulse disorders, by definition, are present-oriented phenomena, represented by the motto to live by, "I want this *now!*" To present-oriented individuals, the past and the chance to learn from it are long gone from awareness, and the future seems both unknowable and unimportant in this moment of reflexive responding. All that matters is the desire of the moment, whether it's for a drink, a drug, a comfort food, a desire to hit someone who's making them angry, a sexual conquest, a chance to win some money at the card table, a chance to blame someone else for their bad choices, and on and on. The number of ways impulsivity can lead someone down a destructive path are seemingly infinite. What someone does impulsively is the content of their problem, but how someone responds to an impulse is the process. The development of impulse control is a highly desirable self-regulation skill across countless life situations, and process-oriented hypnosis can facilitate the teaching of that skill.

## How Now Attains Ascendance

When the culture encourages a do-it-now philosophy along with other structurally similar messages (e.g., "Don't hold back your feelings," "Feel free to say or do whatever you want," "Just do it," and "Who cares what others think?"), there is no reason to develop restraint, the essential ingredient of impulse control. In America, and other places too, we have seen a loosening of the social restraints that encouraged people to be more civil with each other. The result has been an escalation in hate crimes and open disdain for anyone perceived as different and therefore less than. Tolerance encourages restraint, a clear emphasis on accepting differences between people based on simple respect.

On an individual level, the lack of a mechanism of restraint leads people to speak without forethought and say things they soon come to regret. They do things on a whim, with no forethought at all about the possible consequences that brings them, and most often the others around them as well, a great deal of hurt. Now is what matters, consequences be damned.

What about the effects of teaching a philosophy of now to such now-oriented people? When therapists are the ones to say, "The past is gone, and the future hasn't happened yet, so all there is is this moment," are they really doing their clients a favor? Some of the most destructive things that humans do are clearly in the name of right now. But it's also true that some of the most valuable experiences human beings can have arise directly from being present in the moment.

## Typical Problems Derived From a Lack of Impulse Control

The types of problems that people might present for treatment that reflect an inability to exercise impulse control can seem quite diverse, and may include such problematic patterns as these:

- A lack of foresight or inability to predict likely consequences
- A poor grasp of linear thinking and cause-and-effect relationships
- A reckless attitude that eschews the need for any self-restraint
- A history of negative experiences from which they learned little or nothing
- A history of making bad decisions in the heat of the moment that they later regret
- A lack of coherent strategy for addressing important issues with no better plan than to just wing it
- A general inability to consider or even care about their effect on others
- Avoidance as a coping strategy (prioritizing immediate comfort over problem solving)
- An ability to justify bad behavior with poor excuses

## Defining the Salient Therapeutic Targets

If a present orientation can be both helpful and harmful, depending on the context, it raises another discrimination question we must be good at answering for our clients: How do you know when to be present in the moment and when you're much better off thinking beyond the moment? The general answer lies in the ability to recognize the consequences of either position in some situation. That highlights what might seem to be a paradox: being future-oriented enough to know whether you can be present-oriented right now.

There are therapists who advocate the point of view that the future can't be predicted. I flatly reject that statement because it's both global and fundamentally incorrect. I accept that aspects of the future can't be predicted, but many things can be predicted. I can predict that if you abuse your kids, they will have some pretty serious emotional problems to contend with as a result. I can predict that if you smoke two packs of cigarettes a day, you're going to suffer some negative health consequences. I can predict that if you think you can just say anything you want to anybody you wish, you're going to face plenty of rejection.

We may not be able to predict everything, but that doesn't mean we can't predict anything. It isn't all or none, and requires of us another type of discrimination: What things can be predicted on a clear-cut cause-and-effect basis, and which things are so multifactorial and context specific that an accurate prediction is unlikely? An ability to make accurate predictions, an obviously future-oriented skill, should be one of the skills we routinely teach in the course of therapy. It is the foundation for teaching impulse control.

To teach impulse control in therapy, one would have to first recognize the merits of thoughtful restraint. Appreciating the pause needed to determine what might be an effective response in some circumstance provides time enough to be deliberate in deciding whether to respond and how to respond. Why is it better to accept the speeding ticket than to strike the cop you're furious with for writing it? Even the impulsive, raging client knows better than to make matters worse by striking a law enforcement officer. In the client who impulsively lashes out, but this time manages not to, where does that unexpected restraint come from, and how can we extend it through process-oriented hypnosis into other contexts?

Impulse control requires a key skill that can be taught in therapy, especially when utilizing hypnosis. That skill is called dissociation. Dissociation features an ability to step outside of the immediacy of your experience, whether it's your physical experience, as in pain relief, or your cognitive experience, as in thought-distancing strategies. Dissociation allows people to step out of the moment long enough to consider other people's feelings or the likely consequences of some contemplated action. Hypnosis is by its very nature a dissociative experience, as is mindfulness and other similarly structured focusing experiences. Dissociation has a much broader clinical relevance than what many clinicians learn if they only study dissociative disorders, particularly when it's structured to help people go beyond the moment.

An interesting example of the ability to separate—dissociate—from an immediate desire in order to go beyond the moment is the psychologist Walter Mischel's famous research from the 1960s on what is commonly called the marshmallow test. In his experiments with young children ages 4 and 5, it became very clear how strong a role future orientation plays in delaying immediate gratification for a greater future reward. The children were given a marshmallow as a treat and then were told the experimenter would be leaving the room for a few minutes. The child could eat the marshmallow right away if they liked, but if they waited for the experimenter to return "in just a little while," they would be given the reward of a second marshmallow. Some kids popped that marshmallow into their mouth as soon as he left the room, and others sat looking longingly at the marshmallow and somehow managed not to eat it, thereby earning the extra one. Mischel (2014) followed the kids who participated in the experiment over the course of their lives. Four decades later, he wrote about the long-term higher-level successes of those children who were best able to delay gratification in his book, *The Marshmallow Test: Why Self-Control Is the Engine of Success.*

The primary target of the process-oriented hypnosis session, then, is to facilitate the client developing the necessary resources to pause before acting or reacting. During that pause, the client can consider what might be the most effective or desirable response in that particular circumstance. Shifting the client's focus from the immediate to the possible consequences imparts a strategy for making decisions with greater insight and foresight. The use of hypnosis and its innate capacity for encouraging automaticity in responding can be a particularly helpful means for making it more reflexive for the client to pause and reflect before acting or reacting.

The result of being more deliberate represents a second target of treatment: It empowers people to act with greater integrity and attain greater success. This can serve to significantly improve their self-esteem, feeling better about what they do and how they do it. A third target, then, becomes apparent, namely the ability to prevent regret. What a lighter load to move through life with when you're not burdened with regrets!

Learning to control your impulses is clearly a pathway to greater success on many levels. As you'll see, process-oriented hypnosis can go a long way in helping people develop that skill set. Table 8.1 suggests a means for helping clients develop greater impulse control.

TABLE 8.1. GENERIC SESSION STRUCTURE
FOR DEVELOPING IMPULSE CONTROL

**Induction**

| | |
|---|---|
| **Response set:** | Impulse control |
| **Theme 1:** | Much of our experience is reflexive, driven without awareness |
| **Theme 2:** | Amplifying the space in between perception and reaction |
| **Theme 3:** | Impulsivity is overcome by anticipating consequences |
| **Theme 4:** | You can become more future oriented |

**Posthypnotic suggestions for integration**
**Closure and disengagement**

## SESSION TRANSCRIPT

### Induction

You can begin by taking in a few deep, relaxing breaths . . . and the very act of slowly breathing in and out . . . is such an easy and rhythmic natural experience. . . . It literally sustains life . . . and encourages a wonderful sense of calm within you . . . a deepening level of relaxation that becomes more pronounced with each breath you take. . . . And when you take the time to sit quietly and focus the way that you are now . . . it's really comforting to just let your eyes close and turn your attention inward . . . so you can notice some of the many different aspects of your own internal experience. . . . And of course, that includes your physical experience . . . the experience of breathing comfortably in, effortlessly out. . . .

### Building a Response Set Regarding Impulse Control

And when it's so basic to your very life . . . there's something quite comforting about knowing how automatic a process breathing is for us. . . . It's one of the many great marvels about the human body. . . . Especially when you consider how many things are taking place within us at a given moment . . . how many bodily functions are going on *automatically* that we tend to not even notice, much less think about . . . such as the blinking of your eyes as they refresh themselves from moment to moment . . . the circulation of blood and distribution of nutrients from the foods you eat . . . the coordinated movement of muscles that help balance you and move you . . . and the rhythmic act of breathing that continues every moment of your life. . . . And thankfully there's no reason for you to have to think about breathing. . . . You can appreciate that the *impulse* to breathe is necessary and wonderful. . . . You don't have to think about it. . . . Your body just responds to the impulse to breathe . . . that automatic signal from deep within to inhale and the automatic signal to exhale. . . . And like the drive to breathe . . . there are so many other drives built into our very makeup . . . drives from deep within us . . . such as the drive to seek out new or stimulating experiences when we're feeling bored . . . or the drive to seek out experiences that soothe us when we're feeling stressed. . . .

**Theme: Much of Our Experience Is Reflexive, Driven Without Awareness**
And it's the automatic nature of experiences . . . those things we do on impulse . . . that I'm drawing your attention to right now. . . . And even as you listen, you might notice the drive within you to *get absorbed* in new ideas . . . that can become reflexive . . . and come to appreciate the ways they can help you in moving through life each day with greater deliberateness. . . . So much of what we experience is driven without any awareness. . . . There isn't any personal sense of us doing it . . . things that we just do that we feel compelled to do . . . something from within us that leads us to react instantly and thoughtlessly . . . to feel and behave in sometimes puzzling and even illogical ways. . . . It's easy to see in ourselves when we just consider simple examples . . . such as going to the grocery store to do your shopping. . . . You don't necessarily realize why you choose this brand over that brand of a product. . . . You just reach for it and place it in your cart. . . . But when we look at the marketing research about the brands that people buy . . . it's probably no surprise to anybody that we are much more likely to buy the brand that we've heard of than the brand that we haven't . . . the brand we have some familiarity with, either through past experience or through advertising we've seen. . . . And when you consider how many billions of dollars get spent on advertising . . . we can ask, does all that advertising really work? And the answer is clearly yes. . . . It builds in us a sense of

familiarity that shapes the way we spend our money without our even realizing it. . . . Other research shows how shoppers can be influenced to make impulse buys just by the way items are placed in the grocery store . . . which ones are on lower shelves and which ones are on higher shelves . . . which items are on the end caps of aisles and which ones are placed on central display. . . . And there's a reason why the candy is placed at the checkout counter . . . to create an impulse to buy candy as a small reward at the end. . . . And when you ask people why they chose that product over the other one, most of the time they say, "I really don't know. . . ." And another easy example of how much of what we experience is driven without much awareness . . . is how often people react to someone that reminds them of someone else they know as if they're that person. . . . So they may take an instant liking to someone that reminds them of someone they like . . . or they may take an instant dislike to someone that reminds them of someone they really don't like. . . . And it's not a conscious or deliberate process of saying to yourself, "I'm going to like this person because of the way they remind me of someone else I like." . . . It just happens automatically as an *impulse to react*. . . .

### Theme: Amplifying the Space Between Perception and Reaction

And when you're sitting quietly, focusing the way you are right now . . . you have an opportunity to discover something really important . . . and it can be a really profound discovery when you start to recognize . . . that there is a space that exists in between a thought or a feeling and a reaction. . . . It's the space, that all-important moment, where someone becomes aware and feels an impulsive drive to say or do something . . . that sometimes may not be the best thing to say or do. . . . But now you discover that there's that important moment . . . that can seem longer and longer as you become more skilled in using that moment. . . . You can develop a sense for that moment where you can pause long enough to choose first *whether* to react to something. . . . And, if so, then *how* to react . . . even in, and especially in, difficult situations . . . that require something more thoughtful. . . . What an extraordinary capacity you are born with to take that space in between a thought or a feeling and a reaction . . . and to use it skillfully . . . to first choose wisely *whether* to say or do something . . . and then, if so, what to say or do that will serve you best in that situation. . . . I can tell you about an experience that a friend of mine had not long ago. . . . He had just gotten a new sporty little car . . . a beautiful car that could really reach high speeds effortlessly . . . and he was driving along happily, not really paying attention to how fast he was going on the freeway. . . . And the next thing he knew there was a siren blaring . . . and when he looked in the rearview mirror, he saw a police car behind him with lights flashing . . . and his heart sank as he knew he had to pull over. . . . He went through a quick series of feelings of being angry, then scared, and then angry again. . . . But he pulled over, and though he felt barely in control of his emotions . . . he prepared himself to face up to whatever would happen next. . . . The police officer came up to his window and made the usual request to see his driver's license and car registration. . . . The officer was very polite but also very clear that my friend deserved and was going to get a speeding ticket. . . . Well, nobody wants a speeding ticket, and everybody tries to talk the officer out of it . . . which is what my friend tried to do. . . . "Gee, Officer, it's a new car. . . . And I didn't really know how fast I was going. . . . And gee, Officer, I was in a hurry and I just wasn't paying attention and I'm sorry and gee, Officer . . ." and all the other excuses he used to try and change the officer's mind. . . . And when the excuses didn't work, my friend got angrier and angrier, and he really wanted to argue with the officer. . . . He really wanted to argue because he was so mad . . . and somehow, as much as he wanted to argue, he soon grew quiet and accepted responsibility for his mistake of driving too fast. . . . And when he was given the ticket, he took it politely, and the episode was over. . . . And when I saw him later that day, he was still angry about the whole thing. . . . He thought he deserved a break. . . . And when he was describing to me how he wanted to yell at this officer and how he wanted to shove the ticket right back in his face, but *didn't* . . . I asked him, "As angry as you were, why didn't you vent? Why didn't you yell at him? Why didn't you get angry? . . . And he thought about it for a moment . . . as if he'd never really considered this question before . . . before he simply said, "Because it would have just made things a lot *worse*." . . . Take a moment now and consider that answer. . . . "It would have just made things a lot worse." . . .

### Theme: Impulsivity Is Overcome by Anticipating Consequences

He was no longer responding to his feelings in the moment, was he? . . . Instead, much to his credit, he was thinking ahead in that angry moment

about the possible consequences of following his impulse to lash out . . .
acting on his impulse to vent his anger. . . . And that *automatic jump
into an awareness of consequences* was what allowed him to contain
his angry impulse and set it aside for a much better outcome. . . . Well,
that's a really interesting shift in awareness from the immediate to the
eventual. . . . And if you think about the people that you know who are
effective . . . they follow that same model. . . . They use their capacity for
thinking ahead and containing the impulse of the moment. . . . You might
find it quite interesting and helpful to know that there's a very famous set
of psychological experiments conducted by a psychologist named Walter Mischel. . . . They are well-known experiments that have come to be
known as the marshmallow experiments. . . . And when he first did these
experiments decades ago, he was working with young children ages 4
and 5. . . . And it was unbeknownst to them, of course, at that young age,
that this was an experiment in studying delayed gratification . . . *the ability to resist an impulse for some greater gain.* . . . So he sat them down at
a table and talked with them a little bit . . . and then he presented them
with a marshmallow, a favorite snack of kids in those days and still a
favorite for some kids. . . . Then he told them, "I'm going to give you one
marshmallow right now that you can eat right now if you'd like . . . but
I'm going to leave the room for a few minutes, and if you haven't eaten
that marshmallow while I'm gone, I'll come back and give you a second
marshmallow, and then you can have two instead of one." . . . Well, there
were some children who gobbled up that marshmallow without even
thinking, as soon as he left the room . . . and there were other kids who
sat and looked at the marshmallow and smacked their lips but managed
to wait until he came back. . . . You could tell they clearly wanted it *right
now*, but they demonstrated even at that young age . . . the extraordinary ability to set aside the impulse to eat the marshmallow now . . . in
order to have two by waiting just a little while. . . . Now, that's interesting
that some kids could do that . . . but what was even more interesting was
how Walter Mischel followed these kids all the way into adulthood to see
how their lives would turn out . . . and then he wrote a book about it that
came out not long ago . . . and what he discovered, to no one's surprise,
is that the kids who could delay gratification . . . who could think beyond
the impulse of the moment . . . were more likely to build careers instead
of just having jobs. . . . Consequently, they were likely to make more

money and live a more comfortable lifestyle. . . . They were more likely to be physically healthy and didn't smoke or drink or overeat . . . and that ability to *think beyond the moment* governs so much of the quality of life. . . . The people who are willing to go to school, trade school, college, whatever, and endure the hours, weeks, and months and years of class time . . . and endure all the demands and stresses of school such as writing papers and exams . . . they give up some comfort *now* because *they want something greater later* in terms of a higher quality of life. . . . Likewise, consider the people who carefully guard their health . . . who have the impulse to eat favorite junk foods or drink lots of alcohol . . . but in that space, that important moment in between the impulse and the reaction . . . is the thought, the deeply held belief, that their longer-term health matters more . . . much more . . . than the impulse to put junk into their body . . . and there's a lot to learn from these experiences and how people handle them with finesse. . . .

### Theme: You Can Become More Future Oriented

And for you now to *be aware of that wonderful moment, that space in between the impulse and the reaction . . .* draws your attention to how *you can become more oriented to the future . . .* more oriented to the consequences, the eventual consequences of the decision you make in that moment . . . than you are to the immediate feeling or impulse. . . . You see, you can have a flash of anger, but you can let it pass in order to handle the situation more calmly . . . and gently. . . . It means you can have a flash of fear and you can quickly set it aside . . . because there's something important to be done . . . something *more important* than just being afraid and lashing out in fear. . . . And it's all about making these sorts of forward-looking choices about the best eventual consequences that you get to make in that special moment . . . in that sizeable space in between your initial impulse and what you then actually say or do. . . . And as you get better and better at using that space wisely . . . that's what allows you to gradually develop a genuine sense of pride in yourself and how you react under pressure . . . embodying the phrase "grace under pressure." . . . The pride that develops in you when you can *think beyond the impulse* and when you can routinely find that space in the moment where you can *jump ahead in your awareness . . .* and handle your feelings and reactions in ways that you respect in yourself. . . . And by making choices beyond the moment, you have the ability to not just feel better, but to actually *be* better. . . . And it might occur to you that there's still another benefit to using that special space in between impulse and reaction. . . . It's the ability to *prevent regret* because you *didn't* say careless words and because you *didn't* overreact emotionally. . . . Instead you were careful . . . and you were thinking beyond the moment. . . . And doesn't it feel wonderful when you can handle a situation well and actually like what you did there because you let your cooler head prevail? . . . The ability to prevent regret is a huge and valuable gift to yourself. . . .

### Posthypnotic Suggestions for Integration

You know as well as I do . . . that everyone has impulses . . . including self-destructive or simply foolish ones. . . . Everyone, in one way or another, wants the marshmallow now. . . . Some people want the drink now. . . . Others want the drug now. . . . Others want the sex now. . . . Others want the freedom to do whatever they want now . . . even if it hurts others or themselves. . . . But what it's really about to *live well* . . . is to *go beyond the impulse* . . . go beyond being driven by emotions and unconscious forces that you don't even understand or don't even recognize until much later, if ever. . . . And so right now, you're learning something really important . . . that you can absorb deeply and use well for the rest of your life . . . that you have the space and the time to make better choices . . . choices that help create the kind of future you'll be happy to live in. . . . And you can use that space and time more automatically . . . in ways that you'll find satisfying . . . letting your cooler head prevail. . . .

### Closure and Disengagement

It's nice to have had the time to explore within yourself and discover abilities you didn't necessarily know you have. . . . And it's these new awarenesses that you can bring back with you when I invite you to reorient yourself in just a little while. . . . But first, it's a good use of time to bring this session to a comfortable close . . . an unhurried time to enjoy the sense of comfort you've developed and bring it with you when you reorient. . . . And when you're ready to bring this session to a close . . . you can begin the process of slowly moving your body as you bring yourself back to your usual state of alertness . . . reorienting fully now and opening your eyes . . . alert and comfortable. . . .

# Chapter 9

# Facilitating Compartmentalization

*In fact, we are each a confederation of rather independent modules orchestrated to work together. . . . There is not one centralized system working to produce the grand magic of conscious experience.*
—Michael Gazzaniga, *The Consciousness Instinct*

## The Case of Bradley

Bradley, age 32, is the father of two young boys, ages 5 and 7. He has come to therapy with the report of being a "self-described wimp as a dad." Bradley describes his marriage to Jeanette of almost 10 years as a happy one. He says there is "nothing deeply wrong" that brings him to therapy right now, but he is aware that if he doesn't get a good handle on one of his troublesome issues, his family might suffer as a result. He'd like to prevent that from happening.

Asked what it means to be a "self-described wimp," Bradley began by first making sure I knew that he wasn't "*always* a wimp *everywhere*." He said he was just a wimp with his sons, an observation that Jeanette had made many times that he brushed off as nothing to take very seriously. He thought he was just being a good dad.

I inquired, "What changed that brought you here?" Bradley again assured me that he wasn't really a wimp but said that he had handled an interaction with one of his sons quite poorly. Jeanette expressed a great deal of disappointment, and it just added to his own poor appraisal of his behavior.

He got to the story that illustrated the problem and led him to see me: His younger son, Timmy, had found a lighter somewhere, who knows where, since neither he nor Jeanette smoke. Timmy was playing with the lighter, and no one was in the room to see it happen, but he set fire to the couch, and it quickly began to fill the room with smoke. The smoke detector went off just as Timmy was screaming for his mom and dad, and pandemonium broke loose. Fortunately, Bradley had a fire extinguisher nearby and was able to get to it quickly and extinguish the flames. Everyone was okay, which was the primary consideration, of course. But in the immediate aftermath, when Bradley should have had lots to say both verbally and nonverbally, he went AWOL. He didn't say anything, didn't do anything, just froze as his mind spun with the question, "What am I supposed to do here?"

Jeanette, on the other hand, went into high gear. She grabbed the lighter, with her face all about a controlled fury, before she erupted into shouting at Timmy about what he'd done and the tragedy that could have happened and the damage that did happen, and so on, and so on. Bradley watched the eruption and said nothing. Timmy was appropriately upset and crying. His brother was conspicuously missing in another part of the house. Jeanette was red faced with anger, and Bradley was all but invisible. It was in that moment, a greatly amplified moment related to other similar AWOL moments, that Bradley wondered about his fitness to be a parent to his boys. Jeanette was sorry to have to admit to him that she wondered the same thing.

Bradley enjoyed the fun of being a dad. He liked the roughhousing, tossing around a ball together, teaching the right way to field a ground ball. But when it was time to provide some discipline, Bradley just couldn't seem to get the job done. He said, "It makes me feel like I'm abusing them if I yell at them or punish them. They're really good boys, so I rationalize their occasional bad behavior as 'Oh well, boys will be boys.'"

So, what's Bradley's issue with providing parental discipline? Is he simply conflict avoidant? Was his relationship with his own father marred by harsh punishments, and he's overcompensating as a result? Is he fearful his boys will withdraw their love from him if he disciplines them and then won't want to be with him anymore? Does he fear honesty and the intimacy that goes with it? Is he afraid he'll scar them for life and be a failure as a dad? Does he have an unconscious ambivalence about being a dad that leads him to withdraw from the tougher parts of the job? Or what?

The content of Bradley's problem is his difficulty with providing necessary discipline to his boys. The process of his problem is his internal orientation, his using his feelings to inform his actions or lack thereof. It doesn't feel good to him to discipline them, so he doesn't.

If you were to get a thousand parents in a room and ask them the question, "How many of you enjoy disciplining your child?," it's a pretty safe bet no one will raise their hand. Hugs and kisses are wonderful; yelling and punishing not so much. But parents do it because it needs to be done. If you want to raise a personally and socially responsible child, meaning they have clear boundaries that define right and wrong, acceptable and unacceptable, then discipline provides those boundaries.

The use of hypnosis to facilitate compartmentalization skills becomes essential in cases such as these, that is, people who don't do what makes them uncomfortable even though it needs to be done. Compartmentalization skills mean breaking a global experience down into its components. In Bradley's case, there are his child's intentions, the behavior arising from those intentions, the message the child is sending through his behavior, the impact on other people and the environment, the message that is sent back if you do or don't react, the absorption or dismissal of that message regulating learning from feedback, the applicability of that lesson in other contexts that will arise, and how that confirms or contradicts previous messages. There's a lot going on in an interaction. And yet another component is Bradley's feeling state in response to his son's behavior.

Of all the things Bradley could be focused on, though, it's his focus on his feelings of distaste for discipline that governs his response. He doesn't want to, doesn't like to, and so he doesn't.

Hypnosis to facilitate compartmentalization was used with Bradley to make one vital point: There are things more important than your feelings. One of those is helping your sons develop a moral code, a greater sense of right and wrong, and the desire to consistently do what's right. The suggestions that dominate compartmentalization sessions revolve around the message that "there are many different voices speaking at one time: the voices of reason, passion, fear, optimism, others' judgments, . . .and so on. And you get to choose—you get to choose—which voice to listen to that will serve best in a given situation."

The problem isn't that Bradley has a voice inside his head that says, in essence, "Look the other way." The problem is that he listens to it. The hypnosis session with Bradley gave voice to these different parts of his experience and the different parts of the interaction and made it really clear to him that he was going to need to consistently respond to the voice that would serve to improve his sons' character rather than responding to the voice that made it easier for him to ignore and thereby indirectly sanction bad behavior.

In the span of just a few sessions, Bradley developed full clarity about what it would mean to set aside (compartmentalize) the voices of fear or convenience and focus on and respond from the voice encouraging good character in his sons instead. From that vantage point, it became instantly clear to him what needed to be said and when. His worst fears about being a disciplinarian never materialized. In his own self-satisfied words, he said, "My wimpy days are over."

## The Role of Compartmentalization in Quality of Life

Every person plays multiple roles in life. One can be someone's child, parent, grandparent, spouse, employer, employee, friend, and so on, living through each day juggling the different, sometimes conflicting, demands that accompany each role. Some roles are chosen; some we are born into. Some endure a lifetime; others are transient. Some are very clearly defined with unambiguous expectations of what that role requires; others are so fuzzy that we stumble through them trying to do our best.

When someone must manage many different roles in relationship to other people and institutions, it helps considerably to know which role(s) one is in at a given moment and what behavior best serves the demands of the situation. Similarly, when each person is made of many different parts on many different levels of experience, how we learn to recognize, develop, and value our different parts is a strong indicator of having a refined self-awareness. How we then come to understand the necessity of knowing which part(s) of ourselves to express and, conversely, which to suppress, in a given circumstance is a powerful force in shaping our quality of life. Having the insight and foresight to know, for example, that "now isn't the time to kick him when he's down" means suppressing anger at some hurtful or self-destructive decision that person made and focusing on expressing compassion instead.

This sophisticated skill is made possible only when someone has the ability to compartmentalize experience. Compartmentalization, discussed briefly in Chapter 4 and elaborated here, is the ability to break a global experience, such as an interaction in which one is feeling emotionally upset or threatened in some way, into its component parts. Instead of responding to the entirety of some experience, whether internal states or external circumstances, since they are two sides of the same coin, compartmentalization skills empower you to determine which part of yourself to respond to and which part of yourself to respond from.

Consider these two common examples: (1) Therapists routinely tell their anxious clients, "Feel the fear but do it anyway." Unless a client has the ability to compartmentalize and set the fear aside sufficiently well to keep their focus on taking effective action, their unrestrained fear can easily paralyze them into inaction. (2) Consider how often the biggest regrets people have result from their "moment of weakness" when they gave in to the part of themselves that enabled them to cross a line that shouldn't have been crossed. Whether the part that proved destructive was anger, lust, greed, need for approval, selfishness, or some other part, focusing on it, rather than away from it, and thereby giving it greater power had unfortunate consequences.

The ability to compartmentalize allows for a skillful divide-and-conquer strategy, an ability to deliberately detach from one element of experience in favor of connecting to another element that will be more beneficial. It stands in direct contrast to entire therapy approaches built on the self-limiting one-dimensional notion, for example, that you should always focus on the cognitions or on the emotions of the client simply because that is your preferred treatment approach. It is a simple truth that each part of a person is valuable someplace, sometime, but not every place all the time.

## Compartmentalization and Dissociation in Hypnosis

Compartmentalization is the everyday term for dissociation that practitioners of clinical hypnosis use in their professional nomenclature. From the earliest days of hypnosis as a therapeutic tool in the late 19th century, advanced by the famed neurologists of that era, including Pierre Janet, Jean-Martin Charcot, and Hippolyte Bernheim, the process of dissociation was a primary focus of inquiry. The use of hypnosis revealed remarkable displays of compartmentalization, or splitting off, of core elements of mental experience including memory, perception, sensory and motor functions, and even personal identity. Normal individuals, while dissociated during the experience of hypnosis, could isolate and amplify elements of experience, increasing or decreasing their magnitude of influence in response to suggestion. Dissociation is now the basis of modern inquiry for this reason.

One of the more influential models of hypnosis that refined Janet's pioneering work is called the neodissociation model. It was primarily developed and advocated by experimental psychologist Ernest Hilgard, who, along with research psychologist André Weitzenhoffer, founded and ran the famed Stanford Laboratory of Hypnosis Research. Their lab was the center of the hypnosis universe for decades, producing some of the highest-quality research into hypnotic phenomena. Hilgard's research into what he perceived as hierarchically organized networks of functionally specialized and reciprocally connected neural processes set the stage for today's cognitive neuroscience. Through the use of technologically sophisticated brain-scanning devices (fMRI, PET, SPECT, etc.), serious neuroscientists are now addressing basic but utterly fascinating questions raised by hypnosis such as, What goes on in the brains of people capable of experiencing suggested anesthesia sufficient to tolerate surgery without a chemical anesthetic? The ability to detach from painful sensory cues and maintain comfort is a remarkable display of dissociation in hypnosis. It highlights Hilgard's insight when he concluded that "the concept of a totally unified consciousness is an attractive one but does not hold up under examination" (1994, p. 38). Researching how the mind influences the brain makes for endless fascination.

In the early days of hypnosis, however, dissociation was viewed only through the lens of pathology. Unfortunately, it is still true today that most clinicians' training includes consideration only of the pathological forms of dissociation, such as dissociative identity disorder (DID), depersonalization, psychogenic amnesia, fugue states, and the like. There is a sharp distinction to be made, though, between pathological and nonpathological dissociative experiences. Psychiatrist Richard Chefetz summarized this point well when he wrote the following:

> Dissociation is not just a marker for life experience gone poorly. Dissociative process is something we use every day as we unconsciously sort salience in the flow of consciously and unconsciously perceived mental input. Associative process alerts our awareness that something is worth noticing. Dissociation tells us we need not pay any attention. The healthy result of this sorting is a coherent mind. (2015, p. 1)

Dissociation and association inevitably coexist across all experiences because, as we pay attention to (i.e., associate to) this, we no longer pay attention to (dissociate from) that. The general function of any hypnosis session then, process oriented or otherwise, is to use the dissociated experience of hypnosis to help the client detach from whatever needs to be detached from (e.g., a hurtful memory, a physical pain, a cognitive distortion, a destructive impulse) and attach to some other element of experience that will be helpful.

## The Role of Detachment (Dissociation, Compartmentalization) Across All Therapies

It can be especially enlightening to recognize the essential and therapeutic role dissociation plays in all forms of treatment, whether the practitioner realizes it or not. Consider the 10 different therapies below and how a primary message of that model reflects a need for dissociation from what isn't helpful in order to suggest a new reassociation that can be.

- Cognitive-behavioral therapy (CBT): "You are not your thoughts" highlights the standard practice in CBT of helping you detach from cognitive distortions you hold and then reattach to a more objective, rational perspective.

- Emotion-focused therapy (EFT): "Focus on the feeling beneath that behavior" is the standard practice of EFT, encouraging you to separate from the surface emotion in order to become aware of and associate to the underlying emotion.

- Ego state therapy: "Which part of you tells you that?" is a standard question that encourages identifying a part that can be detached from the whole and given its own identity and purpose to address in treatment.

- Psychodynamic: "Your unconscious need has motivated you to do that" suggests detaching from the need-driven dynamic and associating to new insights to guide future responses.

- Gestalt: Suggestions such as "It seems your hand is trying to tell you something" encourage the client to detach from the lack of personal awareness and associate to messages from within that can guide reactions with greater self-understanding.

- Mindfulness: "You can focus on forgiveness" is a typical suggestion to detach from anger or the desire for revenge and instead focus on and associate to a higher-level response of compassion and forgiveness.

- Acceptance and commitment therapy (ACT): A suggestion that "you can focus on acceptance" encourages the client to detach from their unrealistic expectations and subsequent disappointment and associate instead to the perceptions that life isn't fair and acceptance will serve you better than fighting against that which you cannot change.

- Dialectical behavior therapy (DBT): "You can watch the impulsive message go by as if on a sign carried by a parade marcher" is a typical suggestion for detaching from your thoughts, especially the ones that drive hurtful emotional responses, and instead associate to the imagery of thoughts being outside of you in the comfortable distance.

- Ericksonian hypnosis: "Your unconscious is smarter than you are" is an indirect suggestion to detach from a reliance only on your conscious mind and instead associate to or recognize that you have other, hidden resources that can surface from your unconscious when needed.

- Strategic therapy: "When you carry out the task, you'll discover something important" is a standard line that helps detach the client from the passivity fueled by negative expectancy and associates the client to the belief that effort will be rewarded with a new and valuable understanding.

Each approach differs in the content of what it strives to dissociate in the client's experience as well as what it strives to associate them to that would be helpful to them. But the process of dissociation and association is clearly evident in each approach.

## Dissociation Is Evident Even in Routine Hypnotic Suggestions

Beyond the role that dissociation plays in psychotherapy in general, you can see its role in many of the most basic suggestions commonly used in the clinical applications of hypnosis. Consider the following examples:

- "Focus on your breathing" suggests separating one's attention on breathing from other ongoing elements of experience that can recede into the background.
- "Focus on your experience as it unfolds right now" suggests separating one's attention from the past or future.
- "Your unconscious can listen even while your conscious mind drifts off" suggests separating conscious from unconscious processes.
- "You can be willing to experiment with new experiences" suggests separating yourself from an attitude of certainty.

Suggestion in treatment is, of course, inevitable. In the practice of hypnosis, suggestion is especially well-recognized, and as soon as we say, "Here . . . focus on *this*," we're encouraging not focusing on *that*.

## Typical Problems Derived From Either Over- or Undercompartmentalization

The types of problems that people might present for treatment that reflect compartmentalization issues can seem quite diverse. In part that's because the compartmentalization can take either of two primary forms: experience that is undercompartmentalized or experience that is overcompartmentalized. Undercompartmentalization is reflected in global or overgeneralized responses where it is clear the person can't separate out the different components of their experience. Global cognitive style, almost by definition, precludes effective compartmentalization. Some examples of undercompartmentalization patterns would include the following:

- The inability to separate the past from either the present or the future (as in PTSD and depression)
- Emotional overreactions (as in rage or panic or too much "feeling *your* pain")
- A lack of emotional differentiation (as is typical in self-harm)
- Taking things personally that aren't personal
- A lack of critical thinking, impairing the ability to separate facts from feelings
- A lack of personal boundaries or recognition of others' boundaries

Overcompartmentalization means the boundaries that separate one experience from another are overly rigid, thereby preventing an effective crossover of learning from one experience to another. Someone who overcompartmentalizes generally fails to recognize how experiences are similar or related, and responds to them unrealistically as a result (e.g., behaving badly but thinking you're still a good person and it shouldn't affect how others see you). Some examples of overcompartmentalization patterns would include the following:

- An inability to detect gradations or degrees of experience (as in not recognizing rising stress levels until they reach a critical point)
- An inability to consider or learn from past experiences
- Emotional underreactions and lack of empathy (as in, "That's your problem . . . tough luck!")
- An ability to rationalize or justify bad behavior
- A global perfectionism (as though anything less than perfect is terrible)
- Rigid personal boundaries or rigid expectations of how others should behave

## Defining the Salient Therapeutic Targets

When formulating a treatment plan, the clinician is likely to be contemplating an answer to these two questions: What do I want to help the client dissociate from? And what do I want the client to associate to?

Every experience has a variety of components. The essence of people's problems is that they associate to parts of their experience that work against them. This makes it easy to appreciate how people's problems are largely problems of focus: The person focuses on the unchangeable past instead of the possibilities that can exist in the future, or focuses on what's wrong and never seems to notice what's right, or focuses on their feelings when they would be better off thinking rationally (or vice versa), or focuses on others when they'd do well to focus on themselves (or vice versa).

This is one of the primary reasons why hypnosis is such a valuable treat-- ment tool. What hypnosis does so very well is grab people's attention, wherever it is directed, and redirect it to some element of experience that will serve them better. The primary goal of compartmentalization is to shift focus toward (i.e., "give voice" to) a specific element of experience previously either underrepresented or ignored altogether. To shift someone's focus from what's wrong to what's right, for example, can have lasting impact on the person's outlook, as techniques like the empirically validated gratitude journal (writing down at least three positive things, however big or small, that happen each day and doing so for at least 6 months) show us. Hypnosis can increase the magnitude of the perceptual shift to noticing what's right as well as the emotional impact of doing so. The dissociation from the old and the association to the new—the compartmentalization of past perspective away from the new—reflects good therapy.

A second reason why hypnosis is so valuable also relates directly to compartmentalization and has to do with the client's resources. Therapists routinely talk optimistically about their clients' innate personal resources and the role of therapy in helping people connect to and develop them. That raises a fundamental question: If people have resources, then why don't they use them? The answer should be apparent: Because the resources are dissociated—meaning there is no link, or trigger, to associate to them in some desired context (i.e., overcompartmentalized). Clinically, the goal is to connect people to their resources and place them in context. Hypnosis is especially well suited for that task, since people in hypnosis can readily access personal resources that they didn't know they had. You can imagine what it's like for someone in pain, for example, to discover their ability to generate hypnotic anesthesia during a hypnosis session. Once again, dissociation and association must be viewed as the core elements of effective psychotherapy.

Thus, the goal in a process-oriented hypnosis session is to help the client dissociate from whatever they are currently associated to that is working against them. What they're associated to (e.g., their specific feelings about some person or situation) is the content of their problem or issue. How you dissociate them from that element of experience and reassociate them to some better, more adaptive element of experience is the process. As long as it's clear what you want to bring into the foreground of the client's awareness (e.g., effective action) and what you want to help recede into the background (e.g., exaggerated fear), this process-oriented hypnosis session can be most valuable. Table 9.1 offers a generic structure for helping clients evolve compartmentalization skills.

---

### TABLE 9.1. GENERIC SESSION STRUCTURE FOR FACILITATING COMPARTMENTALIZATION

**Induction**

| | |
|---|---|
| **Response set:** | Specific components of global experience |
| **Theme 1:** | Every experience is composed of multiple components |
| **Theme 2:** | What you focus on—or away from—shapes your reactions |
| **Theme 3:** | Prioritizing helps compartmentalize what's unhelpful |
| **Theme 4:** | Compartmentalizing your feelings when difficult choices need to be made |

**Posthypnotic suggestions for integration**
**Closure and disengagement**

## SESSION TRANSCRIPT

### Induction

You can begin by taking in a few deep, relaxing breaths . . . and as the experience of focusing your attention becomes increasingly familiar to you . . . you can more easily and more readily . . . begin to build a deep sense of growing quieter inside . . . your thoughts slowing down . . . your inner voice gradually quieting to a gentle whisper. . . . Each breath . . . can relax you.. a little more deeply. . . . It's easy to enjoy the simple rhythm . . . the symmetry of breathing . . . each breath in . . . taking in a deeper level of comfort . . . and each breath out . . . letting out . . . what you really don't need. . . . And so each time you inhale . . . it can allow your body . . . to grow more comfortable. . . . Each breath out . . . provides a soothing release . . . allowing you the comfort . . . of knowing that this time is for you. . . . This experience is for you . . . and that you've created this time . . . to just . . . provide some space . . . space to relax . . . some room to learn . . . and grow . . . perhaps from things you hear me say . . . but more importantly . . . from things you come to realize. . . . And when you have a calming experience like this one . . . there's a moment-by-moment . . . flow . . . to your thoughts . . . a moment-by-moment . . . flow to the session . . . and at the same time . . . there's a purposefulness to the session . . . that goes well beyond being just a relaxation session. . . . Although it certainly is wonderfully relaxing . . . it's more . . .much, much more. . . .

### Building a Response Set Regarding Specific
### Components of Global Experiences

Because when you have an experience like this one . . . there are so many different aspects to it . . . just like any experience that has some complexity in its makeup. . . . There are different facets to the experience. . . . So in this experience right now . . . one facet is your internal dialogue, the things you say to yourself as different thoughts pass gently through your awareness . . . the ongoing conversation in your mind that is simply the process of thinking . . . and perhaps even going from thinking to realizing. . . . There's also the facet of the external dialogue . . .my voice . . . my words . . . reassuring you . . . encouraging you . . . providing you with possibilities for feeling better . . . and *being* better. . . . There's also the facet of the external environment . . . such as the everyday sounds of the routine aspects of life that go on around you . . . whether it's the sound of the wind in the trees . . . or birds singing . . . or the distant sounds of traffic . . . or the sound of a dog barking or the sounds of kids playing . . . or even just the sounds of the stillness of the environment. . . . But all of that is outside of you . . . such routine background sounds that they're hardly worth noticing . . . and simply pass through your awareness as you grow even more absorbed inside . . . and at the same time you begin to recognize these facets of experience as you grow more focused. . . . There's also the facet of your internal environment . . . the quality of feelings . . . that you experience as your body relaxes . . . the sensory awareness of what it's like to have your breathing slow down . . . the pleasurable feelings of your muscles relaxing as you become more still. . . .

### Theme: Every Experience Is Made of Multiple Components

And as your thoughts continue to slow down . . . and you experience the comfortable flow . . . of just being with yourself in a way that's . . .easy . . . and relaxed . . . you can come to an important realization . . .that *whatever* experience you happen to be in . . . there are many different components . . . many different components that combine to make up the full experience. . . . When you do something as routine as watch a movie . . . you're not *just* watching a movie. . . . You're processing experience on many other levels as well . . . even if you don't realize it . . . because there are many different components to a movie. . . . Certainly there are the visual images that flash across the screen . . . the things you watch . . . but those images . . . are a trigger . . . a catalyst . . . for your emotional reactions . . . the way you react to the things you're watching. . . . So when you watch a really funny comedy . . . there's obviously a quality of humor that leads you to smile and laugh without effort . . . the silliness or perhaps the wittiness or maybe the absurdity . . . whatever that quality is that makes something seem funny to you . . . and it isn't just images that trigger feelings. . . . There's the carefully chosen music in the soundtrack . . . and also the sound effects . . . that make it abundantly clear . . . that it's a comedy. It's meant to be funny and taken lightly . . . or that it's meant to be taken seriously when you're watching a drama. . . . And the movie's characters inspire reactions through the way they endear themselves to you or anger or alienate you. . . . So there are the feelings in the moment . . . but movies can also be a catalyst for memories . . . as you remember . . . things from your own experience that might relate to what you're watching. . . . And if you're watching with someone else, there's a relationship component to the experience. . . . The movie keeps you connected to one another by sharing the experience . . . the social side of watching a movie together. . . . So there's images, sounds, feelings . . . reactions, memories. . . . It's much, much more than just watching a movie. . . . And what I'm drawing your attention to in a very deliberate way . . . is that even just watching a movie . . . like countless other everyday experiences . . . has many different components to it. . . . And sometimes people seem to forget . . . or just never really thought about it . . . that when there are so many different components making up everyday experience . . . we choose . . . we *can* choose . . . which component to pay closer attention to. . . .

**Theme: What You Focus on—or Away From—Shapes Your Reactions**
How you view the different experiences you go through each day . . . which facets of a circumstance you pay attention to . . . shapes how you react to them . . . how connected you feel or how *disconnected* you feel from some aspects of the situation. . . . Well, it's not only about what happens in your life. . . . It's not just an event that occurs that you only see one side of. . . . By now you have already come to know . . . that each experience has many different components . . . many different aspects to consider. . . . On one level, there's what objectively happens . . . but on another, far more important level . . . there's your *interpretation* of what happens . . . the meaning that you give . . . to different experiences . . . the part of the experience that you focus on and thereby amplify. . . . When people face some situation that requires a response . . . you can easily see how what they focus on shapes what they experience and how they respond. . . . It's interesting to observe how some people focus on . . . trying to figure out what the most effective response might be to what's happening . . . while someone else gets wrapped up in how it makes them feel. . . . Someone else immediately starts to focus on what to do next . . . and someone else focuses on . . . the uncertainty and feelings of inadequacy when the solution isn't immediately obvious. . . . And so it becomes very important . . . *very* important . . . to remind your-

self . . . at any given moment . . . that you can actually choose which aspect of an experience to focus on . . . what the best response is . . . which is a different focus than how it makes you feel. . . . What the most skillful way of handling something is . . . which is different than how it makes you react. . . .

**Theme: Prioritizing Helps Compartmentalize What's Unhelpful**
And the more that you begin to focus yourself on regularly asking yourself the question . . . "What's the best response here?" . . . focusing yourself on what is going to . . .effectively empower you . . . to say or do something to yourself or others . . . that rivets your attention . . . to a response you can feel good about. . . . Even if it isn't comfortable, necessarily, but is still an effective response. . . . And then you discover how you can *set aside feelings* of upset or fear . . . how they *recede* into the background as you focus on what's best or most helpful right now . . . aware of your feelings, of course . . . but comfortably *distancing* yourself from them as you handle well what needs to be handled . . . instead of simply reacting as if you have no choice but to be upset or anxious. . . . You have a choice to focus inside or outside . . . on feelings or taking meaningful action . . . and much more often than you ever realized before . . . the more that you focus outside . . . with the goal being doing or saying what works best . . . in answering some person or handling some situation effectively . . . the more you can appreciate your own skills in recognizing what to shine your spotlight on in some situation and what to let recede into the darker background. . . . And if you think about the people who are effective people and high-powered people . . . you watch them do exactly that. . . . Watch a skilled politician in a debate or press conference. . . . Watch the CEOs of companies . . . who hold meetings in front of voters or stockholders . . . and someone in the audience will ask a pointed question . . . a critical or even rude question . . . and the person with finesse deftly sidesteps the criticism and rudeness. . . . That's *not* the part of the question they respond to. . . . Instead the part that they respond to is the opportunity to provide information . . . the opportunity to provide perspective. . . . And so they sidestep the criticism . . . even though you can be quite sure . . . that on the inside . . . the criticism or rudeness irritates

them. . . . They have feelings . . . but they let them quickly recede into the background as they shine their internal spotlight on the opportunity to calmly explain and to nondefensively clarify . . . because that's what is more important in responding in that public arena. . . . And I can give you a thousand examples of that same kind of effective responding . . . such as a really good parent . . . whose child has just done something wrong that angers them . . . or frustrates them because they were just so careless. . . . And even though they have that initial surge of anger and want to . . . punish this child . . . they recognize that this is an import-ant opportunity . . . to teach . . . and to teach in a way that's loving and patient. . . . Now not everyone has ideal parents like that. . . . Maybe you did or maybe you didn't. . . . But the point I'm making . . . is that you can have . . . a flash of anger . . . a flash of fear . . . a flash of doubt . . . a flash of cynicism . . . a flash of pessimism . . . but what can take hold of you almost instantly is . . . the realization that that's *not* the part of you . . . that you want to respond from. . . . You'd rather respond from a differ-ent part of you . . . perhaps by recognizing that you can also have a flash of understanding . . . a flash of tolerance . . . a flash of compassion . . . a flash of kindness. . . . And so you can set aside the anger or the fear or the frustration . . . and focus yourself intently . . . on providing an effec-tive response . . . of saying what needs to be said . . . what explains and clarifies what needs to be explained and clarified . . . what needs to be taught and demonstrated. . . . And when you grow more comfortable . . . with breaking situations down into their components . . . so that you're perfectly clear . . . that, yes, there's an emotional reaction . . . yes, there's concern . . . or anger or even fear . . . but what's more important. . . . what you keep your focus on . . . is that there's quite often something more important . . . than getting caught up in your feelings. . . .

### Theme: Compartmentalizing Your Feelings When Difficult Choices Need to Be Made

Often there's a difficult task at hand . . . a situation to be managed that will have implications or consequences that will endure beyond the moment, that matter more than the feelings of the moment. . . . And if you think about every movie you've ever seen where there was a hero . . . a hero that stayed focused on . . . the dangerous and even life-threatening mission they couldn't turn away from . . . the hero was clearly afraid. . . . You could see it in their face. . . . Anyone could see it. . . . The hero may even have said it out loud . . . "I can't do this" . . . when going through those agonizing moments of self-doubt. . . . But it was their perseverance, their tenacity in focusing on the challenge. . . . Their fear or self-doubts . . . receded into the background when they shone their spotlight on the path they knew they had to follow. . . . Now you know that courage isn't about not feeling fear. . . . Courage is about staying focused on the goal . . . and it's a powerful realization when you come to know that the only time you *can* show courage is when you're afraid. . . .

### Posthypnotic Suggestions for Integration
Every day, then, you have many opportunities to recognize the different components of your interactions with others . . . and the situations you face. . . . And as you can discover to your great satisfaction . . . you can find it getting easier and easier to stay focused on the mission. . . . And I say the mission . . . but that might make it sound much too important when all you're really trying to do is . . . teach a colleague or a friend . . . or a child . . . or a relative . . . how you want to be treated . . . or what you want them to know about something . . . or what needs to be done. . . . But it can really be helpful to you to know that all through each day . . . you have an opportunity . . . to notice in the world around you . . . what's effective . . . what works . . . how people achieve things. . . . They were motivated to achieve . . . even as they were scared to achieve them. . . . And as you come to more deeply understand and appreciate . . . that anxiety, concern, fear, anger, worry . . . is only one part of you . . . and a part of you that's growing smaller and smaller day by day . . . as you make more satisfying choices about which part of you you'll respond *to* and respond *from* . . . as you grow stronger and more focused . . . more oriented toward recognizing what your best and most effective response can be . . . and so being able to appreciate now that every experience has many different components . . . what you're learning is a way of *dividing and conquering* . . . reducing concerns . . . as you focus on and amplify . . . in your awareness . . . what you want. . . . I think you'll enjoy discovering . . . how much calmer . . . and more focused you are. . . . And you can remember . . . this wonderful saying I learned a long

time ago . . . that *obstacles are what you see, when you take your eyes
off the goal. . . .* And so you can be calm . . . and focused . . . and aware
of the opportunities . . . to handle situations with skill . . . and purpose . . .
keeping your eyes on the goal . . . and letting the obstacles recede into
the background. . . .

## Closure and Disengagement

You can take some time now to quietly absorb . . . these deep messages . . . and remind yourself many times throughout the day to focus
on . . .which components of any experience . . . will best serve . . . your
needs . . . in ways that will strengthen . . . and build your confidence. . . .
And then when you've had enough time for now . . . to process all these
different ideas and possibilities . . . you can begin to bring this session
to a comfortable close . . . at a rate that's gradual and easy. . . . And in
a little while . . . when you're ready . . . you can reorient yourself completely . . . bringing back with you that sense of knowing . . . knowing. . . .
And when you're ready, you can reorient yourself completely . . . fully
alert . . . fully refreshed. . . .

# Chapter 10

# Encouraging Acceptance

*Now that I've given up all hope, I feel much better!*

—Popular bumper sticker

## The Case of Kathryn

Kathryn knew something was wrong when she found the lump in her breast. She had found lumps occasionally before, but they always turned out to be benign cysts. This time, though, it felt different, and an icy feeling of dread came over her immediately. The hoarse throat and persistent cough she'd had for weeks now suddenly seemed ominous. She had assumed it was a low-grade cold and that her fatigue was also part of fighting it off. Finding the lump, she told herself not to jump to any conclusions. Perhaps it could just be a differently shaped cyst or one of a different texture, but still just a benign annoyance like the others. Despite telling herself not to jump to any conclusions, she found herself jumping anyway. Her anxiety level rose sharply as she called her doctor to get evaluated as soon as possible. Amazingly, she was able to get in the next day because of someone else's cancellation. She hoped this might be a sign of impending good fortune but didn't really believe she'd be so lucky this time.

By the time she and her husband, Kevin, arrived at the doctor's office, Kathryn was barely holding it together emotionally. She was afraid, and no amount of reassurance from Kevin could reduce her anxiety. When she was called in to see her doctor, she was examined thoroughly. The doctor ordered a biopsy taken, and when it eventually came back as malignant, her doctor ordered a breast MRI to determine how far the cancer had spread. She was referred to an oncologist for treatment. Kathryn was in shock at the use of the "c" word, the very diagnosis she had spent too many years fearing was inevitable given her history and her family history. Inevitable had now come to pass. Now what? She could see the fear in Kevin's eyes even though the words that came out of his mouth were meant to be reassuring: "We'll deal with it, honey. We'll deal with it."

She was given the news by her oncologist that she would need to have a total mastectomy of the one breast where the lump was found, but it was also recommended that she have a preventive (prophylactic) mastectomy of the other breast to reduce the risk of additional cancer. She went instantly numb. What was she feeling now? Her brain was racing at top speed, too many thoughts shooting back and forth to even know what she was thinking, much less feeling. Kevin held her hand tightly, actually too tightly, and she had to loosen his grip. When she looked at him, he had tears in his eyes but a forced smile as he said, "We'll deal with it, honey. We will, and you'll be okay." Her oncologist watched this interaction she'd seen a thousand times before but was still touched by their connection. She was glad Kathryn had a loving husband's support.

When Kathryn came for therapy, she had already had the double mastectomy. She'd had it only a short while before and was having great difficulty coping with what had happened to her. She felt the body she'd lived in for the past 52 years was now unrecognizable to her. Beyond that, it was also unacceptable to her. She had always overreacted, it seemed, to every little sign of her body aging, but that was small stuff by comparison. Following the double mastectomy, she felt she lost so much of herself and that she could never look at herself in a mirror again without feeling revulsion. She had always felt good about her body, and took pride in her appearance, felt attractive to Kevin, and together enjoyed a rewarding sex life. Now? She was sure all that was gone.

As Kathryn described her despair and her inability to move on, she also expressed anger at well-intentioned people who said, "Focus on the positive. You're alive. All you lost was some tissue, and doing so saved you. You should feel lucky!" She understood they were trying to be supportive, but it wasn't their body that had been "mutilated," as she thought of her own.

Kathryn's feelings are understandable. She had been through a lot, and it had forever changed her in some painfully obvious ways. Why couldn't she accept what happened more readily? Is it because she defined her self-worth by her body's appearance? Is her sexuality determined by her breasts? Is it a symbolic loss of herself, and she no longer knows who she is and fears finding out? Is she jumping to the scary conclusion that her husband will be turned off to her, and she'll lose his love? Is she so dichotomous in her thinking that if she's not perfect, she's worthless? Or what?

The content of Kathryn's problem is the loss of her breasts and her associated feelings of grief. The process, though, is about adjusting to the reality of circumstances beyond your control. Consider how many more times she could feel betrayed by her body in her lifetime: another wrinkle on her face, another varicose vein on her leg, another brown spot dots her hands, her hair becomes thinner and grayer, and so on and so on.

The reality is, if you're lucky enough to live a long time . . . you get old. And the older you get, the more physical challenges you'll face, from cosmetic to structural, from wrinkles to arthritis and worse.

Hypnosis is particularly helpful when logic is doomed to fail. Kathryn already knew at some level that she was lucky to be alive, and she knew she was lucky to have caring and skilled doctors as well as a loving, supportive husband. She could acknowledge "how good Kevin has been through all this." But as much as Kathryn might know intellectually about these things, she was still asking, "Why me?" and still wanted to fight back even though the surgery was already done.

Hypnosis to gently encourage acceptance of a harsh reality can allow the reality to seem much less harsh. Such sessions need to go slowly and move only gradually from less to more direct. I did hypnosis with Kathryn several times before ever speaking directly about her loss and the process of reconstruction she'd be undergoing. The early sessions spoke about human nature in a general way, speaking of the unrealistic and idealistic wishes people have for a world population living in peace, the ways that most people strive to live better lives, how people everywhere love their families, and how creative and artistic people can be in the way they see the world.

Kathryn could easily relax and focus in these sessions, but more than that, she was starting to expand her views beyond herself, an interruption to the self-absorption she naturally had during all she'd been through. Examples of people adjusting to less than ideal circumstances, whether noisy neighbors or an economic downturn or their aging bodies, held her interest, and at times she even smiled at the absurd conditions people have to deal with, things they can't really do anything about. She was getting calmer, less self-rejecting, and getting much better at believing Kevin when he told her he loved *her*, not just her breasts. There came a moment during one hypnosis session where she really grabbed onto that realization with both hands, and a transformation in her view followed soon after. She understood at a much deeper level that she's more than her body, much more. Over the span of a month, her attitude went from revulsion to excitement about her eventual reconstruction. Curiously, she said, "It'll be nice to look more normal, but unexpectedly, I'm not feeling all that urgent about it."

## The Role of Acceptance in Quality of Life

Who doesn't wish for some things in their life to be different? Who wouldn't love to have a magic wand to change the things they think are terribly unfair, heal themselves or the people they love from sickness, or obtain something deeply desired, whether it be material wealth, power, fame, special knowledge, world peace, or spiritual enlightenment? How much focus or mental energy people give to their wish that something will change can have a profound impact on their general outlook on life, encompassing their relationships, level of life satisfaction, productivity, physical and mental health, and even their political views.

Discontent with the status quo is a double-edged sword. In its favor, a desire to change something deemed unsatisfactory provides the motivation that might well give rise to taking action that results in an improvement. Necessity might well become the mother of invention. Innovation almost inevitably begins with a question: How can we do this better? That's true in the world of technological innovations, where we want the product to be faster, cheaper, more efficient, more something. It's equally true in the social realm when we strive for better: fighting against prejudice, striving for better care and more humane treatment of members of our society, generally working to create pathways of improved quality of life for people. Inspiration to want more than what we have was captured perfectly in this popular quote from Robert Kennedy: "Some men see things as they are and ask why. I dream of things that never were and ask why not."

The other side of discontent, though, is when, instead of inspiring us, it leads to bitterness and suffering. If you want to find someone's dissatisfaction with some aspect of themselves or with life itself, you won't have to look very hard in most cases. When people don't have as much money as they think they should, or don't get the lucky breaks that undeserving others seem to get instead of them, or don't get to do something they feel they should be able to do, whether others like it or not, or aren't treated the way they think they deserve to be treated, it's easy to understand where the frustration comes from and how it can lead to anger, disillusionment, and even go as far as lashing out against the perceived injustice. The extraordinary political divide we see in America today came about from a desire to break a government-as-usual system that was the basis for too many people's discontent.

The key question that we as clinicians need to address, then, is this one: When faced with a problem, any problem, how shall we decide whether to strive to accept the reality of those circumstances or strive to change them in some meaningful way instead? This is not an easy question to answer but is a constant factor that literally defines the direction therapy will take. It is quite different to employ approaches that strive to help someone accept some distressing circumstance than to employ approaches that encourage a transformation of oneself, of the circumstance itself, or a combination of the two.

## Fighting Against Reality: Acceptance as a Starting Point . . . or an End Point

I'd like to share a story here that is special to me for a number of reasons. It's a story I first shared in my book *Mindfulness and Hypnosis* (Yapko, 2011). It says a great deal about acceptance and the quality of one's outlook.

I was in Africa a few years ago and had the occasion to visit a small village in Zimbabwe. The people were economically terribly poor but spiritually rich, generous in sharing their way of life with my small group of visitors. Only a year before, the village had been lent a hand when an international relief organization dug a well for them. For the first time ever, they could go to the well at their leisure and pump clean water to drink. It was a daily ritual for the village women to take their containers, walk the long mile to the well in the heat and dust, pump vigorously to get the water into the container, then carry the heavy container back to the village balanced on their heads. I imagined a sudden rise in neck problems among the village women but saw no evidence of this.

I was amazed at the amount of hard work a woman had to go through to get a bucket of water back to her home. In talking with one young village woman about this, I asked with an expression of both awe and respect in my voice, "How can you walk a mile each way to get water?" It was really meant as a rhetorical question indirectly expressing admiration for her enduring the associated difficulties, but she looked at me with a gentle smile and replied simply, "Because that's where the water is."

This young African woman had no anger in her, no hint of sarcasm in her voice in her reply to me. She modeled equanimity—she was peaceful, compassionate and accepting, both of me as a visitor and of her life conditions as well. (Can you imagine how easily she could have worked herself into anger and bitterness by resenting having to walk so far to do the prescribed chore of fetching water?) When I think of what a powerful example of acceptance looks like in real-world terms, I invariably think of this young African woman. (She, of course, has no idea that I think of her often and in this special way.)

What acceptance means in the broadest sense is an ability to accept the reality of something, whether it be an external situation that affects you personally, or a personal situation that is challenging at least, excruciating at most. Fighting against reality, those factors that objectively regulate the distressing circumstance, can be seen as a desperate flailing away with no possible path of resolution, resulting in further desperation. Or it can be a methodical and sensible plan of attack that yields tangible positive results. In either case, acceptance is a critically important starting point. If you accept that there's nothing that can be done to change whatever is distressing, then the wisdom of the bumper sticker quote at the top of this chapter becomes apparent. If you accept that the reality is what it is, but your awareness of that reality leads you to develop a motivation and means of changing it, the benefit is obvious. This is the basis for a process-oriented hypnosis session that strives to encourage acceptance as a starting point and, perhaps, an end point as well.

## Typical Problems Derived From a Lack of Acceptance

The types of problems that people might present for treatment that reflect a lack of acceptance can seem quite diverse, and may include such problematic patterns as these:

- A chronic and deep-seated anger over the fact that life isn't fair
- An inability to distinguish well what is and is not controllable in some, perhaps many, circumstances
- An oft-expressed wish that things would be "the way they used to be"
- An ability to justify or rationalize bad behavior with the retort, "Why should I be the one to have to change?"
- Criticism of and disregard for viewpoints other than one's own
- Criticism and rejection of others who are different (prejudices such as racism, etc.)
- Exerting pressure on others with the destructive message, "You should be more like me"
- Exerting pressure on themselves to be things they can't be (e.g., perfectionism)
- Rejection of inevitable parts of themselves (e.g., anger, fear)
- Inability to acknowledge, much less own, mistakes
- Inability to agree to disagree agreeably
- Inability to distinguish accepting from agreeing with

## Defining the Salient Therapeutic Targets

Australian psychologist George Burns quoted the Dalai Lama, addressing the power of acceptance in this way: "If you have a problem that you can change, you don't have a problem. And if you have a problem that you can't change, you don't have a problem" (Burns, 2010, p. 310). The Dalai Lama has a very good point. What complicates the issue, though, is the considerable skill that goes into making an accurate determination as to whether a problem can or can't be changed.

Remember the children's book *The Little Engine That Could* by Watty Piper (the pseudonym of author Arnold Munk)? It's a beloved classic tale of a little train engine that, despite its small size, perseveres up a mountain in order to deliver its cargo of wonderful things to children on the other side. As it struggles to make the climb, it repeats the mantra, "I think I can, I think I can, I think I can." It's a story of perseverance in the face of adversity that culminates in a happy ending.

The cartoonist Gary Larson drew a cartoon that is a sad but funny follow-up to the little engine: He is now a down-and-out beggar on a street corner holding a sign that reads, "I thought I could, I thought I could, I thought I could." This cartoon speaks to the issue that naturally arises in therapy: What if either the clinician or the client thinks they can but really can't? Or, conversely, what if they think they can't but really can?

Thus, one of the most important—arguably the most important— discrimination someone has to make is about controllability, that is, how much control someone has in a given context. Given how much of depression originates in misperceptions of hopelessness and helplessness and how often the anxious person tries to avoid seemingly threatening realities, the perception of controllability is obviously vital to these and many other disorders.

An insightful clinician would have to examine their beliefs about the issue of controllability and how they influence their style of clinical practice. Specifically, how do you determine what is and is not controllable in a given situation? How do you determine when a client is limited in some way, and those limits should be accepted and respected, versus when the client should, in your judgment, instead strive to transcend them? (This topic and some guidelines for making such vitally important discriminations are discussed in detail in my book *The Discriminating Therapist* [Yapko, 2016].)

Beyond controllability, another repetitive theme of therapy related to acceptance is a pattern of self-rejection. It's evident when people identify parts of themselves that they are constantly fighting with. They report such things as, "I hate myself for never standing up for myself," or "I hate myself for not being able to get over what that person did to me." People can be terribly harsh with themselves, judging themselves mercilessly in the most negative ways imaginable. It's one thing to say, "I really blew that one," a specific criticism, but quite another to say, "I'm a total loser," a global condemnation. When people see in themselves things they don't like and then globally condemn themselves, it's a valuable opportunity to remind people that they are much more than that part of themselves they hate so much.

When people ask you to use hypnosis to "Help me get rid of that part of me. . . . Help me get rid of my sweet tooth" or "Help me get rid of my neediness," it's an important opportunity to help people absorb the deeper message that you don't get rid of parts of yourself. Rather, you learn to first accept them as inevitable and then redefine your relationship to them. When you provide the reframing in hypnosis that even the parts of themselves they hate have a potentially positive role to play in their lives (e.g., anger that is skillfully used to address an injustice), they can reach an acceptance of that part and move to the next stage of how and when to integrate it so that it functions usefully rather than destructively. For as long as it is viewed as a part of them that they devalue, the lack of acceptance of its inevitable presence ensures that part will remain dissociated and destructive.

A primary message among the many messages in this process-oriented hypnosis session, then, is that each part of you has value when you employ that part in the appropriate context. The problem isn't the part of you that you labeled as bad. The problem is when you give indiscriminate expression to that part in a way and in a context that doesn't support that expression. It requires flexibility, then, to develop another part that would be more effective in that context. This chapter's process-oriented hypnosis session helps facilitate that process.

Acceptance is one of the core foundational elements of mindfulness-based approaches. Instead of trying to change, improve, modify, or fix things, which is viewed as a certain path to unhappiness, cultivating an attitude of acceptance can provide a means of detaching from focusing on problems. Acceptance is a means of getting off the seemingly never-ending treadmill of striving for self-improvement and getting on a path of greater compassion, tolerance, and patience toward the self and others. Buddhist teacher Tara Brach (2004) uses the term "radical acceptance" in her book by that name to emphasize the fuller benefits to be obtained when a global compassion is the vehicle of relationships with self and others.

The inherent paradox regarding acceptance, which I first articulated in my book *Mindfulness and Hypnosis* (Yapko, 2011), may be evident in how promoting acceptance—essentially a message of "Don't change!"—becomes the catalyst for change. On one level, the therapist says, "Don't try and change anything; instead accept the inevitable." On another level, the therapist says, "By *not* trying to change things, you will change." Paradoxes can't be resolved logically. They are experienced. One of the many advantages of using hypnosis in treatment is that the message doesn't have to be logical: people in hypnosis can absorb messages and have meaningful experiences even with entirely illogical suggestions, a phenomenon known as "trance logic" (Yapko, 2019).

More than half a century ago, the late psychiatrist Milton Erickson wrote, "The purpose and procedures of psychotherapy should involve the acceptance of what the patient represents and presents. These should be utilized to give the patient impetus and momentum so as to make his present and future be absorbing, constructive and satisfying" (1954b, pp. 127–128). Erickson is unambiguous in his stated perspective: Acceptance is the desirable foundation for defining the therapeutic relationship and precedes the ability to utilize elements of the client's experience in a goal-oriented fashion.

Although both mindfulness and hypnosis emphasize the importance of accepting reality for what it is, hypnosis generally pays more attention to acceptance as a precursor to making deliberate and meaningful change. Both mindfulness and hypnosis are clear that acceptance has to precede change, but in hypnosis a well-defined therapeutic target lies one step beyond acceptance. In hypnosis, there is an implicit or explicit suggestion to do something. The client is encouraged to make specific cognitive, behavioral, perceptual, sensory, and/or relational shifts in the direction of a goal. In contrast to mindfulness, which is often described as paying attention without intention, hypnosis may best be described as paying attention with intention. In the world of psychotherapy, this is especially appropriate, since therapy is itself necessarily—and appropriately—a goal-oriented process.

The primary therapeutic goals of a process-oriented approach, therefore, are to (1) help the client distinguish between what is controllable and what is not; (2) reframe the value of parts the client has rejected as bad as having merit when expressed insightfully in appropriate contexts; (3) help the client detach from distressing realities in order to reduce emotional reactivity and greater acceptance; and (4) help the client attain a greater level of compassion

---

### TABLE 10.1. GENERIC SESSION STRUCTURE FOR ENCOURAGING ACCEPTANCE

**Induction**

| | |
|---|---|
| **Response set:** | Acceptance |
| **Theme 1:** | Some challenges in life are inevitable |
| **Theme 2:** | There's no sense in fighting against the inevitable |
| **Theme 3:** | It helps to know what's inevitable before fighting against it |
| **Theme 4:** | Making judgments is not only desirable, but necessary |
| **Theme 5:** | Shifting your focus to notice what's right |
| **Theme 6:** | Accepting and utilizing your different parts skillfully |

**Posthypnotic suggestions for integration**

**Closure and disengagement**

---

for and tolerance of differences in relationship to others. Table 10.1 can be a helpful strategy for encouraging acceptance in clients of circumstances that can't be changed.

## SESSION TRANSCRIPT

### Induction

You can begin by taking in a few deep, relaxing breaths . . . and orient yourself now to what can gradually and comfortably . . . become a familiar and welcome experience . . . of simply allowing yourself the luxury of taking a few minutes to focus yourself . . . and to clear yourself. . . . You know as well as I do . . . how the pace of life seems to just keep getting faster and faster for many of us. . . . So much to do, so many responsibilities. . . . That's why it can be especially nice every once in a while . . . to take a few minutes to *just breathe* . . . and to just be . . . a human *being* instead of a human *doing* . . . to get really comfortable in your thoughts . . . in your body . . . and even in your very soul. . . . In this session . . . you can just enjoy the inner sense of calm that slowly evolves . . . when you make a point of focusing on something meaningful. . . . Of course, each time you experience these focusing sessions . . . whether we're doing a session together in person . . . or you're spending time focusing when you're on your own . . . it's a little bit different from one time to the next. . . . Sometimes your thoughts will drift in one direction . . . while other times your thoughts will naturally drift in other directions. . . .

## Building a Response Set Regarding Acceptance

And yet each time you focus . . . no matter what direction your thoughts may take . . . there is an underlying sense . . . a really *deep awareness* . . . for the value of being with yourself in a calm, gentle, and deeply beneficial way . . . an *easy acceptance* of your *growing depth* of appreciation . . . for your abilities and *deeper self-awareness* . . . an *easy acceptance* for the natural tendency of your mind to wander at times . . . and an *easy acceptance* that there's a lot to *get absorbed* in right now . . . especially the things you discover that can really make a difference in how you feel about things that take place in your life . . . and how you make judgments about yourself and your life experience . . . and how some of those judgments naturally change over time . . . as you develop a greater clarity about your own capabilities. . . .

## Theme: Some Challenges in Life Are Inevitable

And how you make judgments as you move through life . . . will powerfully shape your reactions to the challenges you face . . . and the actions you take as a result . . . and it's easy to understand why. . . . After all, life goes on, people change, situations change, things happen. . . . Even just the process of getting older makes this point. . . . The challenges you faced when you were a child having to learn the most basic things . . . such as how to walk and run . . . how to read and write . . . how to attend school . . . and year by year life became more complex. . . . Adolescence came along and your body changed. . . . You didn't choose it, but it happened. . . . And as you grew into young adulthood, you started to face the pressures of people expecting you to take on more adult responsibilities. . . . You didn't choose it, but it happened. . . . And all the life changes that unfolded over time . . . from working jobs to developing friendships . . . things that might seem to have just happened . . . from dealing with births and deaths among relatives or acquaintances . . . and the ups and downs of the economy . . . and the need to do laundry and go to the grocery store . . . all just keeping up with the inevitable respon- sibilities and everyday challenges that are simply part of life . . . things you don't necessarily choose, but have come to accept as inevitable . . . an easy acceptance that comes from knowing what life requires of us . . . whether we chose it or not. . . .

### Theme: There's No Sense in Fighting Against the Inevitable

Sometimes, though, people don't choose their battles very well. . . . They fight against things they'd do much better to simply accept. . . . For example, I have a friend who has a young daughter. . . . She's only 8 years old . . . and she's been getting some of her questions answered lately about where babies come from. . . . She had asked her parents for the sex talk . . . and they're attempting to answer her sensitively and without more detail than she seems ready to handle . . . especially because they know she's not one who usually cares much for change. . . . She much prefers the familiarity of experience over the novelty of experience. . . . And when they talked about reaching puberty and the changes her body would go through . . . and especially what menstruation was all about . . . she threw a tantrum . . . yelling at them because she didn't want to go through puberty. . . . She didn't want her body to change . . . and she was really disturbed about this and announced quite matter-of-factly that she *refused* to go through puberty. . . . She declared it simply was not some- thing she would tolerate and advised her parents not to expect it in her case. . . . And I wonder what you would have told her . . . how you would have responded to her wanting to fight the inevitable changes that are biologically programmed into human DNA. . . . And I wonder how you would explain when it is sensible to fight against something you can't accept and want to change . . . and when it is sensible to simply accept the inevitable with insight and grace . . . and how valuable it can be now to recognize that some battles just aren't worth fighting. . . . And it gives you a chance to determine which of your own fights can give way to a calm acceptance. . . .

**Theme: It Helps to Know What's Inevitable Before Fighting Against It**

Before fighting against something . . . and wasting valuable time and energy . . . it really helps to know something about what, if anything, you can do to make a difference in that situation. . . . Sometimes people fight without realizing they're in a fight they can't win . . . like fighting against aging . . . or fighting against ever dying . . . or fighting against the need to sleep or eat. . . . These aren't noble fights. . . . They're fool- ish ones. . . . But other fights are indeed noble . . . fighting against your self-limiting fears or doubts . . . fighting against others who underesti- mate you by succeeding in ways they didn't think possible . . . fighting against injustices you see unfolding before your very eyes by modeling fairness and integrity. . . . And you're discovering now how important it is to make clear and sound judgments about what is in your control and what isn't in your control . . . what you can strive to change in yourself or others and what you simply cannot . . . and can come to accept for what it is . . . even if you don't particularly like it. . . . And even within your- self . . . you face the same need to make a clear-headed judgment . . . as to whether to strive to change some aspect of yourself . . . or whether to accept it with grace as just a part of who you are. . . . It may not be your idea of perfect . . . but it may be embraced as simply inevitable . . . like your height . . . or your shoe size . . . or your love of a particular type of music. . . .

**Theme: Making Judgments Is Not Only Desirable, but Necessary**

Now, making judgments about people, about situations, and even about yourself . . . is so natural. . . . It's how we decide on a desirable course of action . . . deciding what to do based on how we see and eval- uate things . . . and consider what it takes to develop good judgment . . . the ability to see things realistically and make good decisions accord- ingly . . . making good decisions about who is worth bringing into your life . . . good decisions about managing your money . . . all kinds of decisions in life that need to be made . . . and that includes the abil- ity to see yourself realistically . . . knowing yourself and your strengths and what you're capable of doing well. . . . It's all too easy for many of us to become self-critical at times . . . getting down on ourselves when we don't live up to some expectation or standard that we've set for ourselves . . . instead of being accepting of what it means to be inevitably human . . . and come up short sometimes. . . . It's all too easy to be doubtful about ourselves at times. . . . And for as long as you care what others think . . . an important aspect of being socially responsible . . . and for as long as you want to perform well . . . an important aspect of taking pride in what you do . . . you'll naturally make judgments about yourself . . . too many of which may be unfairly harsh at times. . . . And it's worth asking how you know when a criticism is justified and when it is simply pointless. . . .

### Theme: Shifting Your Focus to Notice What's Right

But such negative judgments aren't constructive . . . simply because they don't teach anything positive that highlights what can be done better. . . . They're just harsh and uncomfortable . . . punishing someone for doing wrong doesn't teach them how to do what's right. . . . And when you begin to move away from those judgments . . . and begin to shift your focus from what's wrong to what's right . . . you'll begin to notice things in yourself and others that would have escaped your attention previously. . . . What a relief when you take the time . . . to remind yourself that no one experience and no one part of you defines you . . . and how that realization can lead to a greater self-awareness and self-acceptance than you ever thought possible. . . . What a pleasure it can be when you take the time . . . the way you can right now . . . to remind yourself about the richness of your experience . . . the interesting people that you've met along the way . . . the special places that you've been . . . the valuable things that you've experienced. . . . These are the personal riches. . . . They're the ever-present reminders of some of the extraordinary opportunities that come our way in life. . . . One of the things that I most like about this kind of focusing experience . . . is that it can be such a kind and gentle way of reminding people of their strengths. . . . It can be such a generous way of helping people find and acknowledge their hidden talents, talents you perhaps didn't even know you had . . . talents that you're rediscovering . . . that you'd forgotten about. . . . It can be such a supportive and realistic way of reaffirming to you that you don't have to be perfect in order to be really good. . . . I like that. . . . I like the positive recognition that comes from acknowledging people's strengths and resources. . . . Too often people overlook their own strengths or the strengths of others . . . or take them for granted. . . . So I'm encouraging you to enjoy these wonderful capacities of yours . . . and to notice much more of what people you encounter have to show as valuable . . . that you can appreciate . . . a much deeper acceptance of the inevitable differences that exist between people . . . that have a greater value than you might ever have realized before . . . making it so much easier to acknowledge what's right with them . . . and what's right with you. . . .

### Theme: Accepting and Using Your Different Parts Skillfully

It's just a nice way of reinforcing for you what I hope you already know . . . that you have a lot of really great resources inside of you to explore, and to develop further . . . and to enjoy. . . . It's one of the curiosities about perception . . . how something that you hear might seem irrelevant to you at first . . . and then, inexplicably, it gradually starts to grow in relevance. . . . Or how something can seem distant to you in your awareness . . . and then it gradually moves closer until it fills your awareness with something that is pleasing . . . inspiring . . . or perhaps surprising . . . but certainly useful. . . . It's one of the many values of just *being comfortable* and present in a focusing experience such as this. . . . It's also what makes it easy to appreciate . . . and it *is* easy to appreciate . . . how each aspect of your experience has a positive value *someplace, sometime.* . . . It's more obvious when it relates to the things that you really enjoy. . . . But the point is . . . that *every* experience is valuable someplace, but *no* experience is valuable everywhere, or all the time. . . . A simple example: You might love a particular food . . . but you wouldn't want to eat the same thing every day, no matter how much you love it. . . . You can enjoy a particular place to go on a vacation or holiday, but sometimes you want to go somewhere different and do something different. . . . You want to see and experience other things, too. . . . So, no matter how much you love that particular place, you can still prefer to be someplace else today . . . and what you learn along the way is that very important principle . . . that the value of things, the value of experiences, the value of parts of yourself . . . that value depends on circumstances. . . . Consider how great it is to be able and willing to challenge people or even to challenge yourself at times . . . and how wonderful it is at other times to choose harmony . . . to choose tolerance . . . and the wisdom is knowing when to do what. . . . Likewise, the value of being

able to reach acceptance of the current conditions at times . . . and likewise knowing how important it is to go beyond acceptance in order to
create changes. . . . Now, you can easily start to form the impression
that I'm talking about the potential value of each experience . . . and
you'd be right to do so. . . . I really don't know if you've started to take
these ideas to the next level yet . . . whether you've started to appreciate that each part of *you* is valuable someplace, sometime. . . . That even
includes the parts of you that in the past you might not have liked very
much . . . or understood very well. . . . But you can now sense *something
changing* about that viewpoint . . . as you start to become aware that
even the parts of you that you haven't liked so much still have a positive
value at times. . . . They have a positive potential if those parts of you
are used well and in the right circumstances. . . . And isn't that the art-
istry of living well and living skillfully? . . . Learning to use the different
aspects of yourself purposefully . . . in order to create positive possibilities. . . . So often in my clinical experience, I've talked with people who
tell me how bad, how unacceptable a part of them is in their view of
themselves. . . . So they'll say things to me such as, "Help me get rid of
my anger," or "Help me get rid of my competitive nature," or "Help me
get rid of my need for approval." . . . It usually takes people a little while
to really grasp the deeper meaning of my reply . . . when I tell them that
you *don't* get rid of these things. . . . They are a part of you. . . . You don't
get rid of parts of yourself. . . . No, instead you learn how to *use* them
effectively, selectively, and wisely to your own best advantage . . . and
to the advantage of the people you care about. . . . You can be deliberate in choosing . . . when and how you express these parts of yourself . . .
but it's important when you realize that these parts all have a positive
value someplace . . . just not in the places, perhaps, or in the way . . .
that you've been using them . . . when they seem to just pop up in some
context where they really aren't at all useful. . . . It requires a different
perspective . . . to learn how to accommodate all your parts . . . instead
of striving to eliminate the ones you just haven't known how to manage skillfully. . . . When you come to that inevitable realization . . . that
each part of you is valuable someplace, but not every place . . . what a
wonderful discovery to find out that you can actually develop an appreciation for what previously seemed only worthy of your self-criticism
or self-rejection. . . . When you process these ideas on so many differ-

ent levels, it's a really good reason—*a really* good reason—to start to develop that deeper trust for yourself. . . . And isn't that what's evolving at this very moment? The deeper trust in yourself that you can think about experiences that are empowering and transformative. . . . It isn't about controlling the world, or controlling the people around you . . . simply because you can't. . . . Rather, it's about trusting yourself to reach inside yourself and find the part of you that can best help you manage some circumstance and go ahead and use that part skillfully . . . and with a genuine sense of self-acceptance . . . as well as compassion for others. . . .

## Posthypnotic Suggestions for Integration

Now, I've talked about many different possibilities of things you might consider. . . . I've provided a good reminder to you that you don't have to live perfectly . . . as if you could, even if you wanted to. . . . After all, fighting to be perfect just isn't a fight you can win for as long as you live in a human body and have a human mind . . . but you do have lots of opportunities to *live well* . . . to absorb that message certainly translates into a shift about the kinds of things that you can say to yourself . . . and the way in which you say these things to yourself . . . a much kinder, gentler voice in your thoughts . . . and the things that are positive you can see and accept in yourself . . . the things that are valuable . . . and the things that you begin to notice in other people and in the world around you that are worth acknowledging and accepting. . . . You can enjoy noticing those expansive shifts in your perceptions . . . particularly when you realize that you're the one responsible for them . . . they are *yours*. . . . Well, you probably know by now that you can be as attentive to the possibilities presented here as you wish. . . . After all, it's your experience to create and enjoy. . . . You get to decide what you can absorb and maintain in your life from this and each experience . . . because it's worth holding on to even after I invite you to reorient in just a moment. . . . Some people hold on to the physical and emotional comfort. . . . Some people hold on to the feeling of really appreciating the richness of their own experience. . . . Some people hold on to the realization that some life challenges are inevitable, and some life conditions are just not worth fighting against . . . allowing you to hold tightly to the idea that you can be so much more self-aware and self-accepting. . . . I certainly hope that the good feelings you have can be easily memorized and accessed again and again at your leisure. . . .

### Closure and Disengagement

When you've had enough time to process this experience and consider and absorb the deeper messages, then you can start to bring this experience to a comfortable close. . . . Take whatever time you want to . . . to have that sense of completion for right now. . . . And then when you feel like you're ready to . . . you can start the process of reorienting yourself at a rate that's gradual and easy . . . so that in a little while you can reorient yourself completely and let your eyes open . . . feeling alert, fully alert, deeply refreshed, fully reoriented, and feeling just great!

# Chapter 11

# Defining Responsibility

*The price of greatness is responsibility.*

—Sir Winston Churchill

## The Case of Kyle

Kyle's moodiness posed an ongoing challenge to his wife and kids. His 9-year marriage to Karen was generally good but was at times exhausting to her because of Kyle's unpredictable fluctuations in mood and outlook. He could be warm and upbeat one minute, then distant and irritable the next. He was that way when she met him, which she accepted as "that's just Kyle," but lately it seemed to her that Kyle was spending more time in what she called "the down zone" than ever before. Worse, his irritability was often unleashed on their kids. Melissa, age 8, and Martin, age 5, were both so sensitive to their dad's responses to them that they would often grow silent and obviously distressed when Kyle would yell at them for truly petty reasons. Karen secretly wondered if it was a mistake to have kids when Kyle was so easily stressed by them but knew it was a pointless question given the fact that they already had them.

Kyle came to therapy alone at Karen's insistence, which he diplomatically called a "strong recommendation" that he decided to accept. He didn't really see exactly what she was concerned about that made seeing me such a priority now. He thought he was "pretty much okay." But after that less-than-insightful self-assessment,

Kyle went on to disclose that he had always been an introvert and moody and figured "that's just the way I am." When asked about his moods and their impact on his behavior, Kyle admitted that sometimes he wasn't as "nice" as he "should" be to Karen and the kids. When I asked what that meant exactly, he said he would get into these "states" where everything annoyed him. At such times he just wanted to be left alone for a while, and if anyone intruded on his need for space, he'd react with anger.

I asked Kyle if he gave people any kind of warning that he needed space, and he looked at me with genuine surprise. Then he turned it into a joke: "Warning! Warning! Dangerous moody man!" He dropped that demeanor quickly and turned serious again as he described a recent episode that gave rise to Karen's "strong recommendation." Melissa had come to him with a request for her own smartphone, and when she wouldn't take no for an answer, he blew up at her and said some awful things about what a "spoiled little bitch" she'd become. Melissa was momentarily shocked by his intensity and words, and then began crying uncontrollably. Kyle knew this was bad, but he didn't know how bad until he saw the look on Karen's face. It was a look that said, "What the hell is wrong with you? What *are* you that you could say that to Melissa?" Kyle's nonverbal response was to withdraw and go find some space to be alone.

In the next session, I spoke to Karen, first alone and then together with Kyle. She had a lot to say, of course, about what was going on with Kyle. In the following session, I spoke to Melissa alone, then Martin alone to draw out their feelings and observations about life at home; giving kids a voice is such a necessary way of empowering them, especially during times of family distress. The picture of home life was quite clear: Kyle's erratic moods and behavior kept everyone on edge. Hearing Melissa as the older of the two kids describe interactions with her dad that could only be described as nasty was truly disheartening and made it clear what the first target needed to be. Martin echoed what Melissa said in much less sophisticated language.

What about Kyle? Is he just an angry man who needs to "get

his anger out"? Is he depressed and needs to be medicated? Is he carrying the residuals of childhood trauma? Is he just a chronically dissatisfied man who finds fault everywhere he looks? Is it about poor self-esteem and feeling undeserving of what he has? Or what?

The content of Kyle's problem is his moodiness and the need to better manage his moods. The process is how Kyle's internal absorption keeps him focused on himself and his feelings, too often expressing them in an uncensored form. It precludes him from sensing any responsibility for having to protect the people around him from his moody irritability and the way he speaks to them when he's in a bad place within himself. Kyle will need to develop some boundaries that can help him refocus his attention outside himself in order to fulfill his responsibility to his marriage and family. His responsibility, one of the many he has, is to protect them from his moods and verbal assaults.

In introducing responsibility to Kyle as an issue to discuss, I said directly, "Kyle, I'm sorry you struggle with your moods. I am genuinely sorry you suffer these foul moods that distress you so. But, *that doesn't give you the right* to say the awful things you say to Karen, Melissa, Martin, or anybody else. Your mood is going to lift, but they'll be hearing the echoes of the nasty things you said for *years*, maybe even forever." Kyle blurted out, "But that's how I feel! Am I supposed to lie or playact that everything's okay? If I can't be me with my family, then where can else can I?" Kyle had given himself permission to say these things as evidence of his "being honest" with them. When *isn't* honesty the best policy?

Process-oriented hypnosis provides a gentle context for introducing new perspectives and possibilities for meaningful change. In Kyle's case, it was easy to talk about the concept of atmosphere, first with distant examples such as the atmosphere a restaurant strives to create for its diners or the atmosphere a teacher creates for their students. The atmosphere can differ in lots of ways depending on the desired effect. Then it was an easy transition to talk about the atmosphere he created in his job as a project manager in a construction company. Did he encourage his group members to be open with him in expressing their needs or concerns? Did he encourage them to support or compete with each other? Did he treat them harshly when they made a mistake? Then moving it to an even more personal level, he could think about the family atmosphere he grew up in, whether it was emotionally warm or sterile, what was emphasized as important and what was trivialized, what things his own dad said to him that he still holds on to, whether good or bad, and so on.

Finally, it turned more personal when introducing the recognition to Kyle that each person directly affects the others in their sphere of influence. Every interaction is going to lead people to feel better or worse about themselves to one degree or another. What happens when someone denies that power, though, and is oblivious to the effect they have on others? What happens when they're so self-absorbed that they hurt people without even realizing it? Bad moods were reframed into an opportunity to exercise greater self-restraint as the responsible thing to do in a number of different ways over several hypnosis sessions, and Kyle got the point: He can't just do whatever he wants or feels when he has entered into a marriage and created children that he has a responsibility to care for and love. Kyle became teary as the magnitude of his lack of responsibility for his way of treating his wife and kids became clear and painful. In that moment, he vowed to do much better.

Kyle took the responsibility to make sure he could correct his kids without attacking them, to forewarn Karen when he was feeling down and needed some space instead of just disappearing, and took care not to discuss anything of importance if he couldn't give it his full attention and keep his cool.

Kyle listened to our hypnosis sessions often and was moved each time to focus on what it means to be responsible for yourself and what you say and do. Kyle lived up to those responsibilities. And, no surprise, he found he was liking himself much more now as a consequence. He said, "I'm a lucky man. I've got a great wife and kids, and I don't ever want to lose them by acting like a jerk. Thanks for helping me see that with 20/20 vision."

# The Role of Responsibility in Quality of Life

Consider the following two scenarios:

- John drops a glass, and it shatters on the floor. Mary is quick to offer her assistance and helps him pick up the pieces of broken glass. Unfortunately, she cuts herself on a sliver of glass while doing so and bleeds profusely. John feels terrible about Mary getting hurt. How much responsibility for Mary's cut does John bear?
- Mary has asked John numerous times to fix the broken electrical plug at her desk. He always says he will, but many weeks and arguments later, he still hasn't fixed it. Fed up with waiting, Mary finally tells John he has three days to fix it or she's going to call in an electrician to do the job. He dismisses this warning as a frustrated bluff. Five days later Mary calls an electrician, who promptly fixes it for a charge of $180. John is furious with her for hiring someone and paying them so much when he was "planning to get around to it." He berates her and then stops talking to her altogether. How much responsibility for John's anger does Mary bear?

Both of these scenarios raise a difficult question: How do we determine the level of personal responsibility for one's actions and experience? This issue is vitally important in the context of psychotherapy. Every client we treat in whatever manner we treat them has to come to a meaningful conclusion that will help determine whether and how therapy progresses. This is the question one must answer: Am I in charge of my life, or aren't I?

For clients who believe they are not responsible for themselves, victims of genetics or circumstances, why strive to learn anything different? For clients who have agency, the sense that they are at least partially in control of their lives, then using therapy as a means to lead a better life makes sense. Beyond the global beliefs of the client, the content of what they believe, the real challenge in therapy at the process level is to help the client be clear in a given situation where the responsibility for oneself is to be found.

Philosophers have argued over the question, "Am I responsible for my actions, or aren't I?" for centuries. More recently, neuroscientists have entered the debate arena and offered a completely different view, one that has an especially great relevance for practitioners of hypnosis.

# The Unconscious and Free Will:
# Do Either Actually Exist?

Modern cognitive neuroscience no longer focuses on the unconscious as though it is an organized entity; rather, it focuses on the role of unconscious processes governing subjective experience. A sharp distinction is made between automatic and controlled processing. Automatic processing isn't easily explained, as the person isn't really aware of how they made decisions or formed responses and features a sense of effortlessness in responding. Controlled processing features thinking, reasoning, and planning.

What brought neuroscientists into the free-will debate is the recognition of how unconscious processes can be influenced by priming strategies, that is, the introduction of stimuli (e.g., words, images, objects) outside of conscious awareness that have a demonstrable effect on perception and behavior. Famed neuroscientist Michael Gazzaniga, well known for his pioneering work with so-called split-brain patients, tackled the subject of free will in depth in his book, *Who's in Charge? Free Will and the Science of the Brain*: "Our minds are always being unconsciously biased by positive and negative priming processes and influenced by category identification processes. . . .Our very own brain machine runs on its own steam, even though we think we are in charge. Now that's a puzzle" (2011, pp. 69, 8).

The issue of what is and isn't in our control has already come up more than once previously, and once again becomes extremely salient to the current discussion of responsibility. If free will is illusory when in actuality we are pushed and pulled by nonconscious processes, then how responsible are we for our own actions? And, if it isn't me who's responsible for what I do, then who is?

## Attributions and Making Sense of Responsibility

One of the core components of human nature is the need people feel to make sense out of their experience. As we saw in Chapter 5, the meaning of most of the experiences we have throughout life is infused with uncertainty. Most experiences, including the experience of hypnosis, are sufficiently ambiguous to invite our projections about what they might mean. Sometimes the projections make us feel good ("I can tell from the way they stand next to me that they like me"); other times the projections make us feel bad ("I can tell from the way they stand next to me that they don't like me"). Sometimes the projections empower us ("Stand back—I'll handle this!"), and other times they define us as helpless ("There's nothing I can do about it"). Once again, we see how the quality of your projections shapes your outlook and responses.

When some event happens, whether good, bad, or neutral, it is the most natural of tendencies to immediately ask, "Why did this happen?" This question launches the process of making attributions—explanations—for the perceived causes. Embedded within the attribution is the perception of where the responsibility is placed for the event and its consequences. Since the attribution is merely a projection, it may range from reasonably accurate to wildly— and painfully—inaccurate.

Many people reflexively blame others for their own bad decisions and circumstances, while others reflexively accept such mislaid blame and thereby suffer unnecessary guilt and poor self-esteem. How you deal with the issue of responsibility is a powerful factor in shaping your quality of life experiences and, especially, your relationships with others. In fact, it is one of the key factors I encourage people to assess when they're beginning a new relationship with someone: How does this person deal with issues of personal responsibility? Whatever else might be good about someone that attracts you, if this person is irresponsible, the relationship is going to suffer and is not likely to end well.

Perceptions of responsibility exist on a continuum. At one end is the person who readily assumes responsibility for their actions, including blame when they misstep. At the extreme, they may not only take responsibility for their own actions but may even take the blame for the actions of others as well. The heavy burden of an overdeveloped sense of responsibility is just something they live with and rarely consider because it is simply reflexive to attribute blame to themselves.

At the other end of the continuum is the person who accepts little or no responsibility for their own actions. If you confront them about something they did, you get a defensive reaction that can range from simply making silly excuses and irrational justifications to angry counterattacks, threats, and even violence.

A primary factor that helps shape a sense of responsibility is the role you're in at the time of an important interaction. A sense of agency comes with knowing that when you're in a particular role, there are demands that go along with that role. For example, when you're a parent, there are clear expectations about what it takes to fulfill that role's responsibilities well. When you're a therapist, there are clear professional guidelines about what you can and can't do to fulfill that role successfully. Acting in a way that violates the boundaries of that role is an evasion of personal responsibility.

## The Impact of Taking or Refusing to Take Responsibility

Blaming others for your bad behavior or poor decisions is an obvious evasion of personal responsibility, reflecting an underdeveloped sense of responsibility. Making excuses for bad behavior or exercising poor judgment defines one as untrustworthy. Such evasion may benefit someone in the short run by helping them delay or, in some cases, even prevent having to suffer the negative consequences of their actions. That is the short-sighted goal, of course— divert the blame elsewhere so I don't have to take it and suffer anything as a result. It speaks volumes about whether it's more important to someone to get out of a difficult spot or maintain trust. If you're willing to hurt others, perhaps deeply and irreparably, to save your own skin, that is a shocking display of egocentricity.

Being someone who justifies the unjustifiable guarantees that others will perceive you as lacking genuineness and personal integrity. How often this destroys marriages and families is painfully obvious to therapists who work with the hurtful consequences of people who lie, cheat, lead secret lives, and proclaim that they have a good reason for what they've done. There are many ways to approach the issue of the blamers and the bad behavior self-justifiers, but an especially clear, insightful, and entertaining book on the subject is *Mistakes Were Made (but Not by Me): Why We Justify Foolish Beliefs, Bad Decisions, and Hurtful Acts* (revised edition) written by social psychologists Carol Tavris and Elliot Aronson (2015).

Blaming yourself or letting others blame you for things you are not responsible for reflects an overdeveloped sense of responsibility that can lead to the excessive or inappropriate guilt described in the clinical diagnostic manuals. It's worth pointing out the collective wisdom of the field in saying that guilt can be excessive or inappropriate. Guilt can be paralyzing for a relatively small transgression that may have even been repaired through apology or some form of compensation. Proportionality is difficult to gauge, after all—how much guilt is enough and how much is too much? The inappropriate guilt is an acknowledgment that someone can assume responsibility for something they're really not responsible for. Guilt presupposes responsibility, for you don't feel guilty about events for which you don't feel personally responsible. You might have regrets, wishing things had happened differently, but regret is not the same as guilt.

Deflecting personal responsibility away from the self by blaming others is an obvious way blame can be helpful to someone. But guilt can also be a formidable weapon when it is used as a manipulative tool to coerce someone into complying with a selfish demand. "Pack your bags because you're going on a guilt trip" is meant to be a humorous way of describing how someone can attempt to use guilt to coerce you into doing what someone else wishes. Being able to recognize such manipulative tactics and how to short-circuit them without suffering guilt pangs is an invaluable skill set to teach your guilt-prone clients.

It should be apparent that these are discrimination issues that come into clear focus when you ask the client the salient discrimination question: How do you know when something is your responsibility and when it isn't? (For further discussion of this issue see Yapko [2016].)

It's a different issue, of course, when someone feels guilty about having done something that hurt others. They accept the responsibility for it and now suffer the guilt feelings that are proportional and appropriate to the circumstance. What can a therapist do to help in such cases? The goal isn't to take away the person's guilt, simply because that isn't realistic. The person knows what they've done, they know whom it hurt and how much it hurt, and they will forever have to live with this uncomfortable knowledge.

The more realistic goal in such circumstances is to help the client compartmentalize the guilt. That means acknowledging it but not globally defining yourself by it. The compartmentalization strategy provided in Chapter 9 can be adapted for this purpose and used to complement the process-oriented hypnosis session provided in this chapter.

By compartmentalizing guilt, I mean helping the person evolve the perspective that whatever they may have done, they are more than that. It's an acknowledgment that someone can go beyond the destructive label attached to whatever they did and can grow into someone who is better than that. Labels are a sure-fire way to stabilize perspective and thereby make it harder to change perspective. It's one of the principal reasons why I have developed my process-oriented approach that addresses how people generate their problems rather than following a diagnostic label-based approach to treatment.

Too often, people take on a diagnostic label and use it as a basis for believing that their problems are unsolvable. Therapists unwittingly reinforce this when they actually teach the client to define themselves according to a label of one sort or another. As soon as someone learns to say, for example, "I'm a trauma survivor," they have now learned that they can globally define themselves by their unchangeable past. Their history can't change. Only their response to their history can change, and a principal way of helping someone to do that is to encourage them to discover that they are not their history. They are more than their history. And we as therapists want them to be responsible for becoming more than their history.

## Typical Problems Derived From a Lack of Clarity About Responsibility

The types of problems that people might present for treatment that reflect an inability to define issues related to personal responsibility can seem quite diverse, and may include such problematic patterns as these:

- Excessive guilt
- Inappropriate guilt
- Self-justification and a lack of guilt for destructive or hurtful behavior
- Blaming others or external circumstances for one's bad choices
- Conflict-avoidant behavior when confronting bad behavior is necessary
- Taking on more than your fair share of work at home or on the job
- Taking on less than your fair share of work at home or on the job
- Making commitments to others or yourself that you don't honor
- Apologizing excessively and inappropriately or, conversely, never apologizing when appropriate
- An inability to distinguish guilt from regret

These issues represent the kinds of problems clients might present that all reflect a lack of clarity about the issue of responsibility. The content of what they want help with is what they will naturally describe to the therapist (e.g., what they feel guilty about that the therapist recognizes as misplaced self-blame). However, it is up to the therapist to recognize the client's inability to know how to distinguish accurately what they are and are not responsible for as the process needing intervention.

## Defining the Salient Therapeutic Targets

Therapists can easily muddy the waters of responsibility based on their own subjective views or philosophies. There are those who say things such as, "There are no accidents" and "Whatever happens in your life is your responsibility." Such global philosophies work against the client ever learning specifically how to determine when they are and are not personally responsible for something in their life. It leads to a reflex of self-blame even in circumstances where it should be obvious that they're not to blame. If you believe there are no accidents, for example, and you're responsible for everything, then something as absurd as believing you must have caused the driver to rear-end you at the red light because "you had some unconscious need to learn an important life lesson" might actually make sense to you. Philosophies may sound deep, yet still be counterproductive at least, ridiculous at most.

The primary therapeutic goals of a process-oriented approach, therefore, are to (1) help the client be clear about the roles they are in and the boundaries that define their responsibilities; (2) help the client to determine whether it

---

### TABLE 11.1. GENERIC SESSION STRUCTURE FOR DEFINING RESPONSIBILITY

**Induction**

| | |
|---|---|
| **Response set:** | Agency |
| **Theme 1:** | The past need not define us in the present |
| **Theme 2:** | People are more than their one-dimensional labels |
| **Theme 3:** | People are sometimes contradictory |
| **Theme 4:** | Taking responsibility for your mistakes and reducing guilt in the process |
| **Theme 5:** | Recognizing what you're not to blame for even when the finger is pointed at you |
| **Theme 6:** | Being clear about where the responsibility really lies |
| **Theme 7:** | Making better discriminations about personal responsibility |

**Posthypnotic suggestions for integration**
**Closure and disengagement**

was their words or actions that generated the outcome of concern; (3) help the client shake the negative label associated with a past mistake and begin to redefine themselves as much more than that label; (4) help the client develop a means of atonement for past mistakes; and (5) help the client develop a clear recognition of when someone is blaming them inappropriately and have the boundaries and the words to say to resist accepting the blame and deal with any anger that arises as a result. Table 11.1 delineates a generic strategy that can help facilitate reaching these goals.

## SESSION TRANSCRIPT

### Induction

Now would be a good time to arrange yourself in a position that is comfortable . . . and as you find that physically comfortable position . . . you can start focusing yourself now . . . on making yourself comfortable . . . on *all* levels. . . . Now, I know that here at the beginning . . . your thoughts may be going in many different directions. . . . But when you close your eyes . . . as you can now . . . and you start to relax your body . . . by breathing . . . slowly . . . and deeply . . . and by letting your arms and legs . . . just rest there . . . starting to feel heavy and relaxed . . . and getting heavier still . . . you can get so comfortable . . . that even your mind . . . begins to slow . . . down . . . your thoughts . . . getting more focused . . . your mind getting clearer. . . . And little by little . . . your feelings . . . are soothed . . . and comforted . . . so that in the most . . . wonderful of ways . . . you get to just be . . . for a while. . . . No demands right now . . . no pressures of anything else that you have to do right now. . . . This is your time to just be at ease . . . growing comfortably detached . . . from the usual things that take up space in your awareness . . .

### Building a Response Set Regarding Agency

And this is, of course, *your* experience. . . . It's *your* body that's gradually relaxing . . . moment by moment . . . and it's *your* willingness to focus yourself that makes growing comfortable possible now . . . and it's *your* decision to spend time listening to the ideas and possibilities I'll be presenting to you over the next few minutes. . . . And it will naturally be up to *you* to choose what you find meaningful and what's worth absorbing during this time of being deeply attentive. . . . And what a wonderful capacity we each have to make choices so many times each day . . . choices about what to say or do at a given time . . . and to know . . . really know deep inside . . . that the quality of our lives is largely shaped by the quality of the choices that *we* make . . . the *choices we make for ourselves.* . . . And wouldn't it be ideal if every decision we ever made led to great success and satisfaction? . . .

**Theme: The Past Need Not Define Us in the Present**
But, you know and I know that part of growing up is learning from the inevitable mistakes we make . . . things we wish we had handled better. . . . And it's a curious thing how different people come to terms with the things they would love to have a chance to do over again . . . how some detach from it quickly and simply say some variation of, "Oh, well!" . . .and others replay it over and over again . . . as if there's anything more to be gained from riding around that cul-de-sac. . . . And right now you have the time and the space to take a clear step forward in your emotional life. . . . You get to finally . . . come to terms with . . . and create a wonderful sense of detachment from old, outdated feelings . . . that have taken up much too much space within you. . . . And it can be quite comforting to gradually come to realize . . . how many of them are simply no longer relevant . . . certain feelings you had at a time in your life . . . that you now can come to view as simply a piece of history that has receded into the past. . . . And you can use this time to do some emotional house cleaning . . . in order to ease outdated feelings from too long ago . . . out of your system . . . a little at a time. . . . They lose their place in your new and still growing views of yourself. . . . Someone wise once said that "every step *forward* . . . means leaving something *behind*" . . . and you know that's true from your own experience. . . . The things you left behind from childhood like a favorite toy . . . or a favorite game . . . that is now only a distant memory. . . . As you grow clearer and stronger . . . that feelings from the past that are outdated . . . can be left in the past . . . you can grow clearer and stronger about who you are now . . . and what you're about . . . and how you've grown over time . . . and who you are becoming. . . . After all, you're still growing as a person . . . seeking out new experiences like this one we're sharing together. . . .

## Theme: People Are More Than Their One-Dimensional Labels

You have a very important opportunity right now . . . to reach a new level of understanding . . . about your own sense of integrity. . . . And by integrity . . . I mean . . . a moral guide that you strive to live by . . . that shapes what you're willing to do and say . . . and what you're *not* willing to do and say . . . and how you respond to yourself and others when you behave in a way that goes against that moral guide. . . . And one of the most difficult concepts . . . for people to grasp . . . is that . . . no one can be defined by a single label. . . . You might be a young person or perhaps an older one . . . but you're more than that. . . . You may be someone's child or someone's sister or brother . . . but you're more than that. . . . You may be a boss or an employee . . . but you're more than that. . . . No one is one-dimensional, defined only by a single characteristic. . . .

## Theme: People Are Sometimes Contradictory

And so it can become easier for you to understand that someone, *anyone*, can do something . . . that isn't very nice . . . and yet . . . still be a good person. . . . It isn't so simple . . . that a bad person only does bad things and a good person only does good things. . . . Sometimes . . . really good people . . . do something that really isn't very good . . . just as sometimes . . . a really bad person can do something really nice. . . . An honest person . . . can do something dishonest . . . and a dishonest person can sometimes tell the truth. . . . Life isn't quite so simple or easy . . . and it distorts things to think . . . in overly simplistic and extreme all-or-none terms . . . such that if you do something bad . . . it makes you a bad person . . . any more than if you do something good, it makes you a good person. . . . It's just too simple and one-dimensional to be entirely true. . . . Someone can be a pretty sensitive person . . . and a pretty perceptive person . . . who may be good at reading other people . . . getting a good sense of who they are . . . what they're about. . . . And as sensitive as one generally may be . . . every once in a while . . . even sensitive, perceptive people can miss the chance to be sensitive and perceptive and mishandle some interaction or decision. . . . They may say something that wasn't very well thought out . . . that hurt somebody . . . or they may do something that ended up hurting someone else's feelings. . . . Now, it may be a pretty serious breach, but most of the time it may not even be anything all that big. . . . It might just be a snippy reply or a sarcastic barb . . . that someone said that was insensitive. . . . But even if it was relatively small . . . it *did* hurt someone's feelings and it really wasn't the intention. . . . It just came out thoughtlessly. . . .

### Theme: Taking Responsibility for Your Mistakes and Reducing Guilt in the Process

But, since no one is perfect . . . and since nice people can say mean things sometimes . . . the real measure of someone's integrity . . . is that as soon as they realize that they did or said something that injured someone else . . . they'll accept the reality that they did something hurtful to someone . . . and they'll apologize for it . . . and strive to make it right in some meaningful way. . . . They can own up to the fact that it was *their* action . . . and the right thing to do is to take personal responsibility for the hurtful consequences. . . . And yes, they may feel bad about what they said or did. . . . They may feel guilty. . . . But it's good to remember at those times . . . and you can remember so clearly at those times . . . that even a sensitive person . . . can occasionally do an insensitive thing . . . and even a smart person . . . can occasionally do something . . . pretty foolish. . . . And remembering that when you have created a way to live with integrity . . . that you can go out of your way to right any wrongs you've done whenever you can . . . even a simple but sincere apology can go a long way. . . . And taking steps to act with integrity can quickly ease feelings of guilt . . . and allow you a comforting recognition that you're much more than what any mistake you might have made would suggest. . . .

### Theme: Recognizing What You're Not to Blame for Even When the Finger Is Pointed at You

But you know and I know . . . there's another side of this responsibility issue to consider. . . . There are lots of people out there who make bad choices . . . who say things and do things that are hurtful to themselves or others . . . and somehow manage to convince themselves that it wasn't really them who made the choice. . . . It was somebody else's fault. . . . And it's important to recognize . . . and recognize quickly in various life situations . . . that you're *not* always responsible for other people's feelings. . . . You can come to recognize more quickly and efficiently that they're responsible for their own feelings and reactions. . . .

Sometimes the action you take or the things you say can hurt someone . . . but *not* because you were wrong or thoughtless. . . . For example, sometimes you have to tell someone they behaved badly, and they
won't like hearing that . . . but it doesn't mean you were wrong to say
so. . . . And as another example, sometimes you have to end a relationship that isn't going anywhere good, and it hurts the other person's
feelings . . . but it doesn't mean you were wrong to end it. . . . As you
can see, it's a challenge sometimes to distinguish when you are and
when you're not responsible for other people's reactions. . . . Sometimes
someone else may point the finger of blame at you . . . for something . . .
that you're really not to blame for. . . . They may tell you . . . for example,
that it's your fault . . . that they had to stay up all night worrying . . . simply because you went out for the evening . . . or that it's your fault they
were too distracted to remember where they put their car keys. . . . And
if you're not perceptive enough to recognize . . . that they're blaming
you for something you're not to blame for . . . then you could easily take
in that blame and feel bad . . . or guilty . . . unfairly, unnecessarily. . . . It's
easier, much easier . . . to blame others for one's own bad decisions or
bad behavior than it is to take personal responsibility for those bad decisions or behavior. . . .

### Theme: Being Clear About Where the Responsibility Really Lies

It will save you lots of unnecessary guilt if you can quickly determine
who is really responsible for what happened in some situation . . . *before*
accepting blame from somebody else or blaming yourself. . . . And it will
define you as a person with integrity when you accept the responsibility
for your own actions. . . . It's true that some situations are so emotionally
charged that it can take a little while to sort out who's responsible for
what. . . . Here's an example to consider. . . . I've worked with people who
have . . . gotten angry when they were criticized in ways they thought
unfair . . . and behaved in a way . . . that crossed a line that should never
have been crossed . . . saying cruel things in anger that should never
have been said. . . . And when they cooled down . . . they were truly
sorry. . . . They took responsibility for it, learned from it, and never did
it again. . . . And the relationship not only survived but eventually even
thrived. . . . And, other times . . . I've worked with people who crossed
a line by saying nasty things in anger and thoughtlessly blamed the

other person. . . . They actually justified their awful behavior when they said, "Well, if that person hadn't provoked me, then I wouldn't have said those things." . . . And they literally blame the other person for what they said. . . . Such a person *doesn't* take responsibility for their behavior, nor do they feel guilty that they hurt someone. . . . It's appalling . . . and destructive and irresponsible . . . and just plain foolish. . . . What a clear sign of maturity and integrity when you take responsibility for yourself . . . and the things you say and do. . . . But unfortunately not everyone does . . . and some people will be happy to blame you for their bad choices . . . and will try to make you feel guilty, as if you made them say or do something that crossed the line of decency. . . .

**Theme: Making Better Discriminations About Personal Responsibility**
Part of what you're learning here . . . I hope . . . is that the ability to feel guilty . . . means that you have a conscience . . . a higher sense of virtue . . . a moral code you strive to live by that you may have violated in some way and *felt* bad about. . . . And now you can appreciate more than ever before how that can be a good thing . . . and it can teach us valuable life lessons. . . . And if you or I hurt someone . . . then feeling guilty is normal . . . appropriate . . . even desirable . . . but it doesn't need to be a hurtful feeling that lingers too long. . . . When you can remind yourself that smart people can sometimes do foolish things . . . and sensitive people can sometimes do insensitive things . . . and responsible people can sometimes do irresponsible things . . . it's so much easier to lift the burdens of guilt from your shoulders . . . so much easier to let it fade into history . . . when you take *timely* responsibility for your actions and do what you can to make amends. . . . And so, you can let old guilt go . . . day by day . . . let it go . . . living your life at a higher level of integrity now . . . by being more aware of yourself . . . and being more deliberate about the choices that you make . . . and situation by situation, more quickly recognizing the boundary . . . that defines the limits of your responsibilities . . . clearer than ever about what's yours and what isn't. . . . Clear now that it *isn't* your job . . . to keep that person from making bad choices they defend their right to make. . . . And it *isn't* your job . . . to keep that person from getting angry when you tell them something they'd prefer not to hear. . . . And it *isn't* your job . . . to make sure your spouse's report for work or your

child's school report is written and turned in on time. . . . You may want to help . . . but it's a responsibility that belongs to that person . . . and you really don't want to contribute to their pretending it isn't. . . .

## Posthypnotic Suggestions for Integration

And so the clearer you get . . . about the limits of your responsibilities . . . the less often you'll feel guilty inappropriately or unrealistically . . . and the less you'll blame others for your mistakes . . . and the less you'll be willing to take the blame for others' mistakes. . . . And the more quickly and efficiently you can master the skills that go into knowing where the lines are that define responsibility . . . the more you'll be able to appreciate yourself . . . and like yourself . . . for the things that you do . . . and the good ways that you treat people . . . with integrity . . . and respect . . . and the good ways that you treat yourself . . . with integrity . . . and respect . . . and the ways that you make it clear how you expect to be treated with respect . . . and how you make it clear that you are unwilling to take responsibility or blame for other people's bad choices. . . .

## Closure and Disengagement

And notice how good it can feel to you now to go through your day-to-day life . . . without any of the guilt pangs of old. . . . And doesn't it feel good . . . even now . . . to let go . . . and feel good . . . and be so much clearer about what it means to be responsible for oneself? . . . So, enjoy the comfort . . . the relief . . . that you're feeling now . . . and carry it with you . . . throughout the rest of your day . . . and throughout every day. . . . Now, you can finally unpack your bags . . . because you're *not* going on a guilt trip! . . . And when you've had enough time to . . . fully absorb . . . the implications . . . and meanings . . . and learnings of this focusing experience . . . then you can start to bring this session to a satisfying end . . . with a strong, comfortable feeling that's really nice to experience. . . . And when you've done that . . . you can start the process of bringing yourself out of hypnosis . . . at a slow and gradual rate that is comfortable for you. . . . Then when you have brought yourself to a fully alert state . . . you can open your eyes . . . and go about doing the things that you need to . . . to make it a really good day. . . .

# Chapter 12

# Catalyzing Meaningful Action

*Never confuse motion with action.*

—Benjamin Franklin

## The Case of Bart

Bart, age 28, had scheduled and canceled two previous meetings before our first meeting finally took place. I can't say I was surprised when Bart told me his reason for seeking therapy: "I'm a procrastinator. I don't mean to be, but I am. I know there's something I need to do, and I intend to do it, but something always seems to get in the way. I guess I must just be lazy or have ADD or something."

Bart didn't really need to provide examples of his procrastination for my benefit, but he was on a roll, so I let him go on. He said, "I'm super aware of everything I need to do. I mean, you should see my apartment. Well, no, you shouldn't see my apartment because I'd be embarrassed, but you should see what a mess it is. I can't find stuff, I don't know what I did with stuff, and when I think about actually taking the time to get organized, it seems like a great idea but then I don't do anything. It's just so overwhelming. I wouldn't even know where to start. I see what needs to be done. It's too much for me to handle, so I go to a movie or play video games instead. It's kind of the story of my life. I want to do things, or at least I think I want to do things, but then nothing. I manage to hold onto my job, always just barely squeezing my work in under the deadline. It actually causes me a lot of stress, but I don't do anything about it. Can you help me?"

Does Bart have an unconscious fear of success or failure? An unconscious need to suffer? An inadequate personality disorder? Is he suffering with a masked depression? Is he afraid of commitment? Is he just lazy or ADD as he suggested? Or what?

Bart has a cognitive style, or a pattern of thinking, called a global cognitive style. Global cognition, also called overgeneral thinking, generally refers to seeing the big picture at the expense of seeing the associated details. Metaphorically, as in this book's subtitle, the person sees the forest, not the trees. Global cognition is responsible for a number of different emotional and behavioral consequences; anxiety and depression are just two problems associated with it. Procrastination is another manifestation of a global cognitive style.

The content of Bart's problem is whatever he's putting off doing that troubles him right now. The process is about how he decides what he's actually going to do. I asked Bart directly, "How do you decide at a given moment what you're going to do?" His response was most revealing: "I don't know." After a pause he added, "I guess I just follow my gut. I'm pretty spontaneous."

Bart's strategy reflects an internal orientation (i.e., he uses his feelings to decide what to do) but an external locus of control; my question was "How do you decide?" and his answer was that he doesn't decide proactively. He responds reactively. If he's going to react to his gut feelings as the basis for what he's going to do, when exactly he is going to feel like cleaning his apartment when that feeling apparently only comes around once a century? When is he going to feel like suspending his spontaneity to do something that doesn't feel particularly good to do but still needs to be done?

The other part of the process Bart employs in his life concerns his perceptual style. Some people make things bigger than they really are; others make things smaller than they really are. Bart makes even simple tasks seem so big in his mind ("I see what needs to be done. It's too much for me to handle, so I go to a movie or play video games instead") that they seem too formidable to approach.

Hypnosis is all about shifting perceptions. The first principle you learn in studying hypnosis is "What you focus on, you amplify." What elements of a client's experience do we want to amplify, and, in the process, what other elements do we want to deamplify? In Bart's case, it would be important to amplify three things in particular: (1) the means for breaking global and overwhelming tasks into smaller, specific, sequential, manageable steps; (2) the merits of being proactive rather than reactive in living his life; and (3) the greater satisfaction to be enjoyed that comes with fulfilling a task or reaching a goal that outweighs the spontaneity that gives away valuable time to unworthy activities.

The hypnosis sessions with Bart were quite straightforward, weaving these goals into each of the five sessions we had. He was offered numerous examples of breaking globals into specifics (e.g., you don't "take a shower," a global term; rather, you "follow a specific series of steps that culminate in you being clean"), examples of people who waited passively for opportunity to fall into their laps, and examples of times he had been pushed to get something done by some deadline and how much satisfaction he got from the final product, no matter how much he didn't like being pushed to complete it.

Bart was given homework, which was seeded during the hypnosis session. For example, he was given the assignment to break taking a shower down into its component steps. Predictably, he identified only three global steps: get wet, lather up, rinse off. When I added in all the details (How do you find a shower? Do you turn the lights on? Do you take your clothes off? Do you open the shower door or curtain before stepping into the tub or shower? Do you turn on and test the water temperature before stepping in?), Bart said, "Well, yeah, you do all those things. I just never thought about it before." I said, "That's the point: Anything you want to do has a sequence to it, and what makes it seem so overwhelming is when you don't know the sequence." I gave him another assignment as well: Put a chair in front of your apartment door facing the door. Then sit there for 15 minutes every two hours while you're at home. He asked, "What am I supposed to do while I'm sitting there?" I said, "Wait for opportunity to knock." He laughed, but actually did the assignment. He later said, "I think that was a turning point for me. Sitting there, waiting for opportunity to come find me, made me feel really foolish, but in a good way. I've done more in the last two weeks than in the last two *years*! Now every time I think about what I need to do, I think to write out the steps, and it doesn't seem so big anymore, and I think about waiting for someone else to do it for me, knowing nobody will. I really think I finally got it! Thanks."

## The Role of an Action Orientation in Quality of Life

While it is often difficult to know what's in someone's mind or heart, observing what they do and how they do what they do is particularly revealing. It is a basic tenet of communications theory that all behavior has message value. What does someone's behavior tell you? Does it tell you they are impulsive and reckless, or thoughtful and deliberate? Self-absorbed or sensitive to others? Goal-directed or random? Consistent and largely predictable or erratic? There is little room for doubting the wisdom of the maxim, "Action speaks louder than words." The message received from what we do usually comes through loud and clear.

Clearly, though, not all action is meaningful, despite being revealing. People routinely engage in actions that are hurtful to themselves and others. The list of self-destructive behaviors people can engage in is a long one and well-known to psychotherapists. Some are subtle while others are painfully obvious to everyone. Similarly, the list of ways one person's actions can harm others is also a long one and can range from direct (e.g., violence) to indirect (e.g., polluting the environment).

Why would someone engage in self-destructive and/or antisocial behavior? The amount of suffering humans endure from such behavior cannot be calculated but touches all of our lives. These are human tragedies that are anything but logical and are generally looked at by therapists as poor attempts to cope with stressors, both real and imagined, and/or the product of genetic predispositions.

If actions do indeed speak louder than words, and all behavior has message value, the role of action in determining one's quality of life is obvious. Engaging in behavior that is positive and helpful to both oneself and others is our idealistic hope for all people, our wish for world peace on a planet populated by contented and productive inhabitants. At the far more modest level of the therapy context, the clinician's task is to find ways of helping the client do less of this and do more of that. Indeed, of the more than 800 distinct forms of psychotherapy said to be available today, although they vary in degrees of emphasis, all encourage clients in one way or another to do something different. Every therapist has heard the oft-repeated cliché, "The definition of insanity is doing the same thing over and over and expecting a different outcome." Though a cliché it may be, it is a perspective that guides the therapy process. It clearly defines the goal of wanting to get the client to follow a different course of action. The challenge, and it's a formidable one, is how to encourage the client to take action that may be difficult or scary or even just simply unfamiliar and uncomfortable.

Hypnosis as an intervention is especially well-suited for encouraging meaningful action. Hypnosis provides a carefully constructed context in which the client can develop a positive and motivating association to suggested behaviors. The amplification of the benefits of action (the qualities of positive expectancy described in Chapter 6) and the acceptance of personal responsibility for the need to take action (as described in Chapter 11) can be embedded in the type of hypnosis session described in this chapter. What specific action we want the client to take is the content of our intervention. The process is helping the client recognize in any context when purposeful action is required. How should the client know when to seize the moment by doing something that will lead to some desirable outcome or, conversely, when to take the action of insightfully taking no action for the same reason? This represents yet another discrimination issue, a decision-making process that can be integrated into the process-oriented hypnosis session, as you will see in this chapter's transcript.

## Free Will and Social Influence

As discussed in the previous chapter, the question of free will naturally arises when discussing the actions people take. Do we choose our behavior, or are we somehow preprogrammed to act the way we do? How we answer that question for ourselves leads to our self-understandings of why we do what we do: "I take this action because 'it's genetic' or 'wired into my brain,'" or "I take this action because I want to . . . and I *can*."

The field of social psychology in particular has studied the power of situational influences on behavior. Can a peaceful person become violent under certain conditions? Or can an honest person behave dishonestly under the right conditions? The literature of social psychology is filled with fascinating examples of how changes in circumstances give rise to changes in behavior. Consider an example for yourself: If I ask you, "Would you be willing to walk totally naked on a busy downtown street in broad daylight for a distance of half a mile?," most people would say, "No way!" Then I change the conditions when I make this offer: "Would you do it for 5 million dollars tax-free?" In the blink of an eye, what seemed unthinkable a moment ago is now being given serious thought!

The content of the naked stroll isn't the point. Rather, the process of a change in circumstances that gives rise to new behaviors is the point. This is the foundation of strategic therapy approaches that strive to change the client's circumstances through some safe and appropriate means in order to elicit new behaviors that can be helpful. Milton Erickson's use of hypnosis and strategic task assignments earned him a reputation as a creative genius, accolades he richly deserved. Studying his innovative ways of changing the client's problem context in some way, requiring an action of adaptation by the client in the process, is highly recommended.

## Action in Therapy: More Can Be Better

Cognitive-behavioral therapy has become the most widely studied psychotherapeutic treatment for a variety of disorders and has many outcome studies supporting its therapeutic efficacy (Padesky & Greenberger, 2020; Greenberger & Padesky, 2016). As a form of psychotherapy, CBT encourages the depressed client to actively perform a variety of self-awareness and skill-building exercises, which appear to have at least as much therapeutic impact on the client as the focus on changing the client's presumably distorted cognitions. Subsequent research has affirmed that therapeutic change is likely to be greater in those therapies that employ homework (e.g., active skill-building exercises) than in those that do not. The term "behavioral activation" is used to emphasize the importance of getting the client to actually do something rather than merely passively acquire information or contemplate their feelings and circumstances (Yapko, 2010a).

Behavioral activation strategies as a means of promoting experiential learning, skill building, and proactive behavior have been developed into a model of psychotherapy called behavioral activation therapy, known simply as BA. The general goal of BA is to increase the client's frequency of positively reinforced behaviors. It targets many of the most common symptom patterns among therapy clients, including inactivity and, especially, an avoidant coping style. Clients are taught strategies for carrying out goal-oriented behaviors more successfully.

It does not seem coincidental that of the psychotherapeutic treatments with the highest levels of empirical support, none of them focus on analyzing the past; none of them focus on abstract theoretical issues (such as unconscious guilt or existential angst); and all of them emphasize, directly or indirectly, developing skills and using them to take positive actions of one sort or another. It is essential that the client is defined as an active participant in the treatment process, engaged in experiential learning through a variety of mechanisms such as hypnosis (and structurally related processes such as imagery and mindfulness), structured homework assignments, and role-playing.

Researchers and clinicians are virtually unanimous in their belief that hypnosis is an active process, a means of intervention that requires the client to actively attend to, engage with, integrate, and ultimately apply suggestions offered by the clinician or researcher (Yapko, 2019). Hypnosis as a vehicle of experiential learning is already well established. (For a comprehensive review of diverse applications, see Elkins [2017].) Hypnosis as a means of actively encouraging emotional self-regulation through skill acquisition is also well established.

One of the many strengths of hypnosis is evident in its ability to give some definition to the problem. That is especially important when the client doesn't have much in the way of self-awareness or insights into the specifics of what needs to be done. When a client's thinking is overgeneral, then reports such as, "I just want to be happy" are common. As a consequence, the client may be frozen in knowing they need to do something but are unaware of what that would be. Process-oriented hypnosis can help teach the client greater skills in emotional differentiation and the dynamics of breaking global problems into problems that can be resolved with a well-defined plan.

## Rumination Gets in the Way of Meaningful Action

Rumination is a style of coping with life stressors and negative mood states that features a very strong internal orientation, a process of engaging in self-focused attention on one's negative feelings and perceptions at the expense of taking effective action. More concretely, rumination as a coping style means that when the going gets tough, the tough get thinking . . . and thinking, and analyzing, and anticipating, and worrying, and asking themselves the same depressing questions (e.g., Why is this happening to me? What does this say about my life? What does it predict for my future?) over and over again that they're no closer to answering on the 25th go-round than they were on the first. It's the basis for what many understandably call an "analysis paralysis."

Helping to fuel negative expectancy (hopelessness) and helplessness, rumination is a principal catalyst for passivity—the virtual opposite of behavioral activation—and thus must be considered a primary target of intervention, hypnotic or otherwise. As Susan Nolen-Hoeksema, an expert in rumination's effects on anxiety and depression, stated in an interview, "Even when a person prone to rumination comes up with a potential solution to a significant problem, the rumination itself may induce a level of uncertainty and immobilization that makes it hard for them to move forward" (Law, 2005, p. 38).

Asking oneself probing questions such as the above may seem reasonable or even insightful, but instead of getting focused on solving a problem, one may get wrapped up in anxious worrying and depressed feelings, focusing on them, analyzing them, linking them to more and more problems, and thereby making them ever larger and more complicated. This isn't how one will feel better. To the contrary, this is how people get worse by feeling bad about how bad they feel.

Rumination as a coping style, like other coping styles, develops early in life and becomes a deeply ingrained, reflexive pattern for responding to the negative situations one encounters. The research clearly shows that people who ruminate (1) have higher levels of vulnerability to depression; (2) have more severe depressions; (3) have more chronic depressions and more relapses; and (4) are more likely to suffer anxiety in combination with their depression (Nolen-Hoeksema, 2003).

Rumination increases self-doubt, which, in turn, increases one's level of anxiety and behavioral paralysis. If you feel you can't make a decision because you don't know what to do, and even if you did know what to do, you fear it would probably be wrong, then you may freeze into inaction.

As the principle of cognitive dissonance would predict, people who engage in rumination naturally defend it and rationalize it, typically by saying they're not ruminating, merely "analyzing all the possibilities." Thus there's a rationale for rumination that actually serves to keep it going: The people who ruminate tend to believe they're gaining insight through the process of rolling an issue around and around in their minds. Realistically, thinking something through is generally desirable, particularly when it is an exercise in impulse control. But there comes a point when thinking becomes overthinking, and where the ability to solve a problem with decisive action becomes impaired rather than enhanced. If one is too global in one's thinking to be able to distinguish useful analysis from useless rumination, then all analysis will mistakenly seem productive, an illusory step in the direction of problem solving. The goal, then, is to learn to identify where the point is in a given circumstance that distinguishes useful analysis from useless rumination so that one can decide on and then actually take a course of timely and effective action.

## Typical Problems Derived From a Negative Action Orientation

The types of problems that people might present for treatment that reflect an inability to take meaningful action are quite diverse, and may include such problematic patterns as these:

- Rigid perceptions of the unchangeable causes of their behavior
- Negative and self-injurious coping behaviors
- Taking directionless action just for the sake of taking action
- Taking no action for fear of making a mistake
- A history of regretting not taking effective actions
- Believing taking action will be punished or painful in some way
- Believing taking action is futile
- A lack of clarity about what action to take
- Not having a sense of personal responsibility for taking action
- Waiting for more data to analyze to confirm what they already know they need to do
- Waiting for ideal conditions ("a sign") to arise that realistically can't and won't before taking action

These represent the kinds of issues clients might present that all reflect difficulty in being sensibly proactive. The content of what they want help with is what they will naturally describe to the therapist, but it is up to the therapist to recognize the client's inability to recognize when and how to take meaningful action as the process needing intervention.

## Defining the Salient Therapeutic Targets

The primary goal of a process-oriented hypnosis session is to encourage timely and effective action on the part of the client. Hypnotic suggestions can be structured in such a way as to help teach clients to recognize their globally stated concerns (e.g., "I just want to feel better") and develop them into more well-defined problems that can be resolved through a structured, concrete plan that encourages taking appropriate action. How the clinician defines and treats the client's issues matters a great deal. A profound lesson I learned from my friend and mentor Jay Haley, a pioneer in family and strategic therapies, is this: Never define problems in unsolvable terms.

The use of hypnosis to encourage action over rumination involves several factors: (1) The client must come to recognize that action is necessary (even if, paradoxically, the course of action is to take no action other than to strive for acceptance of unchangeable circumstances). (2) The client must come to believe that it is possible to identify a specific course of sensible action that has a reasonable chance of succeeding. Two specific skills make this possible: delineating a specific linear strategy to implement, and an ability to make a realistic assessment of the probability that it will be effective. The individual may need help developing these skills as well. It is an important precaution to acknowledge that building expectancy without a well-defined next step may only serve to increase the client's frustration. (3) The individual must be able to compartmentalize, that is, set aside fears or doubts and follow the action plan to its completion, perhaps modifying it as necessary along the way as new information surfaces (as discussed in Chapter 9).

A process-oriented hypnosis session can also impart these messages: (1) there are more ways to make decisions than just according to one's feelings; (2) pursuing new learning experiences can encourage a revision of old restrictive beliefs and attitudes; (3) there is rarely just one right answer or decision to be made, but rather multiple possible decisions, each with its consequences; and (4) one must learn to discriminate between useful analysis and useless rumination. Table 12.1 offers a structured means for promoting behavioral activation.

TABLE 12.1. GENERIC SESSION STRUCTURE
FOR CATALYZING MEANINGFUL ACTIONS

**Induction**

| | |
|---|---|
| **Response set:** | Taking helpful action on your own behalf |
| **Theme 1:** | Your decisions to act are inevitable, and they shape your quality of life |
| **Theme 2:** | Past actions don't predict future possibilities |
| **Theme 3:** | Good action plans necessarily have steps to follow |
| **Theme 4:** | There's a danger in thinking too much |

**Posthypnotic suggestions for integration**
**Closure and disengagement**


## SESSION TRANSCRIPT

### Induction

You can begin by taking in a few deep, relaxing breaths . . . and begin to focus your attention . . . gradually, of course. . . . There's no reason to hurry as you start to grow more comfortable within yourself. . . . You have the time now to just enjoy the experience . . . of finding and using more of your own internal resources . . . the natural gifts you have to be able to close your eyes . . . and look inside yourself. . . . And as always, you have an opportunity now to create an experience for yourself that's soothing, comforting, and growth oriented . . . in ways you'll discover gradually over time. . . .

### Build a Response Set Regarding Taking Helpful Action on Your Own Behalf

I can slow my voice down to help you slow down as well . . . so you can start to *actively* build the qualities of a gradual absorption. . . . You can *actively* take the time that you need to *build for yourself* an internal atmosphere that makes it easier . . . much easier . . . to consider the possibilities of things you can start to *do* differently . . . and to explore the

*deeper . . . much deeper* implications . . . of what it means to have the
self-awareness . . . that you can easily convert into a plan of action . . . for
feeling good . . . about what you *do.* . . . You've made the choice to allow
yourself this time. . . . You've made the choice of closing your eyes . . .
and you've made the choice to listen . . . good choices and good actions
that can really make a difference in your life . . . in the best of ways. . . .

**Theme: Your Decisions to Act Are Inevitable,
and They Shape Your Quality of Life**
And every day each of us makes so many decisions ranging from
small to large . . . small ones such as what to wear today . . . or what
to have for breakfast . . . or whether to watch this TV program or that
one. . . . These aren't usually serious decisions that carry a lot of consequences. . . . But at the other end of the spectrum, there are sometimes
huge decisions to be made . . . decisions to take actions that can have
a deep and lasting impact . . . such as, "Am I going to stay in this job or
am I going to go?" . . . Or "Do I say something about this person cross-
ing the line here, or do I say nothing?" . . . And so even as you sit quietly,
there are choices you're actively making at this very moment . . . even if
you don't realize it . . . about what to take in . . . and what to use as a new
frame of reference for meaningful *action.* . . . And you can clearly hear
me say that the quality of your life . . . is a reflection of the quality of
your decisions . . . the decisions that you actively make when you deliberately choose a course of action . . . even if, paradoxically, the action
is to deliberately take no action. . . . It's a curious thing to consider how
someone decides whether to take action or choose to take the action
of no action. . . . I remember vividly watching one of my teachers, who
was one of the pioneers of a therapy model called transactional analysis, conduct a clinical demonstration with a man. . . . She knew that he
was an action-oriented person. . . . He described quite clearly how his
first reflex in almost any situation was to want to *do something* . . . to
take some action that was meant to help but sometimes actually back-
fired. . . . How much of his socialization led him to adopt the belief in
the mantra, "Don't just stand there, *do* something!" . . . and it was a real
shock to me when she said quite earnestly to this man . . . the virtually
opposite message: "Don't just do something, *stand there*!" . . . I really
hadn't considered before that powerful moment that there are times

when the decision to act means deciding not to act . . . but the ability to choose and the process of choosing are what I'm encouraging you to focus on now for a little while . . . knowing that even when you choose not to act . . . it's an action plan you've just created . . . that will have consequences for you to consider. . . .

### Theme: Past Actions Don't Predict Future Possibilities

And so I'm curious . . . and perhaps you are, too . . . about your internal atmosphere . . . the environment you create inside yourself . . . as you live your life . . . how you challenge yourself to grow . . . and to *out*grow . . . what's no longer useful to you . . . how you notice . . . and whether you can really appreciate . . . defining what you already do so well . . . recognizing and acknowledging your strengths as a person . . . and how you resolve what can sometimes seem to be contradictions . . . between certain things that you used to believe about yourself . . . and about others . . . and what you're now coming to believe . . . how many of the older perspectives you hold . . . can still be valued . . . and reaffirmed for their merits and contributions to your life . . . and how some of the old . . . can be modified . . . and redefined. . . . You can easily recall actions that you've taken in the past . . . things you've done that turned out really well . . . and others that you would have hoped for a different result . . . times when you took action, and it was the right thing to do . . . other times an opportunity for action that drifted by. . . . And researchers have addressed this very question about decisions and actions . . . and you might be interested to know that on a purely statistical basis alone . . . people are generally far more likely to regret the actions they *didn't* take than the actions they did. . . . And to *actively* open up a future for yourself that will be satisfying to you . . . a future that has so few, if any, regrets. . . . You'll need to know the steps for making a sensible decision to *take action* . . . knowing now more clearly than ever before that making decisions is inevitable . . . and whatever you do or don't do is still your plan of action . . . and learning how to *take sensible action steps* . . . helps you build trust in your own judgment. . . .

### Theme: Good Action Plans Necessarily Have Steps to Follow

It can feel good to know you have choices about what to focus on at any given moment . . . and how your choice automatically leads you to a next step . . . and a next step after that . . . on the path to some well-defined goal. . . . But you know and I know . . . that sometimes people aren't focused on a well-defined goal at all. . . . Instead they simply focus on how they wish things were . . . as if waiting for some magic to happen . . . that will improve their lives . . . without them having to learn anything new or do something different. . . . And I have a good example to share with you of what I mean. . . . I clearly remember working with someone not long ago . . . who asked for my help. . . . He told me that he was dissatisfied with his life . . . that it just didn't turn out the way he had hoped it would. . . . And when I asked him questions about how he ended up in this position of being dissatisfied . . . he said he really didn't know. . . . He said that "it just sort of happened." . . . He couldn't point to any actions he took that landed him in his current place in life . . . and he wasn't aware of any actions he didn't take. . . . He was just living life from day to day. . . . And when I asked him what he wanted in seeking help from me . . . he said quite simply that all he wanted was "to be happy." . . . And he was afraid that being happy "just wasn't in the cards for him" . . . and he felt he must be defective because everyone else seemed happy and he wasn't . . . which made him feel badly about himself. . . . Now I can easily understand someone wanting to be happy. . . . It's what you want and it's what I want, too. . . . But I wonder what you might have said to him . . . how you would have responded to his wish to be happy. . . . It was very clear to me very quickly . . . and might be equally clear to you as well . . . that his way of thinking was so general . . . so lacking in details that it was difficult for him to recognize his own feelings . . . or the decisions that he made and the actions they did or didn't lead him to take. . . . So I gave him an assignment he could do before my next appointment with him . . . I asked him to find at least three things per day that he did that he felt competent to do . . . things he could do successfully . . . simple things like taking a shower . . . or getting dressed . . . or going grocery shopping. . . . And I asked him to pretend he had to teach someone else to do those simple things who had never done them before . . . and had no idea of where to begin and how to do them. . . . And for this assignment he had to articulate a series of steps to follow that would guarantee the person would be able to do the task successfully. . . . And it was his job to identify all the steps involved in, say, taking a shower . . . and bring them to me to discuss. . . . Well, he brought me a list of only three steps: Get wet, lather up, and rinse off. . . . So I asked him how someone who never did it before was supposed to know how to find a shower . . . and did they know to undress first and take off their glasses . . .and did they have a towel to dry off afterward? . . . And how was that person supposed to know how to turn on the water and get the temperature right? . . . And how was the person supposed to know how to use soap or shampoo? And how long were they supposed to wash before rinsing? . . . And with each question I asked, he came to the startling realization that his list of steps would never help *anyone* successfully take a shower. . . . He wasn't able to tell me the steps to follow so that someone, anyone, could successfully take a shower. . . . And then I asked him how someone would feel if they tried to follow his steps for taking a shower and failed to succeed . . . and he understood someone would probably feel bad and even defective. . . . I paused and then I asked him what the steps were to be happy . . . and he got the point instantly. . . . He realized he didn't know . . . and in that moment he became wonderfully aware that he was *not* defective. . . . He just didn't know the steps to follow . . . the sensible *action* to take. . . . And how can you take the next step when you don't know what the next step is? . . . Someone wise once said something I think is worth you remembering . . . "A goal without steps is merely a wish." . . . And learning to define the steps and actively take them is how you can move from the wish to be happy to the genuine experience of liking your life and how you're living it. . . . And I think you'll enjoy discovering you can develop a whole new way of thinking . . . that serves you well . . . a style of thinking that allows you to observe the steps that people take . . . that you may be able to take, too, in your own way . . . to experience something you really want to experience. . . . You're learning now that there are steps to take to build a good career . . . or to have a good relationship . . . things you can do that can work. . . . And there are things to do that will likely never work. . . . And now you're learning to take action . . . but action within a sequence that can likely succeed . . . so that one step at a time . . . you can move forward in ways you feel great about . . . and are happy with. . . .

### Theme: There's a Danger in Thinking Too Much

And how do you grow into thinking in terms of goals instead of mere wishes? . . . What are the steps . . . that you can follow . . . when you

don't know what steps to follow? . . .And when something happens . . .
and you're not sure how to react or what to do . . . it's so natural to want
to contemplate what's going on . . . to consider what it means . . . or
what could be better . . . or what needs to be solved. . . . It's understandable that you would want to understand . . . and even ask why something
is the way it is . . . but as you're discovering . . . there's an important
distinction to be made between useful analysis . . . and useless rumination. . . . How much analysis is needed before some action is needed? . . .
After all, understanding alone isn't enough. . . . It must invite action . . .
*doing* something that can help. . . . And so often the action to take is a
simple, straightforward one. . . . For example, instead of wondering if
someone is annoyed with you about something you said or did . . . you
can *ask*. . . . Instead of wondering what to do . . . when you know you
need to do something purposeful . . . you can *ask* for ideas . . . and you
can take actions you'll feel good about. . . . And instead of analyzing
your past some more . . . you can *do* something to make tomorrow better. . . . And consider again the question I asked earlier: How much analysis is needed before some action is needed? And the more important
question: How do you know when it's useful analysis and when it's useless rumination? . . . And here's my answer: If it doesn't lead you to *take
timely and effective action*, it's useless rumination. . . .

### Posthypnotic Suggestions for Integration

So your too busy mind can slow down . . . and stop its spinning around
of the same old stuff . . . and then it becomes clearer what to do. . . . You
gradually grow clearer about what steps you need to take . . . even if the
first steps are just to find out from trusted others what the steps are you
might take. . . . And I'm happy to help you with that. . . . And gradually
you can find yourself reflexively . . . automatically . . . pushing yourself to
*convert worries to actions* . . . vulnerabilities to strengths . . . worries to
*sensible* actions. . . . You can *actively* convert concerns to decisions and
helpful solutions . . . with a strong sense that there's something good
to be gained . . . an outcome that's clearly worth the effort. . . . And it
eventually becomes second nature to you to be a person of decision
and a person of action . . . and the sense of calm within you grows as
you become more decisive. . . . The quiet in your mind grows as you take
effective action . . . a calm mind . . . and a calm body . . . and a strong

sense of comfort that spreads over you . . . that you may not be able to easily explain in words. . . . And it's wonderful that you don't have to. . . . You can just enjoy it . . . and then really integrate deeply the recognition that what you do matters at least as much as what you think or feel. . . . And the deeper meaning of the saying, "Actions speak louder than words" can have a new and profound significance for you . . . all the while knowing that what you do defines more of who you are than what you think or feel . . . and doing well to feel well . . . comes so much more easily. . . .

## Closure and Disengagement

And as we begin to bring this session to a close . . . it might be more obvious to you than ever that it's your experience here . . . your time of having been comfortably absorbed . . . as you consider what it means to go from a feeling or an idea to taking meaningful action. . . . And even now . . . you get to decide how much time you want to continue being relaxed and focused on these ideas . . . perhaps even as long as another full minute if you wish . . . [pause]. And now you can take the action of reorienting yourself at a gradual rate . . . beginning to move as you become more alert . . . building your momentum for becoming fully alert, fully reoriented . . . opening your eyes . . . feeling ready to do what needs to be done. . . .

# Chapter 13

# Instilling Integrity

*Always try to be the person your dog thinks you are.*

—Popular bumper sticker

## The Case of Jack

Jack started drinking in high school. There were always parties where the beer flowed freely, and if there was a party going on somewhere, *anywhere*, you were sure to find Jack there. Everybody drank, it seemed, but not quite in the way that Jack did. He wasn't aggressive or obnoxious when he was drunk, but his ability to drink great quantities was well known by all his peers.

Despite drinking way too much, Jack was able to do the things he needed to do. He passed all his classes with flying colors, applied to a fairly prestigious university, got in, and formally transitioned from his high school drinking days to his university drinking days. By now alcohol had become so deeply ingrained in his day-to-day life that it really didn't matter what day or time it was, it was time for another drink.

Somehow during his university drinking days Jack found the time to take and pass his classes and graduate with a degree in political science. He didn't know yet what he would do with his degree, but he slowly began his search for what to do in terms of a career.

Jack was fairly oblivious to all the human wreckage he was leaving behind by the time he graduated. He had never been arrested for a DUI, but he had smashed a car or two when driving while intoxicated and managed to get away with it. He had made some true enemies of classmates he begged, borrowed, and stole coursework from. He had made lots of promises he never intended to keep to unsuspecting people he was willing to burn. He had dated some really nice women but was too drunk too much of the time to treat them as anything better than convenient sex partners. He routinely told them what he knew were lies just to hook up, that he "really cared" for them and he'd settle down one day, "But, hey, if you can't party in college, when will you?" More than one woman had left him in disgust and rage, but Jack didn't care. On to the next one. . . .

Jump ahead a few years. Jack found a job working for a political action committee, had a modest but decent income, was still carefully avoiding any real relationships, and was still drinking as much as ever. Then came the unfortunate but all-too-predictable turning point: He was driving while slightly intoxicated, just as he had many times before, but this time he hit and badly injured a pedestrian who was right where he should be, in a crosswalk. For a split second Jack thought about driving away, and he was unsure then and is still unsure now as to why he didn't. But he didn't. He was arrested, jailed briefly, went through a grueling detox, fined, given a community service mandate as well as a therapy mandate, and was then left to pick up the pieces of his life. His victim's injuries were bad, but he survived. In this regard, Jack was lucky, but for the first time in his life, Jack was flooded with guilt.

Jack had already joined AA as a part of his court-ordered treatment when he came for therapy. The story he told about himself smacked of a sociopathic, narcissistic, terrible human being, but the man in front of me was none of those things. He was pensive, fretful, regretful, racked with guilt and self-doubt, and wide open to whatever I might say that could be of help to him. He was clear that he had hit the proverbial bottom and now had to reinvent himself as a much better human than he'd ever been. As he said ruefully, "The party is over."

So, what's Jack's problem? Was he drinking to cover up his true feelings because he doesn't want to feel vulnerable? Or because he hates himself, is depressed and suicidal? Does he have a fragile self-esteem that requires him to be the party-guy center of attention?

Does he suffer an antisocial personality disorder and is so morally bankrupt that he finds using and abusing others satisfying? Does he have buried feelings of resentment he's using alcohol to soothe? Does he have an addictive personality, genome, and/or brain such that he was inevitably going to be an addict of one kind or another? Or what?

The content of Jack's problem is becoming sober and living a life of sobriety. The process Jack now faces is that of becoming a human being, a mensch, somebody with integrity who's worth knowing. He had a long way to go.

Feeling true guilt for the first time he could ever remember gave the therapy some leverage. He didn't want to feel that way, and now it was his constant companion. His involvement in AA encouraged him to acknowledge the wrongs he had committed against the people he hurt through his terrible behavior. He wasn't sure how to do that exactly since so many of the people he hurt were in the distant past, their names and faces lost in the haze of his alcoholism. He and his sponsor, whom he really liked and appreciated, talked about this step of his recovery a lot.

Hypnosis is a great tool for helping people engage in the process of self-discovery as well as self-definition. Each of us has to define ourselves on a variety of different levels simply because we play so many different roles in life: someone's kid, someone's parent, someone's boss or employee, someone's friend, someone's spouse, and so forth. The challenge in life, the road to building integrity, is to define those roles and their boundaries. This is what it means to develop a "code to live by."

In Jack's case, the hypnosis sessions began gradually, introducing the concept of how people become people: the socialization process that we all go through that teaches us what's right and wrong, what's valued and devalued, what you can and can't say or do, and so forth. We all go through a value programming process, the personal values we're encouraged to develop and live by.

But those are outside forces working on us as we grow up. What about someone in Jack's position, an adult who has already lived a significant portion of his life? Is he just who he is, or is he more? Asking rhetorical questions such as these during hypnosis sessions helps launch people into the direction of self-awareness and self-definition. More important, it sets up the greater part of Jack's intervention: developing his own code of honor. His time in AA meetings helps facilitate this as he listens to others' stories of life mistakes as well as sharing his own. He is literally bombarded with stories that can tell him what works in life and what doesn't, and what defines integrity for him.

What values does he profess to have as his life foundation? What specifically does he recognize and value in other people? What gives them worth and dignity, and what must he do to acknowledge their worth and preserve their dignity, as well as his own?

Jack had about 10 sessions, and the combination of hypnosis sessions and exercises in values clarification, empathy, problem-solving skills, and more gave Jack a map to follow, a structure to use to make decisions he could feel good about, knowing he couldn't feel good about any decision that hurt someone for his gain or amusement. He was clear that the time he would feel best and have the greatest self-respect, would be when he set forth his rules for himself and then lived by them, especially when they weren't particularly convenient but were still the right thing to do.

I didn't see Jack again until he came back three years later. He said, "My code of honor required me to come. I want to acknowledge you for what's happened in my life. My legal troubles were substantial, and though I'm still not out of the woods entirely, I'm getting a lot closer. I still work at the same place but have been given more responsibility, more money, and more respect. I'm not feeling deserving exactly, but I am feeling lucky. But best of all, I met a woman about a year ago that is the most kind and loving woman I could ever hope to meet. I am head over heels in love with her, an exciting but scary feeling. We're getting married at the end of the year. I wanted to invite you to the wedding personally. Will you come?"

## The Role of Integrity in Quality of Life

When I was an undergraduate student at the University of Michigan (Go blue!) a long time ago, I took a course in philosophy. While much of the course was loftier and more abstract than is my usual way of thinking, my professor said something once that was crystal clear, immediately relevant, and powerful enough to stay with me all my life. He said, "Integrity is what you will do when you know you *won't* get caught." What he said and the way he said it struck me like a thunderbolt. I was young and was only just starting to develop a deeper quality of thinking, and I just hadn't given the subject of personal integrity much thought up to that time. His words that day launched me in a whole new direction as I began to focus much more of my attention on how I would define integrity for myself.

I have since heard many variations of my professor's words ("Integrity is about how you'll act even when no one is watching you"), and all of them strike a visceral chord. How shall we define ourselves in terms of character strengths and virtues? And as a corollary, how might others regard us in those qualitative terms?

The times when we tend to be the most self-critical and harsh with ourselves, the times we suffer blows to our self-esteem, are when we violate some standard of behavior that we've set for ourselves. It may be a relatively small transgression such as blowing our diet today, or it might be a great transgression such as punching someone out when they enraged us in some way. The feelings of shame and regret we have when we cross some line that we've drawn for ourselves that is not to be crossed can be incredibly corrosive. It can give rise to a level of self-loathing that makes self-preservation seem both undeserved and futile. Instead, it can generate the kinds of self-destructive behaviors (such as alcohol or drug abuse) and/or antisocial behaviors (such as drunk driving or domestic violence) that reveal for all to see how little regard one has for oneself.

## Typical Problems Derived From a Lack of Integrity

The types of problems that people might present for treatment that reflect a lack of integrity can seem quite diverse, and may include such problematic patterns as these:

- Lying to or deceiving others for personal gain at their expense
- Engaging in behavior that is harmful to others with little or no regret
- Justifying bad behavior with no sense of actual wrongdoing

- Having little or no awareness of the situational rules that define appropriate behavior
- Knowing what the rules or expectations are and violating them without regard either for others or for the consequences
- Having little or no insight into what one holds as personal values
- An inflated self-esteem that is undeserved
- A willingness to manipulate others in self-serving ways that are harmful to them

These represent the kinds of problems clients might present that all reflect a lack of integrity. More often than not, if such people show up for therapy at all, it's because they were dragged in by someone they hurt. Sometimes, though, people know they are doing things that lack integrity and need help developing their character strengths. The content of what they want help with is what they will naturally describe to the therapist, but it is up to the therapist to recognize the client's inability to create and live by a meaningful code of conduct as the process needing intervention.

## Defining the Salient Therapeutic Targets: Positive Psychology and Focusing on What's Right

The use of hypnosis in clinical contexts might well be the first application of a positive psychology, preceding by decades the formation of the current science of positive psychology. After all, anyone who practices hypnosis begins with the conviction that people have more resources than they realize. Based on that core belief, the practice of hypnosis strives to connect or associate people with those resources and then help them use the resources in the context(s) where they can serve their needs well.

The orientation to identifying and mobilizing the client's personal resources is the very core of a hypnosis practice. It addresses this basic philosophical question about the nature of therapy: Is the goal of treatment to reduce pathology or expand wellness? The practice of hypnosis, with its emphasis on empowering people to use more of their innate resources, answers this question unambiguously.

Positive psychology has become an influential force in the field, valued especially for its striving to shift the collective focus of the profession from pathology to wellness. By asking profoundly important questions about how we can bring out the best in people as individuals, communities, and cultures, positive psychology has broadened our view of people to consider their strengths and virtues. What do we really know about what defines the best of human potentials?

As a direct response to the pathology-focused classification systems in the field of mental health, psychologists Martin Seligman and Christopher Peterson, leading advocates of positive psychology, undertook extensive cross-cultural research to catalog the best of what humans have to offer. The result was their seminal contribution, *Character Strengths and Virtues: A Handbook and Classification*. In that book, Peterson and Seligman offer an important insight relevant to this chapter:

> *Character strengths* are the psychological ingredients—processes or mechanisms—that define the virtues. Said another way, they are distinguishable routes to displaying one or another of the virtues. For example, the virtue of wisdom can be achieved through such strengths as creativity, curiosity, love of learning, open-mindedness, and what we call perspective—having a "big picture" on life. (2004, p. 13)

One of the primary goals of a process-oriented hypnosis, then, is to associate people to their strengths. That means first creating a context where people can identify their strengths. What about all those people who are so global in their thinking, so lacking in emotional differentiation and insight, that they really don't have a clue as to what their strengths are? Encouraging such people to review situations in their life and then helping them identify and own (i.e., have agency for) personal resources they displayed in those situations can be a powerful lead-in to the process-oriented hypnosis session provided in this chapter.

Likewise, what about those people who are feeling so badly about themselves, who are so filled with self-loathing, who have behaved so badly perhaps or who feel so trapped in their misery, that the very notion of having a character strength seems virtually impossible to them. Well, it might be—at this time. But it points the way to a worthy goal and highlights again the importance of the ideas and methods for building a future orientation, contained in Chapter 6. To structure an intervention that speaks to what can develop, what new strengths and virtues can emerge, is what it takes to build hope. In such cases, hope can literally save lives.

## Defining Integrity: Having a Code to Live By

One of the most inspiring stories I've ever heard is told by astrophysicist and popular speaker Neil deGrasse Tyson. It's his telling of his first encounter with famed scientist Carl Sagan, who was professor of astronomy and space sciences and director of the Laboratory for Planetary Studies at Cornell University. Sagan was known to virtually all Americans through hosting the popular science series *Cosmos* as well as his frequent endearing appearances on late-night television programs.

Neil was only 17 years old, self-described as "just a kid from the Bronx," but was already deeply immersed in his love of physics and astronomy. He had applied to several universities with the intention of studying physics as an undergraduate. One of the schools he applied to was Cornell University. His application was so impressive that it was forwarded directly for review to Carl Sagan. Almost unbelievably, Carl wrote a letter to Neil inviting him to come up on a Saturday for a guided visit to the university and his lab. Neil took the lengthy bus ride and there, ready to greet him, was Carl Sagan! He was taken around while they talked at length about Neil's interests and what his future might look like.

When it was time for Neil to catch his bus home, it had started to snow. Carl said the snow might delay his bus and, if that should happen, he told Neil to call him and he'd come get him and let him stay the night at his home. Neil was, needless to say, quite floored by this man's kindness and generosity to a potential student. In telling this heartwarming story, Neil said, to paraphrase him, "I already knew what kind of a scientist I wanted to be. From that moment with Carl I now knew what kind of a *man* I wanted to be." Here was a moment, a powerful moment, that inspired in Neil a lifetime commitment to be available and generous in sharing his knowledge and support with others. (To hear the full story in his own words, search "Neil deGrasse Tyson and Carl Sagan" on YouTube.)

This story represents the foundation of the worthy goal of instilling integrity. What specifically we want to encourage as worthy behavior is the content, and how that behavior aligns with and reflects the underlying values of the person is the process. It starts with reinforcing the notion that you are responsible for the choices you make and the behaviors you engage in, as discussed in Chapter 11.

The next step, then, is to define and develop a personal code of conduct. By a code of conduct, I mean an organizing set of principles that will define what you can and can't do and what you are and are not willing to do. When someone steps into a role, whatever role that might be, there are rules that define what is ethical, moral, and legal. These rules may be explicit and well defined or only implicit and perhaps even easily overlooked.

Consider some examples: When someone becomes a cop, there are rules of conduct (no, you can't pocket some of the drug money you seized, and no, you can't plant fake evidence on someone you don't like). When someone becomes a psychotherapist, there are rules of conduct (no, you can't sleep with your clients, and no, you can't look the other way while a child is endangered). When you become a parent, there are rules of conduct (no, you can't take a nap while your toddler plays near the swimming pool, and no, you can't teach your 6-year-old how to make and enjoy margaritas).

The code of conduct provides a structure for living. It provides a straightforward way of taking at least a little of the ambiguity out of life while providing clarity and certainty that "this is how I want to live. These are the standards I want to set for myself." We want to help our clients, especially the ones that have behaved badly and know it, to develop a structure that is honest, realistic, and can provide meaningful guidance when they are faced with the need to act with integrity.

That structure is derived from a self-awareness of one's values, what you prioritize and consider important. A whole science has been built around what is termed values clarification, and there are literally thousands of books and workbooks that can help someone gain greater clarity about their values. That clarification paves the way for then honoring those values in your own behavior, doing those things that reflect and give action to those values. Just as important, it helps you recognize the values that others hold that may or may not be quite different than yours. The ability to recognize other people's strengths and virtues is a powerful basis for building good relationships and having realistic expectations for what matters to those folks. Consider how much anger and disappointment that can prevent.

# Self-Esteem and Your Honor Code

Doing things that reflect and give an action voice to your values is how self-esteem builds. Self-esteem is a statement about how you regard yourself. Self-esteem is also a source of confusion for therapists who think that building a client's self-esteem is a goal of treatment. Well, there are lots of people who have high self-esteem . . . who shouldn't! They may like themselves but having high self-esteem doesn't mean you're a good person. Every sociopath in prison for brutal crimes has good self-esteem despite having no legitimate basis for doing so.

Here's the intersection, then, with positive psychology's emphasis on building up character strengths and virtues. So many of the virtues that have been catalogued only surface in the context of our relationship with others. Honesty, loyalty, compassion, generosity, love, and more become manifest only or primarily through our interactions with others. And, consistent with my earlier point that one of the reliable pathways to feeling badly about oneself is to betray a value or virtue, the need to earn respect for yourself is also tied to the need to earn respect from others.

How far should someone go to earn the respect of others? How does one evaluate one's level of integrity or, even more simply, one's effectiveness in the way one has performed? These questions highlight one of the ambiguities associated with trying to live a life of integrity. How well can I live up to my personal code of conduct? How appropriate and realistic are the standards I've set for myself? These soul-searching questions can easily become the basis for ruminations that give rise to higher levels of self-doubt, anxiety, and depression, as discussed in Chapter 12. Here again, the value of a process-oriented hypnosis session to help curtail the ruminations and encourage clarity of purpose cannot be overstated.

It helps to know that one's character strengths represent potentials to be developed and are not fixed, unchanging traits. The client can come to know that whatever mistakes they've made, whatever flaws they've had revealed, there is room to grow into being someone they themselves can respect. It's not about globally raising the client's self-esteem. Rather, it's about the client using their personal code of conduct to say things and do things consistently that allow them the wonderful opportunity to walk away from some interaction, whether in relationship to themselves or someone else, saying to themselves, "I like what I did there." Table 13.1 provides a vehicle for helping your clients evolve a personal code of honor.

---

**TABLE 13.1. GENERIC SESSION STRUCTURE
FOR INSTILLING INTEGRITY**

**Induction**

| | |
|---|---|
| **Response set:** | Changing self-definitions |
| **Theme 1:** | You generate your experiences |
| **Theme 2:** | You can develop a personal code of honor |
| **Theme 3:** | Discover, define, and own your strengths and virtues |
| **Theme 4:** | Rumination and self-doubt cloud self-awareness |
| **Theme 5:** | You can recognize and acknowledge strengths in others, too |
| **Theme 6:** | Integrity means honoring your code of conduct |

**Posthypnotic suggestions for integration**
**Closure and disengagement**

---

## SESSION TRANSCRIPT

### Induction

You can begin by arranging yourself in a comfortable position . . . preparing yourself to focus . . . and relax . . . and listen. . . . It may help you grow more comfortable more quickly when you let your eyes close. . . . This focusing experience can be a welcome opportunity for you to spend a little time with yourself in a way that's relaxed and quiet. . . . It's a quality of time that is free of any particular demands . . . meant for you to simply experience yourself in a comfortable and calm way. . . . Right now you have the room . . . *all* the room you need inside yourself . . . to be with yourself in a way that's easy, gentle, and even generous. . . . And, of course, as you've been experiencing different hypnosis sessions over time . . . by now you have acquired ample experience with allowing yourself the luxury of relaxing . . . and you're wonderfully capable of making a deliberate decision to get internally focused . . . to build a quality of *attention* that also has some *intention*. . . . And here at the outset . . . you might not know exactly what the session's intentions are just yet . . . but there's plenty of good reason to believe that you can expect positive qualities of comfort and meaningful ideas that, as you listen, can feel really good to you . . . knowing full well that you're able to choose what's important to focus upon . . . and consider . . . and make good use of in the future. . . .

### Building a Response Set Regarding Changing Self-Definitions

Well, this session and *every* session . . . provides a forward-looking approach that reminds you in powerful ways that you're much more than your history. . . . You're much more even than who you think you are in this moment. . . . After all, who you are naturally goes through changes over time . . . things you can recognize that used to matter to you that just don't matter much anymore . . . and, likewise, things that never really mattered very much to you that matter a lot to you now. . . . These changes in your priorities and values sometimes arise seemingly quickly . . . and some of these changes evolve gradually. . . . It highlights the point that your view of yourself requires frequent updates . . . considerations of who you were, but much more importantly who you're *becoming*. . . . And embedded within this session is an invitation to begin to use your capacity to look forward in a different way. . . . And whether it's slightly different or greatly different . . . you really won't know until you discover what changes in your experience of yourself in the coming days and weeks. . . . But one of the things that I want to draw your attention to is how easily you can allow yourself the experience . . . of getting absorbed . . . and it becomes even easier with each hypnosis session . . . as you go inside and discover more of your innate resources . . . and update your view of yourself . . . redefining aspects of yourself in ways that you can feel really good about. . . . And even now as you relax and focus yourself . . . I'm encouraging you in the most respectful way that I know how . . . to notice the quality of your experience and the ways it gradually changes as you continue to grow more comfortable. . . . And what exactly you notice as you listen, I obviously have no way of knowing. . . . It might be the physical sensations of relaxing . . . such as the changes in your breathing and muscle tone. . . . It might be the gradual immersion in a deeper awareness of the things you say to yourself through your thoughts . . . as you consider new possibilities. . . . And when you do . . . how easy it can be to acknowledge and appreciate the greater goals you have of developing new ideas and perspectives that can make your life better. . . . It can bring into sharp focus the type of internal atmosphere that you generate that is consistent with wanting to grow as a person and redefine yourself in some important ways . . . the very reason you're taking the time to focus on and experience the benefits of learning through this and other sessions you listen to as well. . . .

### Theme: You Generate Your Experiences

When you're able to go inside yourself . . . and focus yourself . . . and engage with new ideas and possibilities as you are right now . . . it would be easy for you to take that ability for granted . . . as if there's nothing particularly special about it. . . . But I *hope* you can appreciate . . . I *expect* that you can appreciate . . . that doing what you're doing right now . . . is exactly what far too many people don't know how to do. . . . They have no idea that they can alter their physiology and deliberately relax just as you are doing. . . . They have no idea they can enhance their mood and feel better by choosing to get absorbed in ideas that are enlightening and uplifting, just as you are doing. . . . And this is why taking the time you're taking now to generate experiences of comfort like this one becomes so valuable. . . . It says a lot of good things about what you value . . . and you can appreciate the process . . . the *how* of how you go about using what you experience. . . .

### Theme: You Can Develop a Personal Code of Honor

Because *how* you integrate meaningful ideas and perspectives into your life . . . is worth considering . . . *how* your internal atmosphere gradually grows calmer . . . how you develop a greater sense of what really matters to you . . . what your values are and how they guide the choices you make . . . how you evolve a stronger sense of confidence as your personal code of conduct becomes clearer. . . . Now, what do I mean by a "personal code of conduct"? . . .I mean the ever-clearer guidelines you'll define for yourself and then follow . . . the personal code of conduct that leads you to know you're living your life with integrity . . . being true to yourself in ways that keep building your own self-respect. . . . And there are lots of examples of codes of conduct different people live by . . . the code that someone who joins the military adopts to be an honorable part of a greater whole . . . the code that physicians live by in how they treat their patients . . . the code that teachers adopt that guides their relationships with their students . . . and on and on. . . . And you're defining your own code of conduct in the way you live . . . what you prioritize . . . what you are willing to say and do, and what you're simply unwilling to say or do . . . in order to honor your personal code. . . . Now, that doesn't mean you will always say and do the things you feel good about. . . . After all, you're not a robot that can just be programmed. . . .

**Theme: Discover, Define, and Own Your Strengths and Virtues**
But you can aspire to enjoy a level of self-respect that comes from knowing what matters to you . . . and how you can live by that knowledge. . . . And being absorbed in experiences like this one . . . can help people discover important and even life-changing things about themselves . . . especially when they discover their own character strengths . . . and their virtues. . . . Now, I can easily talk about the atmosphere that surrounds you in daily life . . . the way the world and the people in it treat you as you live your life. . . . And sometimes the atmosphere that others create outside of you is wonderfully positive and supportive . . . and other times, not as much when people are thoughtless or worse. . . . But in the same way that I can talk about an external atmosphere . . . I can talk about an internal atmosphere, the atmosphere that you create inside yourself . . . the way you treat yourself . . . the way you talk to yourself through your thoughts . . . the way you choose what you're going to do and what values you choose to live by and integrate into your everyday living . . . and what you choose to show the world about you through the things you say and do . . . that make clear statements to others about what you have adopted as your personal code of conduct. . . . And having learned as much as you have learned about how people will evolve as they strive to rise to the standards that they set for themselves . . . and how people grow into being richer in their internal resources as they explore new possibilities and have new experiences and develop new insights . . . it all really comes together now to help you form and live a meaningful life that you can feel good about. . . . And when I start focusing your attention on *your* character strengths and virtues . . . it's important to know what I mean. . . . I'm speaking about those characteristics that represent the best of human experience . . . the most valuable aspects of what human beings . . . including *you* . . . are capa-

ble of. . . . Some of the virtues people prize most . . . regardless of where
they live . . . or what culture they live in . . . are loyalty, compassion, honesty, empathy, and self-sacrifice. . . . I can add to that list the capacity to
love. . . . These virtues really do represent the best of what humans can
be. . . . And what is especially noteworthy is that all of these virtues . . .
loyalty, compassion, honesty, empathy, self-sacrifice, and love . . . are
all virtues that most prominently surface in our relationships with others. . . . These strengths and virtues are reflected in what we do and say
in our interactions with others. . . . And the quality of the relationships
that you build are so powerful in defining you . . . reflecting clearly what
you value . . . what you choose to say to people and what you deliberately choose to withhold . . . what you focus on and amplify in your
awareness of others and what fades into the background as unimportant. . . . And I wonder, if I had the chance to meet you socially and ask
you what *you* consider to be *your* character strengths . . . your virtues . . .
I wonder how you would answer that question. . . . I wonder whether
you've ever given this important question any serious, in-depth consideration . . . and you might reply with an updated self-awareness . . . or
whether you may have been trained to be so modest that it's hard to
acknowledge your own strengths and virtues. . . . Training yourself to be
so self-aware that you know exactly what your greatest strengths are . . .
doesn't mean being arrogant or full of yourself. . . . It means knowing
your strengths and recognizing that this is the foundation for learning
how to use them sensitively and skillfully . . . in a way that shows personal integrity. . . . And when you take even just a short while to notice
and acknowledge your strengths . . . well, isn't that quality of being able
to acknowledge what's right with you a virtue as well? . . .

**Theme: Rumination and Self-Doubt Cloud Self-Awareness**
The ability to notice and acknowledge what's right in yourself or someone else is, indeed, a virtue. . . . It's an important component of empathy
and compassion for both yourself and others. . . . There's an experience
I had I'd like to share with you that I believe you'll find both relevant and
helpful. . . . In one of the clinical demonstrations I conducted not long ago,
I was doing hypnosis with a bright and kind woman who had recently
retired from her long career as a schoolteacher . . . and she described to
me how she was filled with distressing doubts about whether she had

been a good teacher. . . . And when I began to describe some of the characteristics of good teachers . . . the ones who have a personal investment
of empathy and compassion for their students and treat them as valuable
human beings . . . the ones who want to be prepared in order to use each
lesson hour well because they generously want to impart some valuable
knowledge and experience . . . the ones who have a loyalty to the higher
principles, the *code*, of the profession . . . the ones who actually teach
their students how to think for themselves instead of dictating what they
"should" think. . . . Well, somewhere during the course of that session she
went from wondering . . . from *years* of wondering, ruminating, and having
self-doubts about her effectiveness as a teacher . . . to seemingly all of a
sudden becoming quite clear that she really *was* good at what she did. . . .
She just hadn't ever gotten so specific in her thinking before . . . about what
personal character strengths and virtues she brought to her classroom. . . .
She had never articulated the code of honor that she had lived by all those
years, that she now recognized defined her as a teacher with great integrity. . . . Now, I have no way of knowing what self-doubts you might entertain . . . but when you're in this very different internal space of comfort
and acknowledgment right now . . . it's entirely possible and reasonable to
expect how uncertainty can become certainty . . . and how you can shift
from questioning and doubting to recognizing your strengths . . . a process
which has started by noticing and acknowledging what's *right* with you. . . .

**Theme: You Can Recognize and Acknowledge Strengths in Others, Too**
And how easy it then becomes to notice and acknowledge what's right
with the people around you . . . especially the ones you choose to bring
into your life . . . because you appreciate their integrity as well. . . . What
an extraordinary experience to develop a new layer of confidence . . .
that you have something to say, something to contribute . . . and that
you have the character strength and the virtue to go ahead and say it . . .
to be one of those endearing people that can recognize the positive
in others . . . and being aware of the virtues you hold that allow you to
actually go the next step of actually saying something about it. . . . You
know how very far a kind word can go. . . . And as it becomes easier for
you to recognize your own strengths and virtues . . . as it can and will
over time . . . and those of others, too . . . you might wonder how that
became possible. . . .

**Theme: Integrity Means Honoring Your Code of Conduct**

But it will become increasingly obvious to you . . . that it became possible when you declared your personal code of conduct to yourself . . . your self-defined sense of what is and isn't right for you . . . that allows you to evolve and maintain strong self-respect. . . . It also helps a lot to know that all people, even smart and self-aware ones . . . can be influenced by circumstances or strong feelings to behave in less than ideal ways. . . . But what might be a useful way to regard yourself when you catch yourself acting in a way you really don't much care for? It can really provide you with a great deal of comfort when you step outside what happened . . . and can see more clearly what the situational influences were . . . that gave rise to your response . . . and with the clear thinking of knowing that there may be something valuable to learn from what happened. . . . It helps to be clear that there's a quality of consideration that makes it easier to learn from what happened without being unnecessarily harsh with yourself. . . . When you learn to be specific in your thinking . . . you can more easily recognize that an all-or-none view of yourself isn't an accurate viewpoint . . . because, as you've learned, a really smart person can sometimes make a foolish mistake. . . . A nice person can sometimes do something that isn't quite so nice. . . . A sensitive person can do something that isn't so sensitive . . . just as a mean person can do a nice thing and a dull person can do something bright. . . . And when you're able to hold on tightly to the bigger picture of who you are . . . what you're capable of . . . the code of conduct you've defined for yourself as the basis for living with integrity . . . well, these are things that you've already done and are still doing that highlight your talents . . . your skills . . . your strengths as a person. . . . And it's important that you take the time to notice these things in yourself . . . and to remind yourself that you're actively seeking out ways to continue to improve . . . ways to continue growing as a person . . . to live with values you hold dear and choose to live by . . . because they give your life meaning and provide you with the satisfaction of knowing you're not just living . . . you're living *well*. . . . And it certainly helps to be able to be specific about what your values are . . . what the guidelines are that you set for yourself in striving to live with integrity . . . also knowing that other people prioritize other things that *they* value . . . that you might not . . . just as you

might value things that they do not. . . . And this is what paves the way
for a respectful acceptance of the differences between people . . . but
especially accepting for yourself that which matters to you . . . what your
personal code of conduct requires of you. . . . That's what helps create
the internal atmosphere of self-confidence, a greater belief in yourself
and what you define as important in living your life in a way that's true
to your values. . . . What an easy way to protect yourself and your self-
esteem. . . . What an important way to manage your internal atmosphere
to keep it comfortable. . . . Well, certainly you've learned through all your
years of experience in living that there isn't only one right way to live . . .
only one right personal code of conduct. . . . In reality, there are *many*
right ways. . . . How valuable it is to appreciate that each way has some
value. . . . What a wonderful ability to choose what you're willing to say to
someone else and what you're not . . . what you're willing to say to yourself and what you're not . . . and what you are and are not willing to do in
living your life with integrity. . . . And I've been talking about the value of
the specifics in your self-definition . . . the details that come with experience that help you create a calm, self-respectful internal atmosphere. . . .

### Posthypnotic Suggestions for Integration
And now you're creating the possibility for yourself of shifting your own
focus to be able to notice and acknowledge your strengths as a unique
person. . . . And I'm curious just how many ways across your lifetime
you'll maintain that connection to your strengths . . . and what that connection will bring forth in your life. . . . And you can certainly anticipate
that the future holds countless opportunities for you to act in a way that
reveals your character strengths and virtues . . . as you live by your personal code of conduct . . . as a person with honor that you yourself can
respect. . . . So, having said all of those things I've said now, what you'll
absorb, what you'll stay connected to, as always, is up to you. . . . But if
you find yourself paying more attention to what's *right* with you, well, I
won't be surprised. . . .

### Closure and Disengagement
It's time to bring this session to a close now . . . a *comfortable* close. . . .
And when you're ready to do that because you've had enough time to

integrate these enriching ideas about acknowledging your strengths and virtues . . . then you can start the process of reorienting yourself slowly, comfortably . . . at a rate that suits you well. . . . And then when you're ready, you can reorient yourself completely . . . and let your eyes open whenever you'd like . . . fully alert . . . and feeling *good*.

# Chapter 14

# Evolving Foresight

*For tomorrow belongs to the people who prepare for it today.*

—African proverb

## The Case of Janet and Mark

Janet and Mark arrived early for the appointment, clearly eager to get things going as quickly as possible. Holding hands, radiating an easy comfort with each other, Janet began by saying, "Mark and I have been married for almost five years now. He's 34, I'm 32. We're both healthy and happy with our lives independently as well as together. We each have great jobs, a really good income, a really great lifestyle, and we don't want to screw it up."

Mark jumped in at that moment and said, "We're here because we've been having this ongoing discussion lately that doesn't seem to end, and it's starting to get both tiresome and stressful. We want to hash this out with a professional who can give us a reality check and make sure we're not missing something."

Janet jumped back in and said, "It's about having kids. When we were dating, we were really clear with each other that neither of us wanted to have kids. We got married, and that didn't change how we felt. We both still don't want kids. But we are getting pressure from both our families, who see that we're financially capable, the marriage is stable and healthy, we're good people that could be good parents, and they have started to plant the seeds of doubt about this in us. Actually, more in Mark than in me."

Mark again: "My folks lived for their kids, which I appreciate, but whenever I say, 'That's not for us,' they say, 'This is a big decision. You don't want to regret it later after the time has passed. Why are you being so selfish?' And a lot of other things that make me wonder if am I missing something."

To make an irreversible decision that is so consequential, regardless of what that decision is, poses a great challenge to make the best one possible. Best for what, though?

If you ask which is the best car to buy, the same question applies: Best for what? For speed? For gas mileage? For resale value? For luxury and comfort? For pickup? For cargo space? For what? What is the most important criterion to base the judgment upon?

In the case of Janet and Mark, what are the criteria for making a decision as to whether to have a child? Best to have the experience of parenting together? Best for satisfying their curiosity about what a child of theirs would be like? Best for their financial security? Best for having kids that can take care of them when they're elderly? Best for getting their parents off their back? Best for what?

Pressure from families to have children can be intense. When you're attacked and called defective by your own parents for not wanting to have kids ("Why are you being so selfish?"), you can start to doubt yourself. You can ask yourself why you don't want to have kids and wonder if there's something wrong with you. Is it because you are, indeed, selfish? Is it because your own childhood was so lousy that you don't want to relive it through anyone else? Is it because you are so rigid and orderly that the idea of the chaos of children scares you? Is it because you feel the need to contradict cultural norms to compensate for your fragile ego? Are you afraid your kid will turn out to be a loser and will reflect badly on you? Or what?

This is a serious decision. To make it effectively, Janet and Mark need to consider how well they really know themselves. How well can they predict how they'll react to future circumstances? Their capacity for foresight is going to be tested in this process and further developed through therapy, especially with hypnosis. A primary goal in facilitating a good decision is that it has not only treatment value, but also prevention value. No one wants them ever to regret what they decided to do. Twenty years and 50 years from now, you still want them saying to each other, "I'm so glad that's the choice we made!"

The content of their problem is a decision about whether to have kids. The process is how they make decisions (this one as well as others in the future) based on sufficient self-knowledge and a refined predictive ability.

Hypnosis with the two of them together (couples hypnosis) provided a much-needed break from overanalyzing what they had been ruminating about separately and together for months. During hypnosis, I introduced the topic of how and when self-awareness develops. I used simple examples of being a toddler and starting to learn your body's signals, such as when you're hungry or thirsty or when you need to go to the bathroom. I firmly pointed out that no one can look at you and say, "You're thirsty now. Drink!" This is something you have to learn for yourself, just as you have to learn to take yourself to bed when you're tired and grab a bite when you're hungry. You learn yourself, and as you get older, you learn more complex things, like whether you enjoy sports or reading a book, whether you like lots of friends or just one or two close ones. You learn what matters to you and what brings out the best in you. And no one can tell you that you're wrong to want only one or two friends instead of many, and no one can tell you that you're wrong for liking baseball but not football. You discover many times in many ways what you want your life to be about, and no one else can do that for you.

I added in some suggestions to jump ahead some years (i.e., age progression) and have some detailed experience of what it's like to live with the choice you've made.

Interestingly, when the session was over, the first thing Mark and Janet said to me was, "Wow, that was really a nice experience." The next thing Mark said was to Janet: "If it's selfish, then I'm all for it." Janet smiled broadly and replied, "I'll be glad to be selfish with you!"

Decision made. Some months later, I received a short note from Janet. It said, "We both feel like you took a 10-ton boulder off our backs. Family is still disappointed with our decision . . . but we're not! Thanks so much for your help."

## The Role of Foresight in Quality of Life

One of the exercises I encourage students in my clinical hypnosis training programs to carry out is to take all the case files of every client that they've seen in the last six months and separate them into two piles. One pile is for the clients who are suffering with problems that were not of their own creation; that might include people who were rear-ended sitting at a stoplight and now deal with chronic pain issues, or people who were sexually abused as children, or people who suffered the loss of someone they loved and are grieving, and many other such problems people suffer that they had no hand in creating.

The second pile is for those cases where the client played a clear and direct role in the creation of their problems. That might include the person who persisted in smoking cigarettes who now, depressingly, has lung cancer, or the spouse who had an extramarital affair that gave rise to the marriage and family splintering and their young kids suffering, or the person who drove drunk and killed someone.

Almost invariably, what therapists discover when they do this exercise is that the second pile is bigger than the first. The short-sighted and destructive paths that people take don't need to be nearly as dramatic as the examples above. An insult hurled in anger, a lack of follow-through on a promise made, an apathetic response to an important moment in someone else's life are milder indiscretions that can still yield some very painful consequences for oneself and/or others.

When people are so limited in their ability to anticipate—or care much about—the consequences of their actions, it reveals a startling lack of foresight. Foresight is generally defined as the ability to predict what will happen or to anticipate what actions or materials might be needed in the future. It is obviously an orientation to the future and serves as a complement to the process of building expectancy presented in Chapter 6. Expectancy is about the quality of one's expectations for the future, such as optimism or pessimism, or positive expectancy or negative expectancy. Foresight is about the ability to realistically anticipate and plan for a future event or development, whether good or bad. It features a specific skill: taking some known or possible factors and extrapolating them and planning one's actions accordingly.

## Foresight as a Means of Enhanced Self-Regulation

Psychologists Alan Strathman and Jeff Joireman edited an excellent volume called *Understanding Behavior in the Context of Time*. It includes an illuminating chapter by researcher John Boyd and social psychologist Philip Zimbardo that I recommend clinicians read. It features a review of their research on the Zimbardo Time Perspective Inventory, an instrument that was designed to assess individual differences in temporal orientation.

In their review, Boyd and Zimbardo (2005) highlight the value of a future orientation and describe future-oriented people as tending to be more successful, better at saving money, and better at making healthy lifestyle choices. Foresight leads to greater career planning, encourages saving money for a rainy day (e.g., if you were to become ill or lose your job), and leads to better choices about how you treat the body you're going to be living in for a while.

The lack of foresight thus exerts a powerful influence on one's quality of life. Engaging in risky behaviors that don't seem risky until something goes wrong can land someone in a hospital—or the morgue. The lack of impulse control, as discussed in Chapter 8, speaks to the lack of foresight in a different way, but the two are obviously related. A moment of yielding to a dangerous impulse can generate consequences that will echo throughout the rest of your life.

Every therapist who has been in clinical practice for more than an hour has heard this woeful line way too many times: "But it seemed like such a good idea at the time." The regret that comes with hindsight can be life consuming and the shame emotionally devastating.

Can therapists do more to teach their clients to think ahead? Of course. But the primary limitation of therapy is its past focus: People come in for help when they have already suffered terrible adversities, and the whole focus of therapy then is how to help someone get past the residuals of those adversities. "Healing the past" is the mantra of countless therapists, while many others are advocating that the client be more mindfully present. So the past and the present temporal orientations get a great deal of attention. The future? Not so much.

## Therapy and Its Relationship to Time

Some therapies are clearly past oriented in their structure, placing a heavy emphasis on childhood developmental processes, attachment histories, and significant past events as presumed determinants of current problems in a person's life. Other therapies are more structurally oriented to the present, paying much less attention to historical causes of client problems and much more attention to the here-and-now life circumstances and their consequences. And some therapies, most notably that of the late psychiatrist Milton H. Erickson, are structurally oriented to the future, focusing on variations of this key question: What can I do or say to interrupt the rigidity of this person's symptomatic patterns in order to introduce flexibility and thereby facilitate a therapeutic outcome?

At a time nearly a century ago when the mainstream practice of therapy was almost universally focused on analyzing the patient's past and interpreting the presumed symbolic nature of their symptoms and underlying psychodynamics, Milton Erickson went in a markedly different direction. Erickson made a simple observation that carries profound implications: "People don't come to therapy to change the past. They come to therapy to change the future." I agree wholeheartedly and have integrated that powerful perspective into virtually every aspect of my work.

Consider your reply to this question: In your view, does the future merely unfold, or do we create it? How you answer this question says a lot about you and what you do in your life, especially your approach to therapy. It's important to consider how your personal orientation to time influences the type of therapy you become attracted to and then choose to practice.

Many therapists are genuinely ambivalent about having a future focus. They often express beliefs that "the past is what makes us who we are," or concerns that "the past won't be honored," or "the traumas will be skimmed over," or "the past won't be sufficiently learned from, thereby ensuring unfortunate repeats," and so on. The justifications for maintaining a focus on the past are seemingly endless in the world of psychotherapy. But as the field continues to evolve, and as the future becomes more threatening and anxiety provoking, it's important that we question whether the past orientation is truly the most effective focus for enhancing people's lives. It certainly isn't a helpful focus if the goal is to evolve foresight.

Learning from the work of Milton Erickson, who took on unusual and complex cases and succeeded with them in innovative and sometimes even shocking ways, highlights how much good therapy can be done without analyzing people's childhoods. But despite this nudge to look ahead much more than behind, the ambivalence about a future orientation has largely continued. I wish I had a dollar for every time someone came up to me at one of my workshops and said some variation of, "Gee, Michael, I really like your work a lot, but . . . you're so goal-oriented!" (I think to myself, okay, here it comes!) They say, "Don't you know, it isn't about the destination? It's about the journey!" But—only therapists say that! Clients never say that. Clients never show up for therapy and say, "Uh, hi, I'd like to go on a *journey*."

Therapists lead the way into a sphere of time, a temporal orientation, with the type of therapy they choose to practice and thereby encourage the client to focus upon. Encouraging the development of foresight should be a basic part of clinical practice, in my opinion. Why isn't it?

Because the future hasn't happened yet, it is an abstract potential in our consciousness. It is an ambiguous stimulus. Ambiguity represents a particular challenge to human consciousness, as discussed in Chapter 5. How well we handle ambiguity as individuals directly shapes our vulnerability to some of the most common disorders that we as clinicians are asked to treat, especially anxiety and depression. Substantial research evidence highlights that people who have a low tolerance for ambiguity have a greater vulnerability to these disorders. For them, ambiguity is a risk factor for suffering emotional distress when their negative, scary projections are then responded to in the moment as if they are both true and inevitable. This isn't foresight—it's only fearmongering.

## Foresight and the Ability to Predict

This brings me to one of the most interesting aspects of a consideration of future orientation relative to evolving foresight, a domain of research called affective forecasting. When people look ahead to the future, they not only predict what events will take place, they also predict how they will feel at that time. Both research and real-life examples show us this process is terribly error prone. Some examples:

- Why do people say, "I will love you forever until death do us part" only to divorce soon after?
- Why do so many people think they'll be happy if only they could make more money or go to Tahiti, only to discover that when they do, they're not?

- Why do so many people think "I'll diet and exercise starting tomorrow" and then do neither?

Affective forecasting, the ability to predict how you're going to feel, is obviously important in lots of ways. After all, people base their life decisions on their predictions, ranging from whom they're going to marry, to what career they're going to pursue, to which house to buy, to where to go on vacation. As clinicians, can we teach people to make better predictions and, hopefully, prevent regrets? This is a primary goal of process-oriented hypnosis, as illustrated in this chapter's session transcript.

Many clinicians who utilize hypnosis in their work are familiar with Erickson's (1954a) widely cited article, "Pseudo-orientation in Time." In that article, Erickson described a therapeutic approach with hypnosis that was quite unique. Recognizing that people often, some would argue always, have an idea at some nonconscious levels of where their life is going or what their solution path may be, Erickson used hypnosis to carry out a procedure called age progression. Age regression orients people to their past, while age progression orients people to their future, to experience the future as if it's happening now.

Erickson's pseudo-orientation in time technique was to conduct the age progression to a future time when the problem that brought the patient into therapy was solved, then ask his patient to describe some of the specifics of how they changed or solved the problem. Then Erickson would suggest his patient develop an amnesia for having told him what the path to success would be, and then he carried out the successful intervention just as the patient described it! The patient's ideas of what would be therapeutic were often somewhere within, and Erickson simply created a pathway for bringing them forward and utilizing them. One of his most telling comments related to this was how the patient could be encouraged to "have hindsight *in advance*." That, in a nutshell, is the structure—the process—of foresight.

## Foresight Depends on a Firm Grasp of Cause and Effect

What good hypnosis sessions utilizing age progression strategies do is help people extrapolate, that is, it teaches them to get a better read on where a particular trend or pattern is headed. That is how foresight creates an avenue of prevention, not just treatment.

We as a profession are so pleased with ourselves for learning to think systemically that sometimes we forget how valuable it can also be to think linearly as well. How many times do your clients tell you a "What the heck were you thinking?" story such as, "How was I supposed to know I'd get fired just because I was sleeping with the boss's wife?" People tell you about preposterous things they do that are just like that and you think to yourself, "Gee, who could have seen *that* coming?"

This makes it essential to the endeavor of evolving foresight to help the client develop a full grasp of the relationship between cause and effect. A process-oriented hypnosis session that addresses that relationship is valuable, of course. It is also valuable for the client to be given the associated task assignment of looking for and identifying cause-and-effect relationships in daily life. Instead of life events seeming random, and even magical when there's no apparent cause for something other than divine intervention, the client is being trained in the process of identifying causes and effects. Ten or 20 times a day, the client can see linear relationships: flipping the switch to make the light go on, the traffic light turning red and cars stopping, paying someone a compliment and appreciating their smile, and on and on.

When people don't really grasp the relationship between cause and effect, it's hard to develop a sense of agency. "Things just seem to happen to me" is the explanation you settle on when you don't see the role you play in what happens. Without a sense of agency, a sense of responsibility to take action on your own behalf with a goal in mind, foresight remains an undeveloped human capacity.

It isn't easy to learn to think ahead, and often what foresight would lead to is having to do things that are unpleasant. It's more fun to spend money than save it, it's more gratifying to have the ice cream than follow a restrictive diet, and it's more exciting to take the risk than it is to play it safe. So much of human misery could be prevented but thinking in preventive terms doesn't come easily. We are trained to do treatment, not prevention, unfortunately. But the better we are at understanding and teaching the relationship between cause and effect, the more opportunities there are to behave preventively. So many of the people I've treated over the years could have prevented a lot of their problems but missed the opportunity to do so simply because prevention came disguised . . . as inconvenience.

# Typical Problems Derived From a Lack of Foresight

The types of problems that people might present for treatment that reflect an inability to think ahead and plan accordingly can seem quite diverse, and may include such problematic patterns as these:

- An inability to make detailed future plans
- Subscribing to the global and narrow philosophy that the future can't be predicted
- Difficulty seeing or understanding the relationship between cause and effect
- Believing that things "just happen" but with little or no insight as to why or how
- Routinely picking the path of least resistance in decision making (e.g., easiest, not best)
- A general inability to predict other people's behavior or emotional reactions
- A low sense of agency, thereby missing the role one plays in generating outcomes
- A greater proneness to magical thinking
- An impaired ability to make accurate risk assessments

These represent the kinds of problems clients might present that all reflect a lack foresight. The content of what they want help with is what they will naturally describe to the therapist, but it is up to the therapist to recognize the client's inability to think ahead and plan accordingly as the process needing intervention.

## Defining the Salient Therapeutic Targets

The building of foresight is, of course, a multistep process. As a starting point, it helps to define the client's role in the process in two important ways: first, to declare they have the necessary internal resources to make it possible and, second, that their actions today will be what shapes tomorrow's consequences. We want the client to feel resourceful and also to develop a sense of agency across their experiences.

Consistent with those messages is encouraging the recognition that the future is filled with possibilities and that the client's quality of life will be determined in large part by the decisions they make and enact. This starts to build the awareness for agency as well as a more personal appreciation of cause and effect. Tied to these is the offering of two meaningful rewards for learning to think ahead: greater personal successes and the chance to prevent regrets.

Metaphors can be offered that highlight the bad decisions people sometimes make when they find thinking ahead inconvenient in some way. Maybe it took too much time; maybe it made the workload bigger and harder; maybe it cost more money than they wanted to spend; but whatever the reason, the story ends with how a preventive opportunity was available but missed because it just wasn't convenient.

Learning to think preventively and becoming more skilled at recognizing cause-and-effect relationships go hand in hand. These are elaborated further and encouraged in the client through the suggestions provided in the process-oriented hypnosis session that follows in Table 14.1.

---

**TABLE 14.1. GENERIC SESSION STRUCTURE FOR EVOLVING FORESIGHT**

**Induction**

| | |
|---|---|
| **Response set:** | Thinking ahead |
| **Theme 1:** | You can use your resources as your actions take you forward |
| **Theme 2:** | The future isn't just more of the past |
| **Theme 3:** | Thinking ahead can prevent regrets |
| **Theme 4:** | Thinking ahead means taking preventive action even if it's inconvenient |
| **Theme 5:** | Making prevention a priority of your life |
| **Theme 6:** | Learn to think in cause-and-effect terms when making decisions |

**Posthypnotic suggestions for integration**
**Closure and disengagement**

### Induction

You can arrange yourself in whatever position is comfortable for you . . . a position that you can sit in for a while . . . easily . . . and effortlessly . . . one in which you can be deeply comfortable and yet still remain attentive enough . . . to focus on the things that I'll be talking about . . . so you can easily absorb their *deeper* meaning . . . and recognize their *deeper* value . . . as they relate to your life experience. . . . And when you're ready to focus yourself . . . you can begin by taking in a few deep, relaxing breaths . . . breathing slowly . . . and rhythmically . . . feeling the rise of your chest . . . as you inhale . . . slowly . . . and deeply . . . and feeling your chest gently fall . . . as you gradually . . . exhale. . . . And each breath . . . in . . . and out . . . can relax you more and more. . . . Steady, easy breathing can calm you . . . and reacquaint you . . . with the deeper parts of yourself . . . that you sometimes may get too busy to notice. . . .

### Response Set Regarding Thinking Ahead

You know . . . it's very easy . . . to get caught up in day-today living. . . . There is always so much to do . . . so many obligations to attend to . . . that can keep you occupied in the moment. . . . But, certainly . . . one of the most important things that you're comfortably positioned now to have learned. . . . and really absorbed . . . is that unless you deliberately take some meaningful time for yourself . . . the way you are right now as you focus on this session . . . unless you deliberately take the time to think through and even think preventively . . . it's too easy to miss how being in the moment . . . is a lead-in to the next moment . . . a stepping stone from now to later . . . just as each breath of comfort leads to the next . . . and today gives rise to tomorrow. . . . And how valuable to have the ability to focus on being in the moment at times . . . and how valuable it is to be able to think *beyond* the moment at times. . . . And you have *both* capabilities . . . but this session is going to focus on what's next . . . what's beyond the present moment of your life. . . .

### Theme: You Can Use Your Resources as Your Actions Take You Forward

You know as well as I do how many challenges we face each day on many different levels . . . and we recognize how stress can build up because of the demands we face that can be quite burdensome at times. . . . But with each hypnosis session you experience . . . and learn from . . . you acquire new insights, and new possibilities begin to emerge. . . . You discover and make better use of your strengths and resources . . . and you evolve more helpful strategies for managing your life well. . . . You absorb ideas and get new perspectives . . . and develop ways to respond to the challenges you face that you can feel good about. . . . You're learning that you can take time . . . quiet time . . . to be with yourself in a way that is kind and supportive . . . rather than being harsh with yourself. . . . After all, people grow best in positive conditions . . . the kind that nurture and encourage what's best in you . . . and you're learning to talk to yourself in a way . . . through your thoughts . . . that's helpful . . . and focused on . . . developing solutions . . . and not just identifying problems. . . . And you're also learning that you don't necessarily have to go dredging up the past . . . in order to take steps that help you move forward into the future. . . . You're learning a lot about how to think . . . in terms of what you *want* to have happen . . . and what the steps are . . . that you can courageously take to bring your goals to fruition. . . . You're learning that taking action is vital. . . . *Action* . . . not just thinking . . . not just contemplating . . . not just analyzing . . . but taking *sensible* action . . . action with *foresight* . . . knowing that it's what you do in this moment that helps determine what will happen in the next moment. . . .

### Theme: The Future Isn't Just More of the Past

There are many times each day . . . when you come to a place of needing to make a decision of some significance. . . . And how you did things in the past can still work in some places . . . but in other places the conditions have since changed. . . . And at those times, doing things just as you did before won't work in bringing you the outcome you want. . . . And for you to be able to look ahead . . . *beyond* the moment and *beyond* the familiar . . . is an opportunity to grab with both hands . . . as you keep your focus on what's possible . . . because the future isn't just more of the past. . . . And the future is where you're going to be living. . . . And the decisions you make in the moment that will shape your future . . . are decisions where you can either limit yourself unnecessarily . . . or you can take a *sensible* risk to try something different that offers the potential of a better result. . . . And as you continue to develop yourself . . . and your life skills . . . you can find it so much more automatic to . . . recognize an opportunity to experiment with how you do things and try something new . . . not just anything, of course . . . but something well thought out and planned . . . perhaps based on something you've observed others do that works well . . . or perhaps based on something you simply believe can work as you extrapolate current conditions and anticipate in detail the likely consequences of your actions. . . . You can continue to train yourself to think more clearly in terms of what is possible . . . and what is realistic. . . .

### Theme: Thinking Ahead Can Prevent Regrets

It's an especially important skill to have for living well . . . to recognize the differences that can arise between . . . what is really true . . . and what you have come to believe. . . . Too often people think things, especially self-critical or self-limiting things . . . and then make the mistake of actually believing themselves. . . . That recognition can lead you to be more skilled at looking for credible evidence before you just simply believe something . . . and can lead you to ask more questions . . . and gather relevant information . . . *before* you reach a sensible conclusion. . . . And these are the tools for making forward-looking decisions that can prevent regrets . . . from poorly made decisions or reckless, impulsive actions. . . . How many times people have told me that what is now the source of distress . . . seemed like such a good idea at the time. . . . These are the famous last words of regret: . . . "It seemed like a good idea at the time" . . . and the other famous last words of regret are . . . "I guess I didn't think far enough ahead." . . . Gathering good information and thinking well ahead are two of the most important skills that you need to live life well. . . . And these are the skills necessary to prevent many problems from arising. . . . And you're learning them and gradually mastering them . . . and you can feel good about that. . . . What you've been learning through these hypnosis sessions . . . are skills in thinking . . . skills that are important for relating to others . . . skills in knowing yourself. . . . Your strengths as well as your vulnerabilities . . . and appreciating them and knowing how to manage them with insight and foresight. . . .

## Theme: Thinking Ahead Means Taking Preventive Action Even If It's Inconvenient

You're made up of so many different parts . . . and what you're now in a comfortable position to appreciate . . . is that each part of you . . . can be valuable *somewhere* . . . but isn't necessarily going to be valuable *everywhere.* . . . And knowing which parts of yourself to express and which to purposely contain at any given time is one of the keys to preventing problems from arising. . . . It's what makes it possible to think of possible consequences, good or bad, before you speak your mind. . . . It's what makes it possible to go outside yourself and your feelings in the moment just long enough to read a situation carefully . . . so you can choose *whether* to say or do something and, if so, then *what* to say or do that will be helpful. . . . Learning to think ahead is the essential ingredient in prevention . . . and there are so many examples of prevention opportunities that people have missed . . . sometimes with truly terrible consequences. . . . Let me share an example with you. . . . Not long ago, in a city in the American Midwest, a heavily used bridge handling an average of 140,000 cars per day collapsed during rush-hour traffic. . . . More than a dozen people died, and more than 100 people were injured as their cars fell into the river below. . . . Many years earlier, structural engineers reported the bridge as unsafe and needing repairs . . . but the government agency responsible for the bridge didn't think it was an imminent danger and claimed they didn't have the substantial amount of money that would be needed for such a repair. . . . Yet, when the bridge collapsed and the magnitude of the tragedy was incalculable . . . they somehow managed to find the money virtually right away, and they were able to build a new bridge in record time. . . . And why did there have to be a bridge collapse and a loss of life before sensible action to reinforce the bridge was taken? . . . Well, prevention isn't always easy or cheap . . . but whoever said an ounce of prevention is worth a pound of cure knew what they were talking about. . . . How much misery in the world could be prevented if people would just think ahead. . . . After all, no one has to be psychic to know that if you keep dumping toxic waste into the air we breathe and the water we drink that it's going to be a problem for us all one day. . . . And no one needs to be a fortune teller to know that when you hurt people for your personal gain, there will be a painful price you're going to have to pay one day. . . . And no one needs to be a genius to know that if you get behind the wheel of a car when you're drunk that it isn't going to end well for you and whomever you might injure or kill. . . . The examples of bad decisions that people didn't have to make are endless . . . small and large tragedies that could have been prevented . . . but that would have required thinking instead of reacting . . . thinking *beyond* the moment and anticipating. . . . And what happens when that is inconvenient? . . . Or when it isn't fun to think preventively? . . .Or when it isn't very easy? . . .

### Theme: Make Prevention a Priority in Your Life

It brings into sharp focus now . . . what the role of prevention can be in *your* life . . . how well you develop your ability to think ahead . . . how important it becomes to you to see a step or two ahead on the path you're on. . . . And, of course, not everything can be anticipated. . . . Not all problems can be prevented . . . but there is an important distinction to be made between the problems that find you through no fault of your own . . . and the problems you unintentionally create for yourself by missing the chance to think ahead and take the necessary preventive actions even when they're inconvenient. . . . And one of my favorite newspaper columnists said this really well when she wrote, "Most people's problems could be prevented, but too often the opportunity is missed because it came disguised as inconvenience." . . .

### Theme: Learn to Think in Terms of Cause and Effect When Making Decisions

There are many different ways to think, of course . . . thinking that is concrete . . . and thinking that is abstract . . . thinking that is reflexive, often called automatic thoughts . . . and thinking that is a slow pondering . . . thinking that is one-dimensional and thinking that is multidimensional . . . thinking that is the global big picture and thinking that is richly detailed. . . . And I'm drawing your attention to a linear style of thinking . . . a style that makes the relationship between cause and effect so much more obvious. . . . And how well can you think in these terms . . . to be able to recognize that this action led to that outcome? Or that these words triggered that reaction? Or that thought gave rise to those feelings? Not everything is so obvious in terms of cause and effect . . . but

more than people generally realize. . . . And learning to think linearly . . .
first this, then that . . . can start early if we care to teach those skills . . .
to read to a child and midway through the book stop reading and ask
what they think will happen next and why. . . . And ask a child questions
such as why you put your socks on *before* you put your shoes on, or
why you put the toothpaste on your toothbrush *before* you brush your
teeth. . . . And you start learning early on that *this* leads to *that* . . . an
obviously important skill when thinking in terms of prevention. . . . And
so what does it take to live well and happily? . . . I think it takes being
able to move from . . . situation to situation . . . knowing your different
parts . . . your strengths and resources . . . and using them skillfully. . . .

### Posthypnotic Suggestions for Integration

And to be able to think preventively . . . you can use your ability that is
ever growing in sophistication . . . of being able to think ahead . . . and to
choose paths . . . that take you where you want to go in the long run . . .
and not just to follow the path that is easy and familiar to you but takes
you to someplace you really don't want to go. . . . That's what gives rise
to the self-blame and self-doubt . . . that can be prevented by doing
what's *best* . . . not what's *easiest* . . . doing what will provide a good
result . . . not doing something that may seem okay in the moment that
will only bring unhappiness later. . . . And it can really be quite comforting . . . to realize . . . at a very deep level within yourself . . . that you can
be so . . . tuned in . . . to what it means to live life well. . . .

You can continue learning . . . continue experiencing . . . continue
observing. . . . And all the principles of effective living . . . come down
to you knowing . . . what it means to be powerful . . . in your ability to
choose. . . . You have the ability to choose. . . . *You* get to choose . . . so
much of what happens in your life . . . such as where you go and what
you do that can serve you well . . . and who you bring into your life . . .
that will enhance your life rather than make it harder. . . . And one of the
best preventive tools that you can develop and continually refine . . . is
the ability to recognize ever more efficiently . . . what you are in control of . . . and what you are responsible for . . . and likewise. . . . what
you're not. . . . It's really quite a great and worthy challenge . . . to be
able to keep moving forward with your life . . . seeking out new challenges . . . facing them with courage and integrity . . . rising to them . . .

always bringing out the best . . . of your deeper self . . . through the life that you lead. . . . And so, as you move into the future . . . you can take great comfort in knowing . . . that you carry with you . . . many wonderful skills and resources . . . the things that you've already learned and experienced . . .and other things that are yet to come. . . . You can use these resources . . . to your own best advantage. . . . You can use your power with insight and foresight. . . . And so . . . now you can take some time to process your thoughts and feelings . . . and integrate deeply whatever you need to or want to, in order to start to make thinking ahead . . . and thinking preventively more reflexive. . . .

**Closure and Disengagement**

And then you can start to bring this experience to a comfortable close. . . . And then when you're ready . . . you can begin the process of gradually reorienting yourself. . . . You can begin to refocus yourself now at a rate that is gradual and comfortable . . . so that when you're ready . . . you can reorient yourself fully . . . and open your eyes . . . fully alert and refreshed . . . feeling good . . . feeling *really* good. . . .

# References

American Psychological Association. (2019, November 5). Stress in America 2019. Retrieved from https://www.apa.org

Boyd, J., & Zimbardo, P. (2005). Time perspective, health, and risk taking. In A. Strathman & J. Joireman (Eds.), *Understanding behavior in the context of time: Theory, research and application* (pp. 85–108). Mawah, NJ: Erlbaum.

Brach, T. (2004). *Radical acceptance: Embracing your life with the heart of a Buddha*. New York: Bantam.

Burns, G. (2001). *101 healing stories: Using metaphors in therapy*. New York: Wiley.

Burns, G. (2007). *Healing with stories: Your casebook collection for using therapeutic metaphors*. Hoboken, NJ: Wiley.

Burns, G. (2010). Introduction: Zen and the art of therapy. In M. Richeport-Haley & J. Carlson (Eds.), *Jay Haley revisited* (pp. 307–314). New York: Routledge.

Callahan, J., Maxwell, K., & Janis, B. (2019). The role of overgeneral memories in PTSD and implications for treatment. *Journal of Psychotherapy Integration, 29*(1), 32–41.

Chefetz, R. (2015). *Intensive psychotherapy for persistent dissociative processes*. New York: Norton.

Elkins, G. (Ed.). (2017). *Handbook of medical and psychological hypnosis: Foundations, applications, and professional issues*. New York: Springer.

Erickson, M. (1954a). Pseudo-orientation in time as a hypnotherapeutic procedure. *Journal of Clinical and Experimental Hypnosis, 2*, 261–283.

Erickson, M. (1954b). Special techniques of brief hypnotherapy. *Journal of Clinical and Experimental Hypnosis, 2,* 109–129.

Gazzaniga, M. (2011). *Who's in charge? Free will and the science of the brain*. New York: HarperCollins.

Gazzaniga, M. (2018). *The consciousness instinct: Unraveling the mystery of how the brain makes the mind*. New York: Farrar, Straus and Giroux.

Greenberger, D., & Padesky, C. (2016). *Mind over mood: Change how you feel by changing the way you think*. New York: Guilford.

Haley, J. (1973). *Uncommon therapy: The psychiatric techniques of Milton H. Erickson, MD*. New York: Norton.

Hallford, D., Austin, D., Raes, F., & Takano, K. (2018). A test of the functional avoidance hypothesis in the development of overgeneral autobiographical memory. *Memory and Cognition, 46*, 895–908.

Hilgard, E. (1994). Neodissociation theory. In S. Lynn & J. Rhue (Eds.), *Dissociation: Clinical, theoretical and research perspectives* (pp. 32–51). New York: Guilford.

Lankton, S. (2020, January). Relying on scripts versus not relying on scripts. *American Journal of Clinical Hypnosis, 62*(3), 172–177.

Law, B. (2005, November). Probing the depression-rumination cycle: Why chewing on problems just makes them harder to swallow. *APA Monitor, 36*, 10, 38.

Mischel, W. (2014). *The marshmallow test: Why self-control is the engine of success*. Boston: Little, Brown.

Nolen-Hoeksema, S. (2003). *Women who think too much: How to break free of over-thinking and reclaim your life*. New York: Henry Holt.

Padesky, C., & Greenberger, D. (2020). *The clinician's guide to CBT using mind over mood* (2nd ed.). New York: Guilford.

Peterson, C., & Seligman, M. (2004). *Character strengths and virtues: A handbook and classification*. Washington, DC: American Psychological Association.

Sloman, S., & Fernbach, P. (2017). *The knowledge illusion: Why we never think alone*. New York: Riverhead.

Tavris, C., & Aronson, E. (2015). *Mistakes were made (but not by me): Why we justify foolish beliefs, bad decisions, and hurtful acts* (Rev. ed.). New York: Mariner.

Yapko, M. (1992). *Hypnosis and the treatment of depressions: Strategies for change*. New York: Brunner/Mazel.

Yapko, M. (1994). *Suggestions of abuse: True and false memories of childhood sexual trauma*. New York: Simon and Schuster.

Yapko, M. (2001). *Treating depression with hypnosis: Integrating cognitive-behavioral and strategic approaches*. New York: Brunner/Routledge.

Yapko, M. (2010a, April–June). Hypnosis in the treatment of depression: An overdue approach for encouraging skillful mood management. *International Journal of Clinical and Experimental Hypnosis, 58*(2), 137–145.

Yapko, M. (2010b, April–June). Hypnotically catalyzing experiential learning across treatments for depression: Actions can speak louder than moods.

*International Journal of Clinical and Experimental Hypnosis, 58*(2), 186–200.

Yapko, M. (2011). *Mindfulness and hypnosis: The power of suggestion to transform experience.* New York: Norton.

Yapko, M. (2016). *The discriminating therapist: Asking "how" questions, making distinctions, and finding direction in therapy.* Fallbrook, CA: Yapko.

Yapko, M. (2019). *Trancework: An introduction to the practice of clinical hypnosis* (5th ed.). New York: Routledge.

Zeig, J. (2014). *The induction of hypnosis: An Ericksonian elicitation approach.* Phoenix: Milton H. Erickson Foundation Press.

Zeig, J. (2019). *Evocation: Enhancing the psychotherapeutic encounter.* Phoenix: Milton H. Erickson Foundation Press.

# Index

acceptance
  cancer-related, 130–33
  case example, 130–33
  defined, 135, 139
  encouraging, 130–48, 140*t* (*see also* encouraging acceptance)
  in hypnosis, 139
  lack of, 136
  in mindfulness-based approaches, 138
  power of, 136–37
  promoting, 139
  in quality of life, 133–34
  radical, 138
  as starting point, 134–36
acceptance and commitment therapy (ACT), 30
  dissociation in, 118
ACT. *see* acceptance and commitment therapy (ACT)
action(s)
  amplification of benefits of, 171
  meaningful (*see* meaningful action)
  past, 177*t*, 179
  personal resources and, 213*t*, 214–15
  revealing, 170
  speak louder than words, 170
  taking, 177–78, 177*t*
  in therapy, 172–73
action orientation
  problems derived from negative, 175–76
  in quality of life, 170–71
action-oriented
  passive-oriented *vs.*, 14
"action speaks louder than words," 170

actions plans
  steps to follow in, 177*t*, 179–81
adaptation
  in mental health, 9
affective forecasting, 209–10
agency
  building response set regarding, 159*t*, 160–61
age progression, 210
age regression, 43, 43*t*, 210
airplane phobia, 6–8
ambiguity. *see also* recognizing and tolerating ambiguity
  anxiety and, 13
  case example, 51–53
  as challenge to human consciousness, 209
  coping with, 55–56
  defined, 13, 44, 54
  lack of tolerance for, 56
  mental health issues related to, 54–55
  in quality of life, 53–55
  recognizing, 13, 51–62, 57*t* (*see also* recognizing and tolerating ambiguity)
  responses to, 13
  rumination related to, 55–56
  salient therapeutic targets for, 57–58, 57*t*
  tolerance for, 51–62, 57*t* (*see also* recognizing and tolerating ambiguity)
  uncomfortableness of, 55–56
*American Journal of Clinical Hypnosis,* 35
American Psychological Association (APA)
  2019 Stress in America survey of, 12

# About the Author

**Michael D. Yapko, Ph.D.**, is a clinical psychologist residing in Southern California. Author of 15 books, including the leading hypnosis text *Trancework* (5th edition), he has taught hypnosis in more than 30 countries and received lifetime achievement awards from the American Psychological Association (Div. 30), the International Society of Hypnosis, and The Milton H. Erickson Foundation.